D1329199

THE STORYTELLER'S SECRET

Carmine Gallo is the international bestselling author of *Talk Like TED*. He is a communications coach for a number of widely admired brands – among them Pfizer, LinkedIn, Intel and Coca-Cola – and a popular keynote speaker who teaches the world's most respected business leaders how to deliver dynamic presentations and share inspiring stories. He is a columnist for Forbes.com and Entrepreneur.com, and head of Gallo Communications in California.

THE
STORYTELLER'S
SECRET

How TED Speakers and Inspirational Leaders
Turn Their Passion into Performance

CARMINE GALLO

PAN BOOKS

First published 2016 by St. Martin's Press, New York

First published in the UK in paperback 2016 by Macmillan

This edition published 2018 by Pan Books
an imprint of Pan Macmillan
The Smithson, 6 Briset Street, London EC1M 5NR
EU representative: Macmillan Publishers Ireland Ltd, 1st Floor,
The Liffey Trust Centre, 117–126 Sheriff Street Upper,
Dublin 1, DOI YC43
Associated companies throughout the world
www.panmacmillan.com

ISBN 978-1-5098-1476-3

9

A CIP catalogue record for this book is available from the British Library.

Design by Patrice Sheridan
Printed and bound by CPI Group (UK) Ltd, Croydon, CR0 4YY

Visit **www.panmacmillan.com** to read more about all our books
and to buy them. You will also find features, author interviews and
news of any author events, and you can sign up for e-newsletters
so that you're always first to hear about our new releases.

To Vanessa,

For believing in us

Contents

Acknowledgments

I can't thank the team at St. Martin's Press enough for their support of this project. Executive Editor Tim Bartlett offered invaluable insights and comments to guide the creative process. Editorial assistant Claire Lampen made the entire process run smoothly, and for that I'm grateful. It's been a joy to work with the entire team at St. Martin's Press including Sally Richardson, George Witte, Laura Clark, and everyone from publicity and promotion to editing and design. Thank you for bringing *The Storyteller's Secret* to life.

Roger Williams has always been more than a literary agent. I'm thankful for his mentorship, guidance, and unwavering enthusiasm.

My speaking agents Tom Neilssen and Les Tuerk, along with the entire team at BrightSight Group, play an invaluable role in helping me share this content with groups around the world. They deserve special thanks and recognition.

Mark Fortier and Norbert Beatty at Fortier PR, our outstanding publicists who I turn to for guidance. Thank you for your valuable partnership.

Carolyn Kilmer, community manager and design expert at Gallo Communications Group, is an important part of our team and she does a magnificent job of extending our content far and wide.

My wife, Vanessa Gallo, believes in the story we have to share and works tirelessly to manage Gallo Communications. She also takes a leadership role in our daughters' school by volunteering as president of the Parent Teacher Group. It's inspiring to watch her apply our storytelling content to the field of education. Vanessa is my guiding light.

As always, special thanks to my family for their support: Josephine, Lela, Tino, Donna, Francesco, Nick, Ken, Patty, and my mother, Giuseppina. My father, Francesco, is no longer with us, but his story of struggle and triumph has always shaped my view of the world. My dad's story gave me permission to dream.

Preface

Your Story Is My Passion

was lying flat on my back.

I had slipped on a sheet of ice outside of my 500-square-foot apartment in western Wisconsin. The thermometer hit zero that morning—20 degrees colder if you counted the windchill. I had torn my only suit, an expensive Italian outfit I had proudly purchased in San Francisco a few days earlier before getting in my car and driving 2,000 miles to take my first television job as a morning news anchor.

As I was lying on the sidewalk in the early morning freeze, looking up at a decaying apartment complex in the worst part of town, a number of questions raced through my mind: *Had I made the right decision to give up law school—the "safe" choice—to pursue my passion—a career in broadcast journalism? Would I be stuck making $15,000 a year for the rest of my career? Would my father, who had landed on these shores as an Italian immigrant with $20 in his pocket after World War II, have been proud of my decision, or would the former prisoner of war have felt that his son was squandering an opportunity to make it in America?*

I didn't have an answer to all of my questions at the moment, but I reached two conclusions. First, it's best to buy two-for-one suits, preferably at a discount, if you can barely afford to pay your $400 monthly rent. Second, that following my passion would be really, really tough, even harder than the ice I had just cracked with my head. And with that I got up, picked up my papers, now stuck on the frozen pavement, wiped the snow off my suit, and continued on my way to work. I wasn't prepared for the Wisconsin winter, but I was prepared to face whatever obstacle would come next because, ultimately, you don't choose your passion; it chooses you.

Twenty-five years later I found myself asking the question again: *Why am I here?* In May 2014, I had been invited to speak at an exclusive gathering of entrepreneurs and CEOs attending the Khosla Ventures Summit at a resort at the foot of the Golden Gate Bridge in Marin County. The event's host, billionaire venture capitalist Vinod Khosla, had personally invited me, though initially, I couldn't see why. The other speakers included Bill Gates; Google founders Sergey Brin and Larry Page; Salesforce CEO Marc Benioff; former secretary of state Condoleezza Rice; and former British prime minister Tony Blair. During an elegant dinner on the first night of the conference, as I felt like the only person in the room who needed an introduction, I began to question my role at the event: *I'm not a billionaire. I haven't eradicated smallpox. Or run a country. Why am I here?*

But Khosla immediately put me at ease when he took the stage. Addressing the entrepreneurs in the audience he said, "You're all brilliant, which is why I invest in you, but many of you cannot tell an emotional story, and that's why I invited Carmine Gallo to speak to you."

On the one hand, it struck me as I looked around the room that every person there was already a storyteller. In fact, I had written about the more famous ones and their effective communication styles. And the impressive young entrepreneurs in the audience were all storytellers, too. Some were more effective than others, but they all had to learn to tell a story if they hoped to change the world with their ideas. In fact, the ones who stood out knew intuitively what neuroscientists and researchers are just beginning to understand: One emotional and vivid customer story is far more persuasive than a data dump in 85 PowerPoint slides. A person can have a great idea, but if that person cannot inspire others to buy into that idea, it doesn't matter.

What struck me even more as I interacted with that group was the degree to which the most successful entrepreneurs and thought leaders—people who are already in many ways master communicators, many of who seem like born storytellers—were hungry to learn more about this most elemental—and crucial—part of presenting ourselves, ideas, and businesses. They realized the exponential potential of even incremental improvements.

At the time of the Khosla event I had been thinking about the subject of my next book. I had been on the speaking circuit promoting *Talk Like TED*, which unlocked the presentation secrets of the world's great thinkers and entrepreneurs who have dazzled their audiences on a TED conference stage. As I made my way around the country talking about the book, I found again and again, no matter who the audience was or where I was speaking, that one chapter seemed to resonate most strongly: how the best TED speakers master the art of storytelling; how great stories seemed to be the foundation of all great communication. As I engaged in back and forth with my audiences, I realized as never before that storytelling held the key not only to the perfect TED talk, but also to the larger mission of realizing one's potential.

And it wasn't just while I was promoting my book; I found the subject of storytelling coming up in a range of other contexts. When I interviewed the famed venture capitalist Ben Horowitz, he noted that among entrepreneurs, "storytelling is the most underrated skill." Richard Branson wrote a blog post on how storytelling can be used to drive change. On a plane flight I sat next to a sales professional for Salesforce who said, "We have a new way to capture customer testimonials on video, but we're struggling with how to use those endorsements to tell a story." On another plane flight, this time to Paris, I met a manager with the global tech giant SAP, who told me, "My company just hired a new marketing manager. Her title is 'Chief Storyteller.' While my company is simplifying its story on a macro level, I'm struggling to simplify my story in PowerPoint. We've been told that no presentation must last more than a TED-like eighteen minutes."

The push for both effective storytelling and brevity strikes many as a significant challenge. On another trip, I met with the top executives of a global energy company, who told me their CEO had a new mandate: Every new business pitch must contain no more than 10 slides. "How do we tell our story in 10 slides?" he asked. On the same trip an executive having a meeting with the prime minister of Vietnam the following week asked me, "In 20 minutes how do I tell him the story of who we are, why we do what we do, and why the country should partner with us over our competitors?" I've met senior leaders running the world's largest companies and young entrepreneurs preparing for the pitch of a lifetime on ABC's *Shark Tank*. They ask the question: *How do I tell the story behind my idea?*

We're all "storytellers." We don't call ourselves storytellers, but it's what we do every day. Although we've been sharing stories for thousands of years, the skills we needed to succeed in the industrial age were very different from those required today. The ability to sell our ideas in the form of story is more important than ever. Ideas are the currency of the twenty-first century. In the information age, the knowledge economy, you are only as valuable as your ideas. Story is the means by which we transfer those ideas to one another. Your ability to package your ideas with emotion, context, and relevancy is the one skill that will make you more valuable in the next decade.

Storytelling is the act of framing an idea as a narrative to inform, illuminate, and inspire. *The Storyteller's Secret* is about the stories you tell to advance your career, build a company, pitch an idea, and to take your dreams from imagination to reality.

When you pitch your product or service to a new customer, you're telling a story. When you deliver instructions to a team or educate a class, you're telling a story. When you build a PowerPoint presentation for your next sales meeting, you're telling a story. When you sit down for a job interview and the recruiter asks about your previous experience, you're telling a story. When you craft an e-mail, write a blog or Facebook post, or record a video for your company's YouTube channel, you're telling a story. But there's a difference between a story, a good story, and a transformative story that builds trust, boosts sales, and inspires people to dream bigger.

In these pages I will introduce you to some of the greatest brand storytellers of our time: Richard Branson, Howard Schultz, Sheryl Sandberg, Joel Osteen, Herb Kelleher, Gary Vaynerchuk, Mark Burnett, Oprah Winfrey, Elon Musk, Steve Wynn, Tony Robbins, Steve Jobs, and others whose names you may be less familiar with, but who have managed to become leaders in their fields on the basis of their ability to tell a transformative story. Many of the people in this book have given TED talks that have gone viral, not because of the data they presented, but because of the stories they told. Ideas that catch on are wrapped in story.

I've personally interviewed many of the storytellers in this book. They've all mastered the art and science of storytelling to inspire, motivate, and, ultimately, to persuade others to take a desired course of action. But they also share one other common trait—they've also faced hardship and are eager to share the lessons they've learned.

One of the major findings in this book is the fact that most great storytellers have struggled in their life and they've turned their adversity into victory. Their failures make them more interesting because, as you'll learn, we are hardwired to love rags-to-riches stories.

Struggle is part of nature, which is why we find stories of adversity nearly impossible to ignore. Pearls, diamonds, and award-winning wine represent nature's conquest over adversity. Pearls are formed as an oyster protects itself from irritating grains of sand. Diamonds are formed under crushing pressure and intense heat in the Earth's mantle. And the best grapes come from steep mountain slopes or rocky soil that stresses the roots and creates grape clusters bursting with flavor; they have the most "character." We especially like stories with a diamond at the end, a satisfying resolution to the struggle. Inspiring leaders often speak in the story of adversity to create an emotional bond with their audiences. Embrace your history because it's the stuff from which legends are made and legacies are left.

Storytelling is not something we do. Storytelling is who we are.

THE STORYTELLER'S SECRET

Introduction

Richard Branson, Dopamine, and the Kalahari Bushmen

The art of storytelling can be used to drive change.
—Richard Branson

On a tiny speck of land in the British Virgin Islands, a group of ambitious entrepreneurs share their terrain with its year-round inhabitants: flamingos, a red-footed tortoise, and 35 Madagascar lemurs. "There are only 200 lemurs left in the world," Sir Richard Branson explains as a lemur attempts to jump from one tree to another. "And if he doesn't make it, they'll only be 199," Branson jokes.

While the rare species of animals are a gift to behold, the entrepreneurs are hoping for a financial gift from Branson, the island's owner. The Virgin Group founder owns all 74 acres of this lush, tropical paradise called Necker Island. It's his home and his hideaway. On this day it's also the setting for the Extreme Tech Challenge, one of the most unusual pitch competitions the world has ever seen. The finalists—some of whom I coached to tell their product story more effectively—are here to sell Richard Branson on their ideas.

Bill Tai, a career venture capitalist and a sponsor of the pitch competition, has been investing in companies since 1991. Tai has seen several waves of technology in Silicon Valley and he believes that now, more than ever, the ability to communicate ideas simply and clearly and to tell compelling stories is critical to standing apart in the marketplace of ideas. Technologists and scientists no longer talk to just their peers. If they can't explain the benefits of their products to consumers, their ideas won't catch on. They must translate the language of bits and bytes into a story every consumer understands. Tai has found a kindred spirit in Richard Branson, who strongly believes in the art of storytelling to drive change. "Telling a story is one of the best ways we have of coming up with new ideas, and also of learning about each other and the world,"[1] Branson says. Branson intuitively knows what neuroscientists are confirming in the lab—our brains are wired for story.

In order to understand Branson's belief that storytelling can make a positive impact in the future, we must look to the past. One million years ago humans gained control of an element that was critical to the survival of our species. The element helps explain why some pitches fail miserably while others succeed at launching a brand. It explains why many ideas fail to gain traction, while others trigger global movements. It explains why many leaders fail to inspire their teams, while others persuade people to walk through walls. The element is fire.

Firelight and the Kalahari Bushmen

Anthropologists point to fire as the spark that ignited human evolution. It makes sense because once our ancestors got control of fire they could cook food, which radically increased the size of human brains. Fire also warded off predators at night, another positive if you wanted to live to see the sun rise. Until recently, however, few scientists studied one of the most profound benefits of fire—sparking our imagination through storytelling.

Firelight extended the day, providing more time for purposes other than hunting and gathering. As people shared their personal experiences around the fire, they learned to avoid danger, to hunt more effectively as a team, and to strengthen cultural traditions. Social anthropologists believe storytelling made up 80 percent of the fireside conversations of our ancient ancestors.

In Namibia's Kalahari desert, a group of nomads known as the Bushmen still spend their days foraging for food such as melons, nuts, seeds, and antelope. They are hunter-gatherers by day and storytellers at night. When the sun sets on the Kalahari, the Bushmen light fires and tell stories just as their ancestors did thousands of years earlier. During the day the Bushmen's conversations are focused on survival: hunting strategies, resource management, mediating disputes, etc. Only 6 percent of their conversations involve stories.[2] By night it's a different story, literally. As the embers of the fire extend the day, the Bushmen devote 81 percent of their conversations around the campfire to telling stories. Men and women tell stories, mostly about people the other villagers know and humorous or exciting adventures. For the Bushmen storytelling triggers the imagination, creates bonds between groups of people who don't know each other, and conveys information about institutions that are critical to the Bushmen's survival.

Not all communicators have the skill of storytelling, even in tribal societies. Among the Bushmen, as among TED speakers or business leaders, the best speakers leave the audience rolling with laughter, still with suspense, or inspired to seek their own adventures. Camp leaders were often good storytellers. And the best of the best—the most admired storytellers—use "multimodal communication" such as gestures, imitations, sound effects, and songs. The Kalahari storytellers learned that they had to deliver information, convey experiences, inspire, and entertain. If people aren't entertained, they stop listening and go to sleep, not unlike what happens in millions of business presentations given every day. Humans evolved to perceive stories as entertaining because if they didn't pay attention, they might be a lion's lunch.

"Stories told by firelight put listeners on the same emotional wavelength, elicited understanding, trust, and sympathy, and built positive reputations for qualities like humor, congeniality, and innovation,"[3] says University of Utah anthropology professor Polly Wiessner. "Through stories and discussions people collected experiences of others and accumulated knowledge of options that others had tried. Night talk was critical for transmitting the big picture." Wiessner, who spent three months living with the Kalahari in northwest Botswana and recording their conversations, says that "appetites" for fire-lit settings remain with us to this day.

The public's appetite for story is what makes some people very, very rich. More than 2,500 years ago a rhetorician named Gorgias learned that great storytellers can inspire audiences. He traveled around ancient Greece teaching rhetoric, specifically arguing that adding emotional stories in one's speeches can "stop fear and banish grief and create joy and nurture piety."

Gorgias helped people craft stronger arguments, which won him many admirers. He became one of the wealthiest citizens of Greece on the strength of his storytelling. Telling great stories still makes people wealthy, especially entrepreneurs with an idea to sell.

The Tools Have Changed

Back on Necker Island, Richard Branson has a smile on his face as he listens to entrepreneurs leverage the power of story to make him laugh, make him think, and inspire him to invest in their idea. The stories give Branson a new way of looking at the world and ultimately spark his imagination that world-changing innovations are not only possible in his lifetime, but that Branson himself can play a role in their development. Branson so loves storytelling around a campfire that he commissioned a local artist to build a beautiful hand-carved metal sphere to hold a giant fireball.

The firelight talk might have started 400,000 years ago, but our brains are still wired for story today. Of course, the stakes have changed. Instead of hunting for food the entrepreneurs pitching Richard Branson are looking for cash. And the tools have changed, too. PowerPoint has replaced drawing pictures on a cave wall. But one thing hasn't changed, and it's our desire—a craving—to hear captivating stories. Those who have mastered the skill of storytelling can have an outsized influence over others. According to Princeton University neuroscientist Uri Hasson, a person who tells compelling stories can actually plant ideas, thoughts, and emotions into a listener's brain. The art of storytelling is your most powerful weapon in the war of ideas.

On Necker, in the 10 minutes that each entrepreneur is given to articulate the vision behind their idea or product, they must grab Branson's attention, convince him that the idea has the potential to positively impact the world, and inspire him to make a substantial financial commitment to the company. Most people who are given 10 minutes to pitch their idea mistakenly assume that potential investors want to hear all about the financials, the numbers, and the data. They are only partly right. These entrepreneurs are neglecting the core findings of neuroscience: Emotion trumps logic. You cannot reach a person's head without first touching their heart and the path to the heart runs through the brain, starting with the amygdala.

The Amygdala: A Storyteller's Best Friend

For many years medical researchers believed that people could only get addicted to drugs and alcohol. Then, neuroimaging technologies emerged that allowed researchers to see blood flow in the brain revealing that humans are also addicted to activities like sex, gambling, food, and shopping. Some activities hijack the brain just as powerful drugs do. Drugs like heroin produce an especially powerful surge of dopamine—one so intense that a single hit can hook a person for life. Scientists are finding that the very same reward centers in the brain are also involved in persuasion, motivation, and memory. These findings have profound implications for your success.

For example, researchers now know that a thought can elicit a "somatic state," meaning the thought triggers the same regions of the brain that would be activated if you were actually experiencing the event in real life. Let's say you win $20 million in a lottery. You'd be euphoric because your brain's amygdala—an almond-shaped mass of nuclei in your frontal lobe—would release a rush of the neurotransmitter dopamine, the pleasure chemical. Now close your eyes and imagine yourself winning the lottery. Picture the sights, sounds, and feelings around the event. Who's with you when you learn the news? What is their facial expression like? What are all of the things you can now do with the money? You might not realize it, but your mouth will gently curl up into a smile. You're getting a small shot of dopamine that's making you feel good because you are activating the same regions of your brain that would be triggered if you had actually won. That's the power of the amygdala. A great story releases a rush of chemicals like cortisol, oxytocin, and dopamine.

Thanks to neuroscience we've learned more about storytelling in the last 10 years than we've known since humans began painting pictures on cave walls. We now know which brain chemicals make us pay attention to a speaker (cortisol) and which make us feel empathy toward another person (oxytocin). We also know what triggers those neurochemicals. We know what stories work, why they work, and we can prove it scientifically.

Addiction to story isn't a bad thing. If inspiring storytellers didn't exist the world would be a far different place, and not for the better. For example, in a series of six speeches in 1940, British prime minister Winston Churchill succeeded in completely turning around public opinion in World

War II. A nation that had resigned itself to appeasing Nazi Germany just 14 days earlier had decided to take up the sword and fight to the end after listening to Churchill's powerful argument. Although Germany had conquered large parts of Western Europe, Churchill masterfully painted a picture of the British successfully defeating Hitler's army. "What is our aim?" Churchill asked rhetorically. "Victory. Victory at all costs, victory in spite of all terror, victory, however long and hard the road may be; for without victory there is no survival." Through the storyteller's gift, Churchill radically altered the destiny of an entire civilization. Interestingly, Churchill wasn't born with the storyteller's gift. Like mastering any art, he had to work on it. Churchill had stage fright early in his political career. So did Richard Branson, and the famous pastor Joel Osteen. Billionaires Barbara Corcoran and Warren Buffett had a fear of public speaking, too. Great storytellers look effortless because they put a lot of effort into being great.

History's most inspiring leaders were storytellers: Jesus, John F. Kennedy, Martin Luther King Jr., Ronald Reagan, Nelson Mandela, Henry Ford, and Steve Jobs. Many of today's most inspiring entrepreneurs and leaders are also storytellers: Richard Branson, Bill Gates, Mark Burnett, and Sheryl Sandberg. Many of the storytellers featured in this book changed the course of history. Some are business heroes. Some inspired movements. Above all, they are all dream makers. They reach for the stars and inspire the rest of us to create our own moonshots. This book is about the visionaries and risk-takers who have mastered the art of telling stories and who inspire us to live better lives. Some make us laugh. Some make us think. Some make us change. Through artfully telling stories that inform and challenge, they build companies, drive the world forward, and make us feel like we, too, can achieve the impossible.

We're All Storytellers

Storytelling is the fundamental building block of communication. In a world where people are bombarded by choices, the story is often the deciding factor in whom we decide to do business with. We're all storytellers. We tell stories to sell our ideas. We tell stories to persuade investors to back a product. We tell stories to educate students. We tell stories to motivate teams. We tell stories to convince donors to write a check. We tell stories to encourage our children to reach their full potential. Learn to tell a story and your life and the lives of those you touch will be radically transformed.

The Storyteller's Secret features more than 50 storytellers who have changed the world or impacted business thanks in large part to mastering the art and science of storytelling. Each storyteller falls into one of five categories intended to inspire you to think differently about your own narrative, and how you can build storytelling into your everyday communication:

- Storytellers Who Ignite Our Inner Fire
- Storytellers Who Educate
- Storytellers Who Simplify
- Storytellers Who Motivate
- Storytellers Who Launch Movements

Each chapter is divided into three sections. First you'll learn about the storyteller's own story. Most of the men and women profiled in this book were at one time common people who used storytelling to achieve uncommon results. The second section of each chapter examines the storyteller's tools in more detail, why they work and how you can apply them. Finally, each chapter concludes with a short summary of the lesson learned—the storyteller's secret.

Once you learn the storytellers' secrets and why they work, you can apply the techniques to almost any type of communication: public speaking, PowerPoint presentations, blogs, e-mail, advertising and marketing, or simply pitching an idea over coffee at Starbucks. You will learn to frame an idea to inform, illuminate, and inspire.

In the next 10 years the ability to tell your story persuasively will be decisive—the single greatest skill—in helping you accomplish your dreams. Since the next decade marks the greatest promise civilization has ever known, the story you tell yourself and the story you share with others will unlock your potential and, quite possibly, change the world. Isn't it time you shared yours?

PART I

Storytellers Who Ignite Our Inner Fire

1

What Makes Your Heart Sing?

People with passion can change the world for the better.

—Steve Jobs

As the sun was setting over the Hudson River on a brisk October day two men stood on the terrace of a luxury apartment overlooking New York's Central Park. One man, a rebellious 26-year-old, dressed in a mock turtleneck and blue jeans, stared at his running shoes for a long time without saying a word. Then, as quickly as a light switch moves from off to on, he turned to the man by his side—a successful corporate executive who was one month shy of his forty-fifth birthday—and delivered the words that would transform the careers of both men and change the business world forever.

On the balcony of the San Remo apartment building in March 1983, Steve Jobs turned to John Sculley and challenged him with a simple but devastating question: "Do you want to sell sugar water for the rest of your life or do you want to come with me and change the world?"

Sculley had just turned down Jobs's offer to run Apple, saying that he intended to remain in his position at PepsiCo. Jobs's question, however, forced him to do some serious soul-searching. "I just gulped because I knew I would wonder for the rest of my life what I would have missed," Sculley recalls of the question that landed like a "punch to the gut."

The punch to the gut. The "wow moment." The "aha" moment. Whatever you choose to call it, radical transformation can happen in an instant. But an idea can only catch on if the person with the idea can persuade others to take action. Otherwise, ideas are simply neurons firing off in a person's brain. The greatest waste is an unfulfilled idea that fails to connect with audiences, not because it's a bad idea, but because it's not packaged in a way that moves people.

This is a book about ideas that *did* capture our imagination and change the world. It's about dream makers, visionaries, and risk-takers who mastered the art of storytelling to bring those ideas to life. Steve Jobs was undeniably the greatest business storyteller of our time.

On the apartment balcony back in 1983 Sculley had witnessed the famous Steve Jobs "reality distortion field," a phrase coined to describe Jobs's mix of charisma and his ability to convince people that they could accomplish the impossible. Upon hearing the news of Jobs's passing in October 2011, Sculley said, "Steve Jobs was intensely passionate at making an important difference in the lives of his fellow humans while he was on this planet. He never was into money or measured his life through owning stuff. . . . A world leader is dead, but the lessons his leadership taught us live on."[1]

Jobs's lessons do live on in the careers of former colleagues such as Apple chief designer Jony Ive, Apple CEO Tim Cook, Nest Labs founder Tony Fadell, or Disney's chief of animation John Lasseter. Jobs inspired them to communicate differently, to sell their ideas in a way that captured the public's imagination. Jobs revolutionized computer design, of course, but he was also a persuasive storyteller. Every public presentation that Steve Jobs gave resembled a Broadway play and had all the classic components of a great narrative: sets and surprises, heroes and villains. Nearly every major technology leader—and darn near every young entrepreneur—now tries to create "Steve Jobs–like" presentations. While anyone can copy the minimalist design of a Steve Jobs keynote presentation, it won't get them very far until and unless they learn the real secret to Steve Jobs's gift as a storyteller. And that gift wasn't on a slide. It was in his heart.

The Storyteller's Tools

In March 2011 the visionary who made "one more thing" a signature catchphrase took the stage one last time to reveal Apple's secret sauce. Steve Jobs, thin and weak from the cancer that would take his life a few months later, made an unexpected appearance to introduce a new product, the iPad 2. Few people in the audience expected Jobs to make an appearance because he was on his third medical leave. "We've been working on this product for a while and I didn't want to miss it," he told the cheering crowd. Jobs closed the presentation with this observation:

> It's technology married with liberal arts, married with the humanities, that yields us the result that makes our heart sing.

In one sentence Steve Jobs captured the essence of what made him an inspiring storyteller. As it turns out Sculley had nailed it, too, when he said that Jobs was passionate about making a difference. Passion is everything and Jobs had plenty of it.

Since he cofounded Apple in 1976 with his friend Steve Wozniak, Jobs combined passion, logic, and emotion to make a profoundly meaningful connection with his audiences. Jobs's ability to inspire a crowd is legendary. After interviewing Jobs's colleagues, presentation designers, and the people who knew him best for my book, *The Presentation Secrets of Steve Jobs,* I discovered that Jobs's secret to captivating an audience was not in the slide design, though the designs were beautiful. Many leaders now try to mimic Steve Jobs's presentation style (current Apple executives use the same design template for major product launches). Jobs captivated our imaginations because he had a wild and wondrous appreciation for how technology could change the world and he had the courage to express it.

Your story begins with your passion. You cannot inspire unless you're inspired yourself. Passion is a puzzle. Most people know it when they see it, but they have a hard time discovering it for themselves. Steve Jobs discovered it by asking, *"What makes my heart sing?"* The answer to the question: *What makes my heart sing?* is a lot different than the answer to the question: *What do I do?* Steve Jobs made computers; building tools to help people unleash their creativity made his heart sing.

The question of what makes one's heart sing goes to the core of Apple's DNA. Apple CEO Tim Cook repeats a version of the phrase in his keynotes and product launches. Cook once asked, "What do our hearts beat for?" On another occasion, the launch of a new iPad Air in October 2014, Cook was talking about the product's high customer satisfaction scores. "This is what makes our hearts sing," he said.

Steve Jobs wore passion on this sleeve. In 1997 Steve Jobs returned to the company he had cofounded after being fired 12 years earlier. Jobs held a staff meeting where he talked about the role passion would play in revitalizing the brand.

> Marketing is about values. This is a very complicated world. It's a very noisy world and we're not going to get a chance to get people to remember much about us. No company is. And so we need to be really clear on what we want them to know about us. Our customers want to know who is Apple and what is it that we stand for. What we're about isn't making boxes for people to get their jobs done, although we do that well . . . But Apple is about something more than that. Apple's core value is that we believe that people with passion can change the world for the better.[2]

On June 12, 2005, Steve Jobs gave one of the greatest college commencement speeches in history. Jobs delivered the 2,250-word speech in 15 minutes. Steve Jobs, the storyteller, crafted the speech as a three-part narrative supporting one central theme: Do what you love. "Have the courage to follow your heart and intuition. They somehow already know what you truly want to become," Jobs told the graduates.

The profoundly moving speech garnered well over 20 million views on YouTube. Apple employees say Steve Jobs's passion continues to live in Apple's DNA and they mean it, literally. When Apple released a new version of its operating system, OS X, they secretly hid a gift, knowing that someone would discover it. Embedded in the Mac's word processing application—Pages—is the entire text of Jobs's commencement speech. Passion is contagious. Passion is irresistible. Passion fuels the inner fire.

Ask Yourself, *What Makes My Heart Sing?*

Your passion is not a passing interest or even a hobby, but something that is intensely meaningful and core to your identity. For example, I play golf as a hobby. While I like the game—love it, actually—it is not core to who I am. It is, however, core to international PGA golf superstar Rory McIlroy. Asked to describe his love for the game McIlroy once said, "It's what I think about when I get up in the morning. It's what I think about when I go to bed." For McIlroy, golf isn't just a passing interest; it's the verse that makes his heart sing.

I was invited to deliver a keynote speech at the prestigious LeWeb conference in Paris, a gathering of the world's most passionate entrepreneurs for several days of sharing information on technology, innovation, and entrepreneurship. Backstage I met Ferran Adrià, the visionary chef who created the world's most famous restaurant, El Bulli.

"What is the one quality that all successful entrepreneurs share?" I asked Adrià.

"That's impossible to answer," he responded. "There are so many paths to success."

Adrià turned away and I figured it signaled the end of our conversation. Adrià then turned to me and said, "I take it back. There is *one* thing that all successful entrepreneurs have in common, and that's passion."

"How do you know it when you find it?" I asked.

"Let's put it this way. When you see a glass of wine, what do you think of?"

"A drink," I said.

"Exactly. You see a beverage. I see a vineyard. I see an ingredient. I see joy. I see family. I see friends. I see celebration."

I enjoy wine, but for Adrià it makes his heart sing in celebration.

Several years ago I interviewed Chris Gardner, the man portrayed by actor Will Smith in the movie, *The Pursuit of Happyness.* Gardner recounted his story of being homeless, spending nights in the bathroom of a subway station along with his two-year-old son. In the daytime Gardner would put on his one suit, drop off his kid at day care and take unpaid classes to become a stockbroker. You can guess how the story ends. Gardner rose to the top of his firm and became a multimillionaire.

When I worked in San Francisco, I would take the BART train and pass the very subway station where Gardner and his son slept at night. I would look around at the faces of the people seated near me. Very few seemed happy. They were staring at cell phones with frowns on their faces or looking out the windows with glazed expressions of longing. The spark in their eyes had gone out. Somewhere along the way they had lost sight of their passion. I wondered: *How it is possible for a homeless guy sleeping in the subway bathroom to have more excitement for life than those who had a job and rode the subway to work?* I asked Gardner that very question. His answer changed my life.

Gardner said, "The secret to success is to find something you love to do so much, you can't wait for the sun to rise to do it all over again."[3]

Gardner rose from the depths of poverty precisely because he listened to the verse that made his heart sing.

If you have yet to find your passion, ask yourself a better question. Don't ask, *What do I want to do?* Ask yourself, *What makes my heart sing?* Both questions will lead to very different answers.

Before you learn the craft of storytelling and master the specific techniques that will help you inspire the world with your ideas, you must get really clear on what you want people to know about you. Begin the process by asking yourself the right questions. For example, I met with the startup team behind a healthcare company that enjoyed the backing of some of Silicon Valley's largest venture capital firms. The company had developed a blood test to detect cancer. I asked the CEO a series of four questions intended to elicit an emotional response and lead to a message the company could use to tell its story to its key audiences (investors, medical professionals, and the media). Note how each question gets progressively more emotional and triggers a very different response:

1. Why did you start a company? *"To impact patients' lives."*
2. What does your company do? *"We've developed a tool that allows us to fight cancer with a simple blood test."*
3. What are you passionate about? *"Patient care. Every week we see patients matched with therapies that can save their lives."*
4. What makes your heart sing? *"We were working with an oncologist who told us about a patient they had diagnosed with pancreatic cancer. It had spread everywhere. The patient was told she had two months to live. There was no hope. Her oncologist knew about our blood test and decided to give it a try. The test results had successfully found the mutation of the patient's cancer. The mutations were inconsistent with pancreatic cancer. The patient had ovarian cancer. Her oncologist changed the treatment. In twelve weeks she had no detectable cancer. These stories keep me burning the midnight oil and working through the night."*

Reflect on what had happened in the previous conversation. The first three questions elicited factual responses. The fourth question—what makes your heart sing—triggered a story. Facts alone don't inspire. The heart of your story gives facts their soul. Fact-filled PowerPoint presentations do not win hearts and minds; stories do. Well-designed slides complement the story, but the story must come first.

Disney animation chief John Lasseter, who said he owes his career to Steve Jobs, once said that in developing a story, the plot can change dramatically: the characters can come and go, as can the setting. What you can't change is the heart of the story because it lays the foundation for everything else.

A famed venture capitalist once told me that he listens to a pitch as he would a song. He asks himself, *Will its verses click with consumers? Will its emotional hook inspire people to join the hero's journey?* The investor is looking for an emotional connection. He's listening for a pulse, a passion. The first step to telling an inspiring story is to discover your verse, the track that makes your heart sing.

The Storyteller's Secret

Inspiring storytellers are inspired themselves. They are very clear on their motivation, on the passion that drives them, and they enthusiastically share that passion with their audiences. Ask yourself, *What makes my heart sing?* The answer is the foundation upon which all great stories are built.

2

From T-Shirt Salesman to Mega Producer

Life isn't about finding yourself. Life is about creating yourself.
—George Bernard Shaw

Mark had plenty of time to think about his story on the 5,000-mile flight from London's Heathrow Airport to Los Angeles International. He had no job, no place to live, and only a few hundred bucks to his name. On paper Mark didn't have a compelling resume. Although he had served in the British military, Mark was 22 years old and had not gone to college. How could he possibly achieve success in a new country he had never even visited? On the flight Mark decided to write his own story and get really, really good at telling it. While he wasn't American, Mark had two personality traits that would help him achieve the American Dream: optimism and self-confidence.

Mark landed in Los Angeles on October 18, 1982, a working-class kid from London's East End with "no return ticket." Mark's friend, Nick, met him at the airport and brought good news: A wealthy Beverly Hills family was looking for a nanny. Mark interviewed with the family that night. They were initially uncomfortable about his experience, or lack thereof. Male nannies were unusual in Los Angeles and Mark didn't strike them as someone who would excel at domestic chores. But then he delivered a pitch they couldn't resist. Using the effective narrative technique of analogy he told the couple that having a former British paratrooper in the house was guaranteed security, "like hiring a nanny and a bodyguard at the same time."

Mark's performance earned him a job within 24 hours of landing in America. The very first job television producer Mark Burnett performed in America was unloading a dishwasher, a device he had never seen until that day.

In his two years as a nanny Burnett studied the habits of the wealthy and learned a valuable lesson about success, one that would catapult him to the top of the television industry. Burnett came to realize that the story of his life was a blank slate and that he was the author, the one ultimately in charge of crafting the narrative. Second, he learned that he had a storyteller's gift for selling his ideas. And he took that gift to the beach.

Burnett's first business plan—if he had written one—would have fit on a napkin: Buy T-shirts for $2 and sell them for $18. Since he didn't have the money to rent a booth, he rented a fence, and since he couldn't afford the entire fence, he settled for a 10-foot section of it.

Although Burnett had never worked as a salesperson, never attended a sales seminar, nor read a book on sales, he excelled at sales because he knew the storyteller's secret. "Customers buy from people they are comfortable with, people they consider their friends,"[1] Burnett said. And friends don't "sell." They tell stories.

Burnett learned to tell the story behind his shirts and to shape the narrative to match the wide range of personalities who visited the Southern California beachfront town of Venice. He learned that facts and data persuaded "analytical" customers (e.g., engineers, doctors, scientists). "They want to know how the shirt was made and whether the stitching will last. My delivery was no-nonsense, to the point," Burnett writes. He discovered that "emotional customers" were less likely to be moved by fact and more likely to make decisions after feeling the fabric and enjoying the color assortments. Burnett would share the stories of where the shirts were made, who made the shirts, and the craftsmanship that went into their design. "In theater, this would be called playing to the audience," he said. On that sidewalk Burnett learned to read an audience and craft a narrative that would appeal to the way their brain worked.

Burnett spent two years pitching T-shirts to thousands of people from all walks of life and from every part of the world. He was so good at selling he essentially paid off the $1,500 monthly rent in one day of sales each month. Burnett saved much of the rest of his income and parlayed the cash into lucrative real estate deals. Within eight years of landing in America Burnett had made his first million.

In 1998 Burnett bought the North American rights to a British team competition called *Survivor*. He thought it might find an audience in America. As a former British paratrooper Burnett was passionate about extreme sports, and he knew that confining a group of people in challenging circumstances brings out heroes and villains, the building blocks of classic stories. But before Burnett could bring it to television, he would need a network to carry it and that meant he would have to use his storytelling skills to convince network executives to buy into it.

At its core, *Survivor* is a reality TV show where a group of individuals are isolated in a remote location and compete in challenges for a $1 million prize. That's the simple pitch. But as you'll recall there's a difference between a story, a good story, and an irresistible story. Burnett always pitched it as a drama, not a game show. "When I traveled for business I would look about the plane at my fellow passengers and imagine us crash-landing on an island. Where would I fit in into our new society? Who would lead and who would follow? Who would find the ordeal overwhelming?"[2] Burnett recalls. Contestants were "castaways" who were grouped into "tribes" and banished from the island one by one in a "tribal council."

"My best skills have always been telling stories and pitching ideas," Burnett acknowledged in his biography, *Jump In!* "All success begins with the ability to sell something, whether it's a shirt or an idea." Burnett was good at storytelling, but storytelling takes practice and even the most gifted communicators don't get it right the first time. Burnett relentlessly worked on his pitch, using his friends as an audience. He recalled, "At first the pitch came out long-winded and overcomplicated. My dinner companions would lean back in their chairs, heads nodding vacantly as if listening, even as their eyes glazed over and their thoughts wandered."[3] Burnett recognized the "eyes glazed over" look from his days selling T-shirts on Venice Beach. As he simplified the story, the glazed looks turned to excitement. "As I perfected the pitch, however, making it faster and more fluid and always exciting, I noticed my dinner companions leaning in to hear each syllable. Their eyes sparkled. They peppered me with questions all of which I learned to answer with the same polish I used to deliver the pitch itself."

The pitch didn't always work. Discovery Channel turned it down. An executive at USA Network rejected it in thirty seconds. CBS, which ultimately bought the show, turned it down the first time. When it comes to pitching ideas, Burnett believes that a "no" simply means one person doesn't buy into your vision at that moment. Someone else might, but you must learn from the "no" and refine the story for maximum impact so when the opportunity presents itself, you can deliver the pitch of a lifetime.

For Burnett the opportunity arrived when the head of the drama division at CBS liked what he heard and took the idea to the president of CBS. Les Moonves had earned a reputation as one of the toughest executives in television, and he wanted to hear Burnett's pitch in person. "Confidently, my skills polished at all those dinner parties and previous pitches, I walked into Leslie's enormous office and delivered the pitch of my life,"[4] Burnett recalls. Burnett began his pitch by handing Moonves a mock copy of *Newsweek* magazine with *Survivor* on the cover. "Be bold and exude confidence no matter how nervous you may be," Burnett advises as he thinks back to the meeting. The pitch worked and Moonves approved a budget large enough to pay for 39 days of filming on the island of Pulau Tiga in the South China Sea. *Survivor* dominated the ratings and became the number one reality television series of all time.

I caught up with Burnett in February 2014, while another one of his shows was making television history—*The Voice*. If success leaves clues, then it pays to note that every storyteller featured in this book, including Burnett, is an optimist. And they're not merely "glass half full, look on the bright side of things," sort of optimists. They have an unshakable belief in their ability to achieve the impossible. The language they use reveals their intentions. Where most people have "goals," inspiring storytellers see moonshots and they don't let anyone get in their way. Above all, they believe in their ideas and are willing to pay the price to make those dreams a reality. They trust their "gut," their "intuition," their "heart," or, in Burnett's case, the "calling." "In the end you are never going to be certain that you are on the right path,"[5] Burnett says. "You just have to listen to the call and trust that it will all work out. The path isn't clearly laid out. You'll be guided, but if you don't start walking, you won't get anywhere. Start walking, even if you don't know where the path will lead."

The Storyteller's Tools

PayPal founder Peter Thiel would categorize Burnett as a "definite optimist," someone who sees the future as better than the present and works to make it happen. According to Thiel in *Zero to One*, definite optimists are the inventors and visionaries who move their generations forward. They are the ones who, despite current circumstances like economic downturns or uncertainty, make bold plans and make the world richer and healthier.

Relentless optimism is a quality that Burnett has in abundance. Not all optimists are storytellers, but nearly all inspiring storytellers are optimistic. They have what Solomon Snyder calls "The Audacity Principle." Snyder is the director of neuroscience at Johns Hopkins School of Medicine. He has spent more than 40 years identifying the traits of scientists who have made the greatest breakthroughs. While original ideas and creative thinking are the building blocks of scientific achievements, Snyder found that those scientists who change the world have one quality that separates them from their intellectual peers: audacity. Snyder defines audacity as a go-for-it attitude, the conviction and self-confidence to pursue an idea and articulate that idea "even though the world punches you in the nose."[6]

Burnett was punched in the nose plenty of times. No matter how many hit shows he had under his belt, every new pitch was met with a chorus of skepticism. The critics and naysayers would come out in force to tell him why his idea would never find an audience. *Survivor* wasn't expected to survive. And neither was *The Apprentice, Shark Tank,* or *The Voice.*

Burnett told me that he and his wife, Roma Downey, met their harshest skeptics when they produced the biblical cable series *The Bible.* "A huge number of people told me not to do it,"[7] he recalls. "It was a daunting project. There were many reasons why we could have avoided it: too difficult, too expensive, and too enormous. What they failed to realize is, it's not a business for us. It was a calling." *The Bible* was shown on History channel in March 2013 and attracted more than 100 million viewers.

Inspiring storytellers like Burnett don't play it small. They dream in moonshots and have the courage, the conviction, and the confidence to share their ideas, even if they get punched in the nose from time to time.

The Storyteller's Secret

Successful storytellers believe in the strength of their ideas. They know those ideas won't sell themselves, and so they work tirelessly at crafting and delivering an engaging story. If they get rejected they don't give up on their idea, but they learn from it. They see "no" as an opportunity to turn the next pitch into a "yes."

3

Conquering Stage Fright to Sell Out
Yankee Stadium

If a man can write a better book or preach a better sermon the world
will make a path to his door.

—Ralph Waldo Emerson

Joel never thought he'd be comfortable speaking to an audience. His father had started a church in an abandoned feedstore on Houston's north side. After college Joel returned to his father's church to help support the ministry. Joel preferred to stay in the background and, for the next 17 years, he sat behind the camera, recording and editing his father's sermons for television.

Joel's father, who thought his son might have a gift that he was neglecting, tried hard to persuade him to preach just one sermon. But every time he brought it up, Joel would politely decline—again and again and again. He was an introvert and preferred to stay out of the spotlight. The truth was that Joel dreaded speaking in front of an audience and could barely contain his shaking hands when delivering church announcements. On those occasions when Joel faced the audience, for a brief moment he would experience the classic symptoms of stage fright—sweaty palms, racing heart, fast breathing.

But his father continued to encourage him, and finally, on January 17, 1999, Joel gave in. Joel couldn't explain why he decided to preach that week; he simply felt a calling. For a while he thought the caller had reached the wrong number; he was a nervous wreck. "My personality is quiet and reserved. My dad was always the person on the stage. I just didn't think it was in me,"[1] Joel recalls. "When I told my dad I would minister I wasn't looking forward to it. I just did it to make him proud. I was nervous. I spoke too fast. All I remember was how nervous I was and how much I dreaded doing it. It was the worst week of my life!"

The week would get worse. His father was taken to a hospital with complications from dialysis. He would watch his son preach his first sermon from a hospital bed. John Osteen was at peace when he passed away five days later.

Two weeks later, with exactly one sermon under his belt, John's son, Joel Osteen, became the pastor of Houston's Lakewood Church. The church that started with 90 parishioners in the back of a feedstore had grown to 5,000 attendees at the time of John Osteen's death. Today it is the largest church in America with 50,000 people attending services each week in Houston's former Compaq Center. More than 10 million viewers watch Osteen's sermons each week in the United States and millions more watch in the 100 countries where the program is broadcast.

Growing into a confident storyteller doesn't happen with the flip of a switch. Osteen preached every week for two years before he began to feel comfortable in his preacher's shoes. The early days were tough: He once overheard two congregants say, "He'll never be as good as his father." It was hard to shake the feeling that he couldn't possibly fill his father's shoes. If words are like seeds, Osteen was planting the wrong ones for the new season in his life. Osteen dwelled on those words, allowing them to take root. He replayed the negative labels over and over in his mind: *You're not good enough. You don't have what it takes. Those women are right; you'll never be as good as your father.*

He was certainly motivated to improve: he began a practice that he keeps to this day: writing his own sermons and rehearsing each one for six hours before delivering it to a live audience. Practice helped Osteen refine his words and delivery, but he still had to change his internal dialogue. He had to reframe the most important story of all—the one he told himself.

Osteen decided to replace the internal negative dialogue with words that would empower him to reach his full potential. He changed the channel playing in his mind's eye. Instead of watching reruns of *I'm Not Good Enough*, he became a loyal viewer of *I Can Do Anything*. Every morning Osteen told himself, *I am strong. I am confident. I am coming into the fullness of my destiny. I am a victor and not a victim.* That, combined with his rigorous approach to each sermon, made all the difference, and once Osteen hit his stride he was unstoppable, inspiring millions in jam-packed stadiums around the world. "Today," he says, "when I walk on stage I feel humbled and rewarded that so many people came out. I now tell myself that I'll give it my best and hopefully move some people in a positive direction."[2]

Just 10 years after the young man with stage fright took to the pulpit, Osteen sold out Yankee Stadium in the first non-baseball event at the new ballpark (he reportedly beat out the Rolling Stones for the inaugural event). "What I thought would be my darkest hour launched me into my brightest hour. I was too comfortable behind the scenes. Sometimes adversity pushes you into your divine destiny,"[3] Osteen told me as he reflected back on his first weeks as a pastor.

It's natural to be stung by criticism. Joel Osteen was hurt when he overheard people suggesting that he wasn't as good a speaker as his father. Osteen may not have realized it at the time, but reframing his internal dialogue reinforced one of the most powerful theories in psychology, self-efficacy.

The Storyteller's Tools

In 1925 the Alberta town of Mundare had a population of 400 people. It's not that much bigger today, having grown to 800 residents. One hundred years ago an immigrant from Eastern Europe was one of the men who helped to lay the tracks for what became known as the Canadian transcontinental railroad. He also cut down trees to build his own home, tearing out the roots with his own hands. He moved boulders with no heavy machinery, just the help of two horses. He built the road to get to his home and helped construct the town's only church and school. The man's wife ran the delivery service in town, taking the supplies that came in on the train and bringing them to the town's residents.

The industrious parents never received public recognition as among Canada's most notable citizens, but their son did. Albert Bandura, the son of a Ukrainian mother and a Polish father with no formal education, would become one of the world's most influential psychologists.

Bandura attended the school his father helped build, the only school in town, with two teachers who taught all the grades, 1 through 12. "Ordinarily these conditions would be viewed as a severe educational handicap,"[4] Bandura explained. "For me, it enabled me to learn to take responsibility for my own educational development. The content of these courses is perishable, but the acquisition of self-directedness has served me very well. In a way my psychology theory is founded on human agency, which means people have a hand in determining the course that their lives take. In many respects my theory is really a reflection of my life path."

In 1977 Bandura published a study that changed the way we view success and motivation. The paper, "Self-efficacy: Toward a Unifying Theory of Behavioral Change," identified a key difference between those people who accomplish their goals and those who fail. The successful people believed in their ability to accomplish a goal. "People with high assurance in their capabilities approach difficult tasks as challenges to be mastered rather than as threats to be avoided,"[5] says Bandura. In other words, if you believe you can do something with every ounce of your being, you are more likely to achieve it.

A person with high self-efficacy believes they can reach their goal and they take the steps required to make it happen. They work harder. They raise their hands more. They ask questions. They practice, get it wrong, and try it again. People with low self-efficacy don't need others to tear themselves down. They do it themselves. They quickly lose confidence. They avoid risk and challenges because, after all, they won't succeed anyway (or so they think). They are much more likely to give up when they hear negative comments.

The good news on self-efficacy, as we've seen in Joel Osteen's case, is that it's not fixed. Osteen started with low self-efficacy ("You're not good enough. You don't have what it takes."), then shifted to high self-efficacy ("I am strong. I am confident."). Instead of tearing himself down, he began to expect a positive outcome, an essential ingredient in Bandura's success formula.

It helps to have someone in your corner. According to Bandura, "People who are socially persuaded that they possess the capabilities to master difficult situations" are likely to put in greater effort. Osteen's champion was his wife, Victoria. Year after year Victoria would encourage Joel to step up. He believes that one of the main reasons he was able to rise to the occasion so quickly was the fact that Victoria believed in him, and she had helped instill that confidence in himself.

Joel Osteen is, above all, a storyteller. He shares stories that plant seeds of hope. Osteen found that the most relatable stories were the ones he told about his own personal transformation. In the following excerpt from one of his sermons Osteen tells the story of how his wife gave him the confidence to take the stage: "One of the first things I did was to cancel my dad's national television broadcast. I thought, *I'm not going to get on television. I don't know how to minister. Nobody's going to listen to me.* I'd told Victoria what I had done and she said, 'Joel you've got to call that man and get the airtime back. People are going to be watching all over the world.' She talked me into keeping that airtime."[6]

In the next section of the sermon Osteen uses his personal story to reinforce the sermon's title, "It's Too Small." In this paragraph he also relies on a powerful rhetorical device called mesodiplosis, the repetition of a word or phrase in the middle of every clause: "I never dreamed the church would grow. There were 6,000 people coming at that time. I thought if we could just maintain what my parents had built, that would be big. But God's big is much different than our big. My big was to maintain; God's big was to multiply. My big was to hold on; God's big was to propel forward. Our big is to pay our bills; God's big is to be debt free and have plenty left over. Our big is to get that promotion; God's big is to own your own company."

After connecting his personal story to his sermon's broader theme and applying it to the lives of his listeners, Osteen concludes by returning to his story: "When my father went to be with the Lord we had an 8,000 seat auditorium. It was a big church even then, but God said that's too small. I have a Compaq center in store. I've got Yankee stadiums to fill up. I've got books to publish. I've got world leaders to meet. All through my life, just when I thought I'd reach my limits, God said, 'That's good, but it's too small.'"

I came across an academic paper written by a graduate student in communication who had studied Osteen's approach. The student wrote that he was originally "perplexed" by Osteen's popularity because the message sounded "too good to be true." After he began reading Osteen's books and watching his sermons, however, he began to feel a sense of calm. The "analytic" side of his brain gave way to a more "emotive response." The graduate student found that he began to let go of the anger and frustration he was feeling at that moment in his life. He began to get a better night's sleep. He faced the world with a renewed sense of confidence and hope, a "lingering feeling that tomorrow would be a better day." The graduate student who set out to explain Osteen's impact on people became transfixed himself.

Unintentionally, the student made a compelling case for the power of story. The student also didn't realize that the storyteller he chose to examine would never have reached his high-profile position had he not reframed his internal dialogue years earlier.

The Story You Choose to Tell Yourself

The story you choose to tell yourself exerts a powerful influence over your ultimate ability to captivate people. Some beliefs limit your potential. If you believe you'll never get hired, you're probably right. If you believe you'll never find your dream job, you probably won't. If you believe that you don't have a story to share, you won't find one. And if you don't believe you'll ever master the art of public speaking, you'll probably be right.

I find that people who are nervous about speaking in public say awful things to themselves, words that they would never say to anyone else:

- *I'm terrible at giving presentations.*
- *I got nervous once and it ruined me. I'm a horrible public speaker.*
- *Nobody wants to listen to me. I'm boring.*

If these are the type of phrases you repeat to yourself day after day, it's no wonder you get nervous! You cannot control what other people say about you, but you can control the story playing on your internal channel. Osteen's confidence grew as he replaced the negative labels with words of encouragement, empowerment, and strength. "Wrong labels can keep you from your destiny," he says.

Academic researchers in the field of communication have found that it's nearly impossible to rid ourselves completely of the fear of public speaking. It's natural and ingrained from thousands of years of evolution where human beings needed to be accepted in social groups in order to survive. Our ancestors who didn't care about the impression they made on others were cast out of the tribe or village. That's not a good thing when a lion is lurking around the corner. It's perfectly acceptable, natural, and understandable to *want to be liked*. In fact, speakers who are not nervous at all are often poor communicators because they don't care about how they come across, nor do they care about improving their skills. Successful storytellers learn to *manage* their fear and not to eliminate it. Reframing your internal dialogue, the story you tell yourself, will help you manage and control your fear.

You have ideas that are meant to be shared, stories that are meant to be told. Too many people keep their ideas locked up because they have a fear of public speaking or a fear of being harshly judged for their ideas. The fear of speaking—the fear of speaking up—is one of the most common fears most of us share. The good news is you can overcome it and, as Joel Osteen has proven, do it in a big, big way.

The Storyteller's Secret

Inspiring storytellers are not always born; they're made. And they make themselves great by reframing the story they tell themselves.

4

A Rock Star Rediscovers His Gift in the
Backstory of His Youth

A great storyteller helps people figure out not only what matters in
the world, but also why it matters.

—Maria Popova

Gordon was born and raised "in the shadow of a shipyard in a little town on the northeast coast of England."[1] His earliest memories were of giant ships at the end of the street, blocking out the sun. Every morning the boy looked out his window as thousands of people went to work, doing the backbreaking labor of building giant vessels that would transport cargo, soldiers, or guests across the world's seas. Many famous ships were launched from the shipyard. The RMS *Carpathia* set sail in 1912 to rescue the survivors of *Titanic*. Ships were built for World War II, including the *Sheffield* and *Victorious,* which helped to sink the *Bismarck,* a Nazi German battleship.

"The shipyard was noisy, dangerous, highly toxic. Despite that, the men and women who worked on those ships were extraordinarily proud of the work they did, and justifiably so. Some of the largest vessels ever constructed on planet Earth were built right at the end of my street,"[2] Gordon recalls.

Gordon's father wanted his son to become a ship worker. His son had dreams of his own, though, dreams that took him far from the grimy port of his youth. He once saw the Queen Mother come to town to christen a finished ship. He and thousands of other kids stood on the side of the streets, waving the Union Jack, the national flag of the United Kingdom, as the royal family passed them in a Rolls-Royce. The event changed Gordon's life. He rewrote the ending of his father's narrative. Gordon decided that *he* would be the person in the car and that his life's work would take him as far away from Wallsend's shipyard as possible. He pictured an extraordinary life. He would meet kings and queens, presidents and prime ministers. Millions would know his name. He would travel to exotic places, and he would return home to his own castle.

Those childhood dreams came true for Gordon Sumner, who would later be known by his stage name, "Sting." Sting had successfully written his life's story, and the stories he told in his songs struck a chord with millions of fans. Sting is one of the world's bestselling artists. In 1977 Sting and his friends formed The Police, a New Wave group that sold more than 75 million albums, making them one of the bestselling bands of all time. The Police disbanded in 1986 and Sting enjoyed a successful solo career . . . until the day the songs stopped coming.

The Storyteller's Tools

Sting ran into writer's block. And not the ordinary kind of block when all it takes is a brisk walk to jump-start the creative process. No, this was chronic. "Day after day, you face a blank page, and nothing's coming. And those days turned to weeks, and weeks to months, and pretty soon those months have turned into years with very little to show for your efforts. No songs. So you start asking yourself questions. What have I done to offend the gods that they would abandon me so? Is the gift of songwriting taken away as easily as it seems to have been bestowed?"[3]

Sting found his missing muse in the stories of his youth.[4] He thought to himself, *Could it be argued that your best work wasn't about you at all, it was about somebody else? Did your best work occur when you sidestepped your own ego and you stopped telling your story, but told someone else's story, someone perhaps without a voice, where empathetically, you stood in his shoes for a while or saw the world through his eyes?*

Sting decided to write about what he knew. He returned to the dreary landscape of the shipyard, the place to which he had vowed he would never return. He told the stories of the people he knew, the stories of their anger, frustration, joys, hopes, and dreams. Sting's Broadway musical, *The Last Ship,* was set in Wallsend. And in that musical he told the story of Gideon Fletcher, who, like Sting, had dreams of a different future and fled town as a rebellious teenager. He told the story of Meg Dawson, a stunning redhead whom Gideon loved and returns to find that the years have changed her and the community. He told the story of the irreverent Father O'Brien, who has a foul mouth and likes to drink, but ultimately inspires the community. "One of the first things I wrote was just a list of names of people I'd known, and they become characters in a kind of three-dimensional drama, where they explain who they are, what they do, their hopes and their fears for the future,"[5] Sting said.

Sting had uncovered his backstory, the story of his origin, the narrative of his life that shaped his identity. Great songwriters are experts at backstory. If you don't know where the characters come from, you won't care where they're going.

The Gift of Your Past Creates a Vision for Your Future

Mary was my first love. I can still hear the screen door slam. I see Mary's dress sway as she dances across the porch. The radio in the background is playing a Roy Orbison song. She broke a lot of hearts, so many in fact, that "there were ghosts in the eyes" of all the boys she had sent away. They screamed Mary's name as they haunted "dusty beach roads in the skeleton frames of burned out Chevrolets." The interesting thing about Mary is that she wasn't a beauty, but hey, she was alright. Of course, I'm talking about Mary the character in what *Rolling Stone* magazine called one of the greatest songs ever written—Bruce Springsteen's "Thunder Road."

Springsteen was only 24 years old when he wrote some of the most enduring lyrics in rock history. The song had characters you wanted to root for, settings, and a backstory. Springsteen, a troubled adolescent who found solace in Roy Orbison songs, once said he wrote stories of the people he knew—the working-class people struggling to make ends meet in the dying factory town of Freehold, New Jersey.

There's something about song, struggle, and New Jersey. Another Jersey rocker, Jon Bon Jovi, is also an expert at backstory. He introduced us to Tommy and Gina. Tommy works on the docks. The union's on strike and Tommy is down on his luck. Gina works at the diner all day and dreams of running away. She cries at night, and when Tommy says, "We've got each other and that's a lot," a stadium full of people can't help but sing the refrain out loud, "Take my hand and we'll make it I swear, whoa-oh, livin' on a prayer." The backstory gives the audience a reason to care about Tommy and Gina. Tommy and Gina are no one, yet everyone can see themselves in their struggle and their quest for redemption.

Every one of us has a backstory. The gift of backstory often comes wrapped in the events or people who have shaped our lives.

A college communication professor once divided the class into groups of two students and asked them to tell a story to the other person, a story of a momentous event in their lives. He told me about a student who came up to him and said, "I don't have any momentous occasions in my life."

"Are you the same person today—as a college sophomore—as you were in the third grade?" he asked the student.

"No, of course not," she replied.

"Then something happened to you that made you grow, that forced you to look at the world differently. That event is your momentous occasion."

The student's face brightened as she began to reflect, perhaps for the first time, on the events and people that led to her personal transformation.

The gift of your past matters most when creating a vision or a culture to take you into the future.

I received a handwritten note one day from the founder and CEO of a fast-growing staffing company. In 12 years Bobby Herrera had built the Populus Group from scratch to $200 million in annual revenue. The letter began with this story:

> When I was 17, my brother and I were on a return trip from a basketball game. The team stopped for dinner and everyone left the bus, except my brother and I. We didn't have the means to have dinner with the rest of the team. We stayed back on the bus. A few minutes later one of the dads came on board. I remember the conversation like it happened yesterday. He said, "It would make me very happy if you would allow me to buy you dinner and join the rest of the team. No one else has to know. All you have to do to thank me is do the same thing for another great kid in the future." It stuck in my heart forever. When I reflect back on all the risks I've taken in my life and everything I've endured to make this company what it is, it's because of the gift I received that day. I've wanted nothing more than to create a vehicle where I can do the same thing for other kids who are just like me on that bus.[6]

That one act of kindness on the bus inspired the young man to build a company to "pay it forward." Today his company and its 3,000 employees and consultants are committed to making a difference in the lives of youth in the nine cities in which the company operates. The company's employees volunteer their time and commit their resources to help some 1,500 kids a year with new school supplies, catered events, and through partnerships with food banks and outreach organizations.

Herrera candidly shares his very personal story of the dad on the bus as a tool to teach his employees about the company culture he intends to create: one that rewards creativity, innovation, and an entrepreneurial spirit.

"A great culture helps to attract great people,"[7] he says. "Culture is to recruiting as service is to customers." Just as customers are attracted by uncommon service, amazing people are attracted by a great culture. Whether we plan it or not, culture will happen. Why not create the culture we want?

A company leader, by definition, sets the vision. But vision falls on deaf ears if not accompanied by a compelling backstory. For example, Herrera tells his employees that "Everyone deserves an opportunity to succeed. It's why we exist." If you didn't know the founder's backstory, the story of the dad on the bus, the cultural vision he espouses would sound like empty rhetoric. The backstory gives the vision its meaning. "Over time culture turns into an incredible competitive advantage that no one can take away from you," Herrera told me. "If your service is any good at all, people will try to duplicate it. But a great culture is practically impossible to duplicate unless you have the same great people."

Pay attention to your past. It holds the stories of where you've been and how you got to where you are. And sometimes, when you feel stuck, the stories of your past and the people you've met might move you forward. Just ask Sting.

The Storyteller's Secret

Inspiring storytellers are eager to share their backstory because it's a gift that shaped their life, career, and business.

5

Change Your Story, Change Your Life

Life has meaning only in the struggle.

—Stevie Wonder

A boy grows up poor, raised by a single mother who struggles with alcoholism and is prone to violence. He finds fame and fortune and becomes a millionaire in his twenties. The good times end and he goes broke. He is forced to live in a tiny studio apartment, washing his dishes in the bathtub. The man regains his fortune, and then some. Today he walks with royalty. For the princely retainer of $1 million a year, he advises kings and queens, presidents and prime ministers, celebrities and business leaders. He has traded that tiny apartment for a 300-acre resort on the north side of Fiji.

If you haven't guessed by now, the story's protagonist is motivational guru Tony Robbins. At six foot seven inches, Robbins is a big man with a big mission: He calls himself a "hunter of human happiness." He's also one of the most successful public speakers of our time. Robbins's TED talk has garnered more than 14 million views, making it one of the top 10 talks in TED history. He brings energy and passion to his herculean 50-hour seminars, which have been attended by a combined 4 million people. Another 50 million people have purchased his books and audios. At the age of 55, Robbins is a motivational powerhouse, but he wasn't born that way. It was a single conversation that set Robbins on his quest for success.

Robbins was writing a sports article for his high school yearbook when he got the opportunity to interview legendary sports anchor Howard Cosell. He asked Cosell what it takes to be a successful sports announcer. Cosell responded, "You have to learn to understand the art of communication, develop it in such a way that it will capture the attention of the greatest number of people."[1]

Robbins took the advice and acted on it. At the urging of a teacher, he ran for student body president. Few people gave him a chance to win, but one well-crafted speech to the student body propelled Robbins ahead of the competition. Robbins's high school classmate Julie Fellinger was there when Robbins took the podium. "He spoke from the heart,"[2] she recalls. "He told a personal story about himself, about his struggle growing up. It was very touching. It was very compelling. It was inspirational. He was elected student body president because of it." When Robbins was 11 years old, his family didn't have enough money to buy a Thanksgiving meal. A stranger knocked on the family's door and left groceries. Robbins never forgot the act of kindness and it influenced the charities he eventually started. More important to the topic of storytelling, Robbins soon realized that by sharing his personal pain, he could make a strong emotional connection with his listeners, many of whom at Los Angeles's Glendora High School in 1977 shared the same socioeconomic background.

In that moment Robbins learned a fundamental lesson that separates the superachievers from everyone else. People who have experienced pain, poverty, struggle, or despair—and many of the storytellers in this book have experienced it all—are only empowered by their experience when they've developed the courage to embrace their backstory, learn from their failures, and share their lessons of struggle with others.

The Storyteller's Tools

"I always say, change your story change your life, because whatever your story is will become the shaper of your life,"[3] Robbins says. The problem, Robbins believes, is that some people are addicted to reliving their story of pain until it becomes a mental prison, preventing them from fulfilling their potential. "Everybody has parts of their life that shape the way they look at today and how they behave today. Everyone has a backstory. They have multiple backstories. The question is, which one is running you now?"

Robbins has consulted and interviewed the most successful people of our time: Bill Clinton, Nelson Mandela, Marc Benioff, and countless others. In his 30-year career of studying personal growth and development, Robbins has discovered that the most successful people share a backstory of struggle and it's the hunger to write a new story that drives them to overcome their limited circumstances. "If you ask 'what's the difference in human beings in the way they perform,' it's not intelligence or ability,"[4] says Robbins. "Almost anyone we know who has done something they're proud of in their life or they feel good about in their life, had to get through the obstacles, their own limiting stories. They had to find something they wanted more. The hunger often comes from a story of frustration or pain or desire. Finding that touchstone and igniting it is how you can take someone who is not driven and hungry and really help them to change their life."

Robbins taps into his hunger story to drive himself and to motivate others. A Google search for "Tony Robbins+400 square foot apartment" will return more than 250,000 links. The story is common knowledge because Robbins doesn't hide from it. He embraces it and uses the pain he felt when he didn't have food to eat or a roof over his head to drive him forward. He also uses the story to connect with his audience.

Success leaves clues and often those clues are right before your eyes. People simply want to know that it's possible for them to live a better life. Through his story, Robbins provides a living role model. *If he can do it, so can I,* they say to themselves.

Robbins is a close friend of actor Sylvester Stallone, who has a similar story of struggle. When Stallone wrote the script for *Rocky,* producers bid up to $350,000 for the rights to the script, with the caveat that Stallone, whom they didn't see as a leading man, not play the lead. Stallone, who had $100 in his checkbook at the time, said no. "It's my story,"[5] he said. He finally negotiated a deal to play the lead for $35,000 and a cut of the receipts. *Rocky* grossed $200 million. Stallone refused to sell the script as long as another actor played the title character because the story of a boxer was a metaphor for *his* personal life story.

The Dramatic Arc

A Hollywood movie producer once told me that the story of *Rocky* is one of the greatest films ever made because it has an irresistible dramatic arc. A skilled movie writer creates a character you want to root for, and Rocky Balboa was the very embodiment of this kind of character. The movie is divided into three parts. The first part of the film builds Rocky's backstory, the struggle he must experience on his road to redemption. Rocky isn't just down on his luck. He's a small-time boxer living in a dark, grimy apartment.

He earns his living breaking thumbs for a loan shark. In the middle section of the movie we are introduced to the movie's emotional hook. Through a quirk of fate, Rocky Balboa gets a once-in-a-lifetime chance to fight the world champion, Apollo Creed. He trains hard, if unconventionally, punching sides of beef instead of punching bags and running up the steps of the Philadelphia Museum of Art, accompanied by Bill Conti's rousing musical score. By the time the audience reaches the third part of the movie—the fight and resolution—they are emotionally invested in seeing Rocky reach his goal, which, by the way, is not to win the fight. He just wants to go the distance. He succeeds and, as he embraces Adrian who stood by his side, it's nearly impossible for moviegoers to stay in their seats. They stand up and cheer for a fictional character because they have been transported into his life and they see something of themselves in his struggle. *If he can do it, I can, too.*

The first rule of emotional moviemaking is to create scenes early in the film that put the hero's life into perspective. Audiences need to build a relationship with a character they like and whose struggle they recognize, otherwise they don't care about the resolution. Just as great movies have dramatic arcs that take the audience on a journey through struggle and redemption, so, too, do most successful storytellers on the business stage. They struggle, find strength in their struggle, and ultimately success or redemption.

The greater the arc, the better the story. And the more likely it is to ignite the passion of an audience. In every public seminar Tony Robbins tells the story of his early struggle because the arc makes people emotionally invested in the outcome. The more dramatic, the more likely it is to ignite the passion of your audience. Some people in the audience may have experienced grinding poverty as Robbins did. Some who were brought up middle or upper class may have experienced the pain of a troubled parent or an event that left them demoralized and disillusioned. They are invested in his story because it's become *their* story.

Nearly every person in this book has faced a significant personal challenge or struggle in their life and has overcome the struggle in part through communicating it and its lessons of empowerment. But make no mistake, the story of struggle they share with the world is only impactful because they've reframed it and embraced it themselves.

We have all experienced seminal events in our lives. In some cases, like

Tony Robbins, it's the experience of grinding poverty, but for you it might be something completely different, such as being turned down by your first choice college or being passed over for a job. You can embrace the event and use it as a growth experience, or allow the experience to run you, usually into the ground. Your potential is not rooted in your backstory; it's formed by how you *interpret* your backstory.

The Storyteller's Secret

Stories have the power to shape our lives and the lives of our listeners. Our personal experience—the stories we've lived through—makes us who we are today. Stories of overcoming obstacles provide a dramatic arc to the narrative we tell the world. Inspiring storytellers don't avoid the difficult parts of their arc, but rather embrace every step as an opportunity to transform, grow, and to make a deeply meaningful emotional connection with their audience.

6

The Power in Your Personal Legend

You have to know what sparks the light in you so that you . . . can
illuminate the world.

— Oprah Winfrey

On January 29, 1954, an unwed teen gave birth to a baby girl in Kosciusko, Mississippi. The young parents didn't love each other, nor had they intended to raise a child. They sent the girl to live with her grandmother, Hattie Mae.

As the baby grew into a precocious little girl Hattie Mae encouraged her to read books, beginning with the Bible. By the age of three the girl began her public-speaking "career," reciting Bible verses she had memorized. At home the girl's family would gather at her grandmother's house to swap stories about the war in Europe. The girl said, "If my sense of storytelling began anywhere, it was in my grandmother's dining room. There I learned to love the sound of language, how words hold a cadence."[1]

The girl grew more comfortable in front of any audience with every passing year and, one day, her skills as a storyteller would make her one of the most influential people on the planet and a role model for millions of women.

But the road to fame and riches wasn't an easy one. The girl had a tough childhood, one that would crush most people. She experienced extreme poverty, neglect, racism, and sexual abuse. She turned her life around at the age of 16 after reading Maya Angelou's autobiography, *I Know Why the Caged Bird Sings*. "With each page her life seemed to mirror mine,"[2] the girl would later write. "Meeting Maya on those pages was like meeting myself in full. For the first time, as a young black girl, my experience was validated."

Inspired by Maya Angelou's way with words, the girl decided that sharpening her gifts as a public speaker would help her leave a mark in the world, and so she began to dedicate herself to the craft. In 1970 she won a public-speaking competition, earning the young woman a four-year college scholarship to Tennessee State University where she majored in speech and drama. The girl, Oprah Winfrey, chose journalism as a career.

Winfrey started as a reporter and television anchor in Baltimore, Maryland. Reporting didn't feel natural to her. She wasn't passionate about the job, but since it paid $25,000 a year—a fortune to her at the time—she stuck with it. As is so often the case, the chain of events that would change her life started with adversity. Oprah soon realized that reporting wasn't for her. It felt like an "unnatural act" and her reluctance to embrace the role showed on the air. Oprah's boss wanted to fire her, but he didn't want to pay out her contract. And so he "demoted" her by making her host of the station's obscure talk show. Her first interview involved asking a Carvel ice-cream man about multiflavor ice cream. While most "serious" news anchors would have been insulted, Oprah instantly felt as though she had found her place in the world: "Everybody has a calling, and your real job in life is to figure out what that is and get about the business of doing it."[3] Oprah left Baltimore for Chicago and got about the business of pursuing her calling.

When Oprah got the call to host a local talk show in Chicago, a television personality named Phil Donahue was the king of talk. Nearly every person in Oprah's life—with the exception of her best friend, Gayle—told her she'd fail. The only voice that mattered, however, was the one speaking to Oprah from her heart. "I am really guided by a force that's bigger than myself,"[4] Oprah once told MBA students at Stanford University. "Every human being comes called. The calling goes beyond the definition of your jobs. There is an innate supreme moment of destiny for everybody."

You cannot inspire unless you're inspired yourself. The secret to mastering the art of storytelling is to first dig deep and identify your true passion, your calling. If you don't buy into your story, nobody else will.

The Storyteller's Tools

One of Oprah's favorite authors, Paulo Coelho, describes a calling as a "personal legend" in his book, *The Alchemist*. When a person chooses a path that fills that person's soul with passion and enthusiasm, he or she is following their personal legend and when that happens, "All the universe conspires in helping you to achieve it."

Oprah discovered that reporting wasn't her personal legend. Neither was sitting in the anchor chair behind a desk. When she started her talk show in Chicago, Oprah was also straying from her personal legend—often doing stories of a kind common to talk shows in those days—stories that felt exploitive of her guests. One episode, one particularly brutal episode, would drive home the need for her to set a different course, and mission, for her show. Three guests—a man, his wife, and his girlfriend—all appeared to talk about infidelity. On live television, the man revealed that his girlfriend was pregnant. The visceral impact of this news on the startled wife provided a "life changing" moment for Oprah: "I looked in her face and I felt her humiliation. I felt her shame. And I said, never again."[5] Oprah decided to take control of her personal legend. She told her producers that she would no longer be used by television. Instead she would use television as a platform to share stories that make a positive impact. She said, "My job is not to be an interviewer or talk show host. I am here to raise the level of consciousness. To connect people to ideas and stories so that they can see themselves and lead better lives."

You will only grow into the fullness of your destiny when you are self-aware and connected to the inner voice. Inspiring storytellers identify their life's core purpose. Their message easily flows from the meaning they attach to their own life story, often a tale of struggle and redemption, of tension and triumph.

Oprah doesn't call herself a "talk show host" because she sees her life story as making a more profound contribution to society. She sees her role as raising the consciousness of her audience. Inspiring storytellers infuse their jobs with meaning that goes beyond a title or a product. Starbucks CEO Howard Schultz isn't in the business of selling coffee; he's in the people business. Steve Jobs didn't build computers; he enriched lives. Richard Branson doesn't sell seats on airplanes; he elevates the customer experience. And Oprah Winfrey isn't a talk show host; she raises human consciousness.

We all have a storytelling platform, a canvas to paint on. Oprah's platform might be bigger than yours, but we all start with a blank slate on which to write our story. If you're a writer, your blog might be the canvas. If you're a parent, you might choose to run for president of the Parent Teacher Group and use that stage as your canvas. If you own a business, the sales floor is your stage. Platforms come in all shapes and sizes, but they all give you a stage to share your story. "Wherever you are, that is your platform, your stage, your circle of influence. That is your talk show, and that is where your power lies,"[6] says Winfrey.

As a storyteller Oprah uses a classic narrative technique to inspire her audience: start with humble beginnings, help your audience see themselves in the story, and turn the experience into a lesson. She can hit all three steps in under two minutes, as she did when she accepted the first Bob Hope Humanitarian Award at the 2003 Emmys:

> I grew up in Nashville with a father who owned a barber shop. I can't get him to retire. Every holiday all the transients were always bumming haircuts from my father and asking for money from my dad. All those guys always ended up at our dinner table. I would often say to my father afterwards, "Dad, why can't we just have regular people at our Christmas dinner?" My father said to me, "They are regular people. They want the same thing you want." And I would say, "What?" And he said, "To be fed." At the time I thought he was just talking about dinner, but I have since learned how profound he really was because we are all regular people seeking the same thing. We all just want to know that we matter.[7]

Classic storytelling structure requires that the narrative begin with a fact, event, or action. Oprah's story begins with an event in her life, the Christmas dinner conversation. The second signature of classic narrative is transformation—the protagonist undergoes a change, a transformation. Oprah's transformation happened when her father offered an explanation for inviting the homeless to Christmas dinner. The third and final step is for the protagonist to learn a lesson that ultimately leads the hero to live a better life.

Oprah is skilled at making a connection with the audience and making them feel as though they are capable of making the same transformation. "The secret to that show's success for 25 years is that people could see themselves in me. All over the world, people could see themselves in me,"[8] Oprah once told Stanford business students.

J. K. Rowling, author of the Harry Potter series, has a lot in common with Oprah. Both women experienced excruciating poverty, both followed their passions, and both became billionaires. Oprah and Rowling also made a decision to rewrite their life's story and, leveraging their struggle, followed the classic narrative structure to inspire their audiences.

In her now famous Harvard commencement speech, Rowling followed the three-part storytelling structure: 1) Trigger Event, 2) Transformation, 3) Life Lesson.[9]

Trigger Event

Seven years after graduating college Rowling experienced an "epic" failure: "An exceptionally short-lived marriage had imploded, and I was jobless, a lone parent, and as poor as it is possible to be in modern Britain, without being homeless. The fears that my parents had had for me, and that I had had for myself, had both come to pass, and by every usual standard, I was the biggest failure I knew."

Transformation

Rowling discovers the benefit of failure: "Failure meant a stripping away of the inessential, I stopped pretending to myself that I was anything other than what I was, and began to direct all my energy into finishing the only work that mattered to me [writing Harry Potter]. Had I really succeeded at anything else, I might never have found the determination to succeed in the one arena I believed I truly belonged. And so rock bottom became the solid foundation on which I rebuilt my life . . . Failure taught me things about myself that I could have learned no other way."

Life Lesson

"You might never fail on the scale I did, but some failure in life is inevitable. It is impossible to live without failing at something, unless you live so cautiously that you might as well not have lived at all—in which case, you fail by default. The knowledge that you have emerged wiser and stronger from setbacks means that you are, ever after, secure in your ability to survive. You will never truly know yourself, or the strength of your relationships, until both have been tested by adversity. Such knowledge is a true gift."

The Storyteller's Secret

The world's most inspiring storytellers align their personalities with their life's purpose to craft a personal legend. By highlighting their struggle in the three-part narrative, they inspire us to work harder, have higher aspirations, or to simply lead better lives. We see ourselves in their struggle. We empathize with their insecurities. We applaud their success because they bring us hope. If they can overcome their obstacles, so can we.

7

A Coffee King Pours His Heart into His Business

The more uninspiring your origins, the more likely you are to use your imagination and invent worlds where everything seems possible.
— Howard Schultz

On a cold January day in 1961 Fred Schultz broke his ankle while working his job as a diaper service deliveryman. He had hated the job, but losing it was worse: It would set him on a downward spiral. Fred's son Howard was seven years old at the time and vividly remembers the accident: "That image of my father, slumped on the family couch, his leg in a cast unable to work or earn money, and ground down by the world—is still burned into my mind."[1]

Fred Schultz and his family had no income, no health insurance, no worker's comp, and nothing to fall back on. Even at a young age, living a hard life in a Brooklyn housing project, Howard found the experience focused his values and his aspirations: "I knew in my heart that if I was ever in a position where I could make a difference, I wouldn't leave people behind." Today, as the CEO and president of Starbucks, Howard Schultz is in a position to make a difference for more than 180,000 employees and their families.

Howard Schultz often tells the story of his father to explain his company's mission and values. His father's story frames the "why" behind the company's initiatives. Shultz's vision was to build a company that treats people with dignity and respect, the treatment his father was never shown. "Coffee is what we sell as a product, but it's not the business we're in," Schultz said. "We're not in the coffee business. Well, we are as a product. But we're in the people business. It's all human connection."[2]

What would a company that's in the people business look like? It would offer comprehensive health insurance benefits to all employees, even part-time workers. It would create a first of its kind profit-sharing plan, offering stock options to all employees. It would commit to hiring 10,000 military veterans in five years. If Howard Schultz had built a company that was solely in the coffee business, the company would look far different than it is today, and most likely be far less successful. "Treating employees benevolently shouldn't be viewed as an added cost that cuts into profits, but as a powerful energizer than can grow the enterprise into something far greater than one leader could envision,"[3] Schultz writes. "Starbucks has become a living legacy of my dad." By framing Starbucks as a living legacy Schultz is not positioning his company as a profit center. Instead it's a story where the employees play the starring role.

While his father's story fueled Schultz's desire to build a company that treated its employees with the respect they deserve, another event transformed Starbucks from a small roaster of coffee beans to a store serving 60 million customers per week. Here is how Schultz recalled the experience in a televised conversation with Oprah Winfrey.

> People think I'm the founder of Starbucks. I was an employee when Starbucks only had four stores. I was sent to Italy on a trip for Starbucks and came back with this feeling that the business Starbucks was in was the wrong business. What I wanted to bring back was the daily ritual and the sense of community and the idea that we could build this third place between home and work in America. It was an epiphany. I was out of my mind. I walked in and saw this symphony of activity, and the romance and the theater of coffee. And coffee being at the center of conversation, creating a sense of community. That is what spoke to me.[4]

The experience "spoke" to Schultz because he saw the story of what Starbucks could become. Schultz has never grown tired of telling the stories of his childhood or his visit to Italy. And it's a good thing he hasn't. There's a direct correlation between his stories, engaged employees, and satisfied customers who view his shops as something more than just a place to get their morning jolt.

The Storyteller's Tools

Schultz studied communication and public speaking as a student at Northern Michigan University, and he learned the role that stories play in rallying a company's employees around a common purpose. He would use the story of his trip to Italy to bring his vision to life. Schultz's vision for Starbucks was to create a "third place between home and work." The story of his trip to Italy fills in the sensory details of what the completed vision looks and feels like.

Schultz tells the Italy story often, remaining consistent in the details, and so it has become part of Starbucks' lore. Here he is in an interview on *The Great Disruptors* on Bloomberg television; pay attention to how similar it is to the story he told Oprah: "A year after joining the company I went to Italy for the first time. You can't walk through any major city or town without running into a coffee bar and seeing the sense of community and romance and theater around espresso. It made me realize that Starbucks was not in the right part of the coffee business. The real business and opportunity was in integrating the beverage to a sense of destination and sense of community in the store."[5]

It takes all of 30 seconds for Schultz to tell the origin story, the backstory, behind the Starbucks brand. The story was critical to the brand's success because in 1987 few people in America had heard of café latte. They didn't quite know what to make of the "third place" concept. Even the original Starbucks founders rejected Schultz's idea at first. Schultz left Starbucks for two years and started his own Italian coffee bar (the founders, facing financial difficulty, came back to Schultz, and, in 1987, sold Starbucks to Schultz for $3.8 million). Only then did Schultz really have the chance to realize his vision fully, to create an experience where people would go to enjoy coffee and conversation and not just to buy beans. The very next year, when, according to Schultz, "employer generosity was hopelessly out of fashion," Starbucks became one of the few companies to cover all of its workers under its healthcare plan, even part-time employees. What drove Schultz then and now is the often-stated goal to treat employees kindly; in return, they will reward you with service and loyalty. Regardless, it's the right thing to do.

Once again we come back to the theme of humble beginnings among the world's great storytellers. Schultz realizes that if his customers can see themselves in his personal story, they'll feel a stronger sense of connection to the storyteller and his brand. "I want to inspire people to live their dreams,"[6] Schultz says. "I come from common roots, with no silver spoon, no pedigree, no early mentors. I dared to dream big dreams. I'm convinced that most people can achieve their dreams and beyond if they have the determination to keep trying."

Authentic Stories Connect People in a Deep, Meaningful Way

Origin stories frame concepts and ideas into a rich, sensory-loaded tapestry that helps listeners process the idea more robustly. Neuroscientists are just now beginning to discover what leaders like Howard Schultz understand instinctively—stories connect two human beings in a deep, meaningful way.

In a 2010 paper published in *The Journal of Neuroscience,* Princeton University researcher Uri Hasson delivered the results of a profoundly important study on the power of story. Using brain scans (fMRI), Hasson recorded the brain activity of a person telling a real-life story, a story of an experience she had at her high school prom. Hasson then measured the brain activity of people listening to the story and also scanned the brains of people resting, without hearing the story. To mirror real-life conditions as closely as possible, the speaker was asked to tell the story as if she were talking to a friend. Hasson took it one step further and asked the listeners to fill out a detailed questionnaire to measure how well they understood the story.

Hasson discovered that "speaker-listener neural coupling is widespread and extensive."[7] Simply put, when telling a story, the brains of both the speaker and the listener showed remarkable patterns of activity in exactly the same areas. The two people were engaging in "neural coupling," having a mind meld. The coupling only occurred when the speaker was telling a story to the listener in a language familiar to the listener. For example, when a speaker told the story in Russian to non-Russian speakers, the coupling did not take place.

When storytellers like Howard Schultz talk about how past events shape their vision for a company, they're connecting on two profound levels: story and authenticity. The stories belong to him.

The founder's origin story is a simple and powerful way to deliver the authentic experience consumers crave. Howard Schultz's stories hit on the three dimensions of authentic brands, defined by marketing professor Julie Napoli as: heritage, sincerity, and commitment to quality. Customers want to know where a product comes from, who the people are behind it, and how committed they are to delivering a quality product. Customers don't buy a brand or a logo as much as they buy into a set of values. And there's no better way to reveal a company's values than through the stories that fueled the people who lead it and continue to ignite the passion of the people who work there.

"Every company must stand for something,"[8] writes Howard Schultz. "A company can grow big without losing the passion and personality that built it, but only if it's driven by values and by people. The key is heart." Yes, the key is heart, but the road to the heart runs through the head and storytelling is the vehicle to get there.

The Storyteller's Secret

Inspiring leaders tell personal stories to bring their vision to life. They'll pour their hearts out because they know that a group of people who share a collective passion around a common purpose can accomplish anything. The storyteller taps into the experience or event that first sparked his or her mission and repeats the story over and over until it becomes part of the company's folklore.

8

We're Not Retailers with a Mission, We're Missionaries Who Retail

Let your heart, sweetheart be your compass when you're lost.

—Lady Antebellum

On Memorial Day in 1981, Shoal Creek in Texas spilled its banks, covering parts of the city of Austin in over eight feet of water. It was Austin's worst flood in 70 years. Six inches of rain fell in four hours, causing streets to become roaring rivers of water that would take cars and people along with them. Thirteen people died and the flood caused more than $100 million in damage in today's dollars.

The 900 block of North Lamar Boulevard was especially devastated. The cars on the lots of three auto dealerships were completely submerged. A natural foods store that had opened just one year earlier appeared to be a total loss. The water destroyed everything in the store. The store's owners didn't have flood insurance and had no savings. Just when all seemed lost, something unexpected happened. The store's employees refused to let it die and its customers refused to let it go. They began to show up with mops, buckets, and shovels. The store's founders were amazed as dozens of people kept coming.

"Why are you doing this?" one of the founders asked a volunteer.

"I'm not sure if I would want to live in Austin if the store wasn't here. It's made a huge difference in my life," the customer said.

An amazing photograph was taken in front of the store three days after the flood. More than 50 of the store's team members posed for a group picture. Although they were covered in mud, each and every one of them had a smile as wide as the Shoal Creek is long. Many of the people in the picture were employees who continued to work for free until the owners could work out a loan and reopen.

Looking back on the event the store's founder asks, "How many 'normal' businesses would attract a volunteer army of customers and suppliers to help them in their hour of need?"[1] Normal companies don't attract love, loyalty, and devotion. Unusual companies do; companies that have an irresistible story to tell.

Today, more than 30 years after the flood, Whole Foods Market has grown from that one store in Austin to more than 360 locations in North America and the United Kingdom. With over $11 billion in sales every year, making payroll is no longer a concern.

Whole Foods cofounder John Mackey never took a single business class in college. He learned philosophy, religion, history, literature, and whatever made his "heart sing." He later said that as an entrepreneur who didn't go to business school he had nothing "to unlearn." Mackey had a blank slate on which to craft the story of the kind of company he wanted to build.

The Storyteller's Tools

In his early twenties John Mackey made a decision that would guide his life and help to create an entirely new category in the food business. He made "a lifelong commitment to follow my heart wherever it led me. I have learned that we can channel our deepest creative impulses in loving ways toward fulfilling our higher purposes, and help evolve the world to a better place."[2]

In storytelling, vision matters and it matters a lot. Inspiring storytellers paint a vivid picture of what the world will look like when they've realized their purpose. According to Mackey, a company's purpose is the difference they're trying to make in the world. "A higher purpose gives great energy and relevance to a company and its brand,"[3] writes Mackey.

Inspiring storytellers ignite the passions of their employees and customers because they have absolute clarity in their higher purpose. "Our purpose is to teach people what they put into their bodies makes a difference to their health . . . and to the health of the planet as a whole," says Mackey.

No customer or employee is going to voluntarily pick up a mop to help you clean up after a "flood" unless they've bought into your company's higher purpose. Your employees come to work for a paycheck; they go the extra mile because they're inspired by your brand story.

In 2015, Millennials, the 82 million young people born between 1980 and mid-2000s, officially became the largest group of employees in the U.S. workforce. Numerous surveys of young people show that what they want out of their company culture is vastly different from that of earlier generations. A competitive salary is important, of course, but Millennials place far greater emphasis on purpose, passion, and meaning. They want to work with teams of like-minded people who are connected to something bigger than themselves. They are inspired by leaders who tell stories that infuse their companies with purpose and meaning.

"Brand is just an abstraction. I use that word sometimes but I'm not a big fan of the word because sometimes when people talk about managing their brand they move away from authenticity,"[4] says Mackey. "Your brand is just the way people think about the company or the product, so I don't think the brand is more important than the purpose or the values of the organization. . . . We're not retailers with a mission, we're missionaries who retail."

Having a clear sense of purpose—and communicating that purpose consistently—is a key attribute that defines inspirational storytelling, especially among leaders who run the world's most admired brands.

Mission as a Competitive Advantage

I recently met a sales professional who had just accepted a director's position with José Andrés, one of the most admired and innovative chefs in the world. Andrés came to the United States with $50 in his pocket, a set of cooking knives, and a mission to make the world a better place through food. "Within two minutes of meeting Mr. Andrés, I wanted to work for him," the salesman said. "His sense of mission was contagious."

The salesman was describing a concept that psychologists call emotional or "mood contagion," the transfer of mood between two people. When you meet people who are genuinely passionate about their mission, there's a good chance that the person's mood will rub off, changing your perception of the person and his or her idea, product, or company. For people like José Andrés or John Mackey, their mission becomes their competitive advantage.

"In a world that is evolving faster than ever, companies must rely on mission to unlock product differentiation, talent acquisition and retention, and even investor loyalty,"[5] according to a *Fast Company* cover story. "The more they focus on something beyond money, the more money they make."

Every year LinkedIn releases its list of the world's most desirable places to work. It's a measure of employee engagement. In 2014 the regular cast of characters made the top of the list: Google and Apple. A surprise came in at number three—the 140-year-old consumer goods company, Unilever. The company receives an astounding 2 million applications a year. Unilever CEO Paul Polman believes the company is such a big draw because it tells a story of purpose that employees want to play a role in telling. "If you peel the onion on that, it really is the pride people have. Putting purpose at the center of everything the corporation does is incredibly motivating for our employees,"[6] says Polman.

Polman launched a "Sustainable Living Plan" that covers Unilever's brands (Dove, Persil, Bertolli, Flora) in all of the 180 countries where the company does business. The plan's purpose is to cut the company's environmental footprint by half in the next decade and to improve the nutritional quality of its food products. "Having a deeper purpose to what we do as people makes our lives more complete, which is a tremendous force and motivator,"[7] says Polman. "What people want in life is to be recognized, to be part of, to grow and to have made a difference. That difference can come in many forms; by touching someone, by helping others, by creating something that was not there before."

Inspiring business leaders often build in the components of story in articulating the company's mission. On June 5, 2015, Walmart CEO Doug McMillon opened the annual shareholders meeting with "At Walmart, we love stories. There is just something about them. We enjoy telling them. We remember hearing them. We repeat stories and pass them down. We also write them. Together, we're writing our company's story."[8] McMillon reminded the audience that a good story has heroes and villains, surprising turning points, and in the end the hero saves the day. In the Walmart story, he explained, the hero is the associates, Walmart's 1.3 million employees. The story has a "love interest," the company's customers. The story has a plot twist: customers are changing the way they shop. The story has a villain: bureaucracy, complacency, a lack of speed. "With the right attitude, teamwork, and common sense, we'll defeat the bad guys and win the customers' hearts," he concluded.

McMillon, Mackey, and other business leaders and legends know that mission and purpose is a competitive advantage. Make it a key component of your brand story and customers, employees, and partners will walk through walls for you—or help you to clean up after a flood.

The Storyteller's Secret

Inspiring leaders ignite passion and loyalty by infusing their brand's narrative with a higher mission. A business, by definition, exists to make a profit and the world's best corporate storytellers acknowledge as much. What sets them apart is what they do next. They wrap their product, service, company, or cause with a vision and a purpose that goes well beyond making money. They spark our collective passion because they speak to the core of what makes us human—a search for meaning.

9

If You Can't Tell It, You Can't Sell It

Stories have a unique power to move people's hearts.
— Peter Guber

Even the best storytellers strike out from time to time. Successful story-tellers readjust their swing to hit the next pitch out of the ballpark. Peter Guber, the chairman and CEO of Mandalay Entertainment Group, vividly recalls making a failed pitch for a new minor league baseball park in Las Vegas.

At the time of Guber's meeting with Las Vegas mayor Oscar Goodman, Mandalay owned several minor league baseball franchises. Guber sought Goodman's support for a new ballpark. "Our success hinged on my ability to persuade Las Vegas's chief politician to lead the campaign for a munici-pal bond to fund this multimillion-dollar civic project,"[1] recalls Guber.

In Guber's mind the baseball stadium was a done deal. After all, Guber had financed the record-setting *Batman* movie and had produced two hit movies based in Vegas: *Rain Man* and *Bugsy*. Guber began the pitch confi-dently, armed with data he was certain would "mesmerize" the mayor. Guber had sales figures, construction costs, schedules, etc. He presented the information on multiple PowerPoint decks full of metrics and "killer data." The data was killer, but not the kind of killer Guber had anticipated. It killed the deal.

"I'd thrown a powerful barrage of raw facts at Goodman—data, statis-tics, records, forecasts—but I didn't organize them in any way to engage his emotions,"[2] Guber recalls. "No wonder he hadn't swung at my offer-ing!" Guber delivered a data dump and had forgotten the core business he was in—the business of producing compelling stories.

Guber is an expert at telling stories on a big screen, but he had failed to bring the same storytelling techniques to the small screen of a computer display. Guber had made the mistake of aiming for Goodman's "head and wallet" instead of his heart. Guber had forgotten the lesson he learned in the movie business: to win market share you must take your audience on an emotional journey. "Stories have a unique power to move people's hearts, minds, feet, and wallets in the storyteller's intended direction," writes Guber.

"After my loss in Vegas, it occurred to me that everybody in business shares one universal problem: To succeed, you have to persuade others to support your vision, dream, or cause. Whether you want to motivate your executives, organize your shareholders, shape your media, engage your customers, win over investors, or land a job, you have to deliver a clarion call that will get your listeners' attention, emotionalize your goal as theirs, and move them to act in your favor. You have to reach their hearts as well as their minds—and this is just what storytelling does!"[3]

The Storyteller's Tools

Guber is now one of the strongest proponents for storytelling in business. "Purposeful storytelling is a game-changer,"[4] he believes. Guber says that anyone can build a story in three steps:

1. Grab your listener's attention with a question or unexpected challenge.
2. Give listeners an emotional experience by telling a story around the struggle that will ultimately lead to conquering the challenge.
3. Galvanize listeners with a call to action.

"Listeners are rarely hooked if they don't sense some compelling challenge in the beginning. They won't stay engaged if they're not excited by the struggle in the middle. And they won't remember or act on the story unless they feel galvanized by its final resolution,"[5] explains Guber.

According to Guber, stories ignite the passion of the audience when they serve as a bridge from what is to what could be. A successful business pitch or presentation is no different than a great movie, and an effective one follows Guber's three steps of story building. For example, in 2007 the world's greatest business storyteller, Steve Jobs, introduced the iPhone. Since the iPhone wasn't the first smartphone on the market Steve Jobs had to craft a seductive story. The following excerpt is a briefly edited transcript of the product story Steve Jobs used to launch the iPhone and to position it in the smartphone category. In doing so he closely followed the three steps of story building that Guber outlines. Jobs delivered the narrative in exactly four minutes; four minutes that proved to be irresistible.

Challenge

"The most advanced phones are called 'smartphones,' so they say. The problem is they are not so smart and they are not so easy to use . . . What we want to do is make a leapfrog product that is way smarter than any mobile device has ever been and super easy to use. This is what iPhone is. So we're going to reinvent the phone and we're going to start with a revolutionary user interface."[6]

Question

"Why do we need a revolutionary user interface?"

Struggle/Narrative

"Here are four smartphones—the Motorola Q, Blackberry, Palm Treo, Nokia E62—the usual suspects. [Steve Jobs uses words associated with villains like "suspects" and "culprit."] What's wrong with their user interface? The problem with them is in the bottom forty. It's this stuff right there [pointing to keyboards]. They all have these keyboards that are there whether you need them or not. They all have control buttons that are fixed in plastic . . . the buttons and controls can't change. How do you solve this?" [Once again, Jobs uses words you'd expect to read in a murder mystery—to "solve" the crime that's been committed.]

Resolution

"What we're going to do is get rid of all these buttons and just make a giant screen. How are we going to communicate with this? We don't want to carry around a mouse? We're going to use a stylus? No. Who wants a stylus? You have to get them out, put them away, you lose them. Yuck. Nobody wants a stylus. We're going to use the best pointing device in the world, a pointing device that we're all born with. We'll use our fingers. And we have invented a new technology called multi-touch. It works like magic. You don't need a stylus. It's far more accurate than any touch display that's ever been shipped. It's super smart. You can do multi-finger gestures on it. And boy have we patented it."

In four minutes Steve Jobs bridged from what is to what could be using the building blocks of compelling narrative—heroes and villains.

According to Guber, a storyteller moves the audience to action by igniting their passion. "The keys to the kingdom" are not purely informational, says Guber. The key is to reach a person's heart and to do so, the storyteller must put him or her inside the experience, not the business plan.

There are many specific techniques to tell an irresistible story and the techniques will be explored in the next sections of this book. For now, consider that Guber has been in the entertainment business for more than 40 years and has reached the conclusion that anyone can learn to tell a good story because it's part of who we are: The capacity for storytelling is in our DNA because humans have been telling stories for more than 10,000 years. "There's a treasure to be discovered, and it's inside you,"[7] writes Guber. Let's go treasure hunting. . . .

The Storyteller's Secret

Inspiring speakers build a story structure for every important pitch, presentation, meeting, or conversation and, in doing so, they introduce three components all great movies share: villains, heroes, and struggle.

Storytellers Who Educate

PART II

Storytellers Who Educate

10

How a Spellbinding Storyteller Received TED's Longest Standing Ovation

What sets TED Talks apart is that the big ideas are wrapped up in personal stories.

—Charlie Rose, *60 Minutes*

At the age of nine, a simple gesture changed Bryan Stevenson's life and set him on the path to become a famed civil rights attorney. While playing with his many cousins, his grandmother singled him out for a pep talk. "I remember this just like it happened yesterday. I never will forget it,"[1] Stevenson says as he recalls the event. "She took me out back and she said, 'Bryan, I'm going to tell you something, but you don't tell anybody what I tell you.' Then she sat me down and she looked at me and she said, 'I want you to know I've been watching you.' And she said, 'I think you're special. I think you can do anything you want to do.'"

Stevenson's grandmother then asked him to make her a promise—that he would never drink alcohol. Stevenson, being nine years old at the time, readily agreed. About five years later Stevenson's promise was tested.

One day my brother came home and he had this six-pack of beer—I don't know where he got it—and he grabbed me and my sister and we went out in the woods. And we were kind of just out there doing the stuff we crazily did. And he had a sip of this beer and he gave some to my sister and she had some, and they offered it to me. I said, "No, no, no. That's okay. You all go ahead. I'm not going to have any beer." My brother said, "Come on. We're doing this today; you always do what we do. I had some, your sister had some. Have some beer." I said, "No, I don't feel right about that. Y'all go ahead. Y'all go ahead." And then my brother started staring at me. He said, "What's wrong with you? Have some beer." Then he looked at me real hard and he said, "Oh, I hope you're not still hung up on that conversation Mama had with you." I said, "Well, what are you talking about?" He said, "Oh, Mama tells all the grandkids that they're special." I was devastated. And I'm going to admit something to you. I'm going to tell you something I probably shouldn't. I know this might be broadcast broadly. But I'm 52 years old, and I'm going to admit to you that I've never had a drop of alcohol. I don't say that because I think that's virtuous; I say that because there is power in identity.[2]

Stevenson told that story in front of a TED audience in 2013 and received the longest standing ovation in TED's 30-year history. Stevenson had to leave before the end of the conference to work on an upcoming Supreme Court argument. He later learned that the attendees in the TED audience on the day of his talk had spontaneously—and without being asked—donated $1 million to Stevenson's nonprofit. Stevenson's stories made his argument so persuasive, he essentially earned $55,000 per minute of conversation.

The Storyteller's Tools

It wasn't the first time Stevenson had told the story about his grandmother. As the director of a nonprofit law firm, the Equal Justice Initiative, Stevenson is constantly fund-raising and sharing stories with his audiences.

"Why do you start with the story of your grandmother?"[3] I asked.

"Because everybody has a grandmother," he replied.

Stevenson's response wasn't meant to be flippant. Stevenson knows a thing or two about persuasion. He argues cases before the U.S. Supreme Court—and wins. If an audience doesn't connect with you early in the conversation and if they don't like you, it's unlikely that you will persuade them to agree with your point of view. And Stevenson's point of view is, at least initially, disagreeable to a large number of people.

Stevenson represents condemned prisoners in Alabama, arguing that, in many cases, those death row inmates were misrepresented at trial or wrongly convicted because they were black and poor. Stevenson's work has resulted in reversing the conviction of 78 inmates on Alabama's death row.

"You have to make it easy for people to connect with what you're saying. You have to get folks to trust you a little bit," Stevenson told me. "If you start with something too esoteric and disconnected from the lives of everyday people, it's harder for people to engage. I often talk about family members because most of us have family members that we have a relationship to. I talk about kids and people who are vulnerable or struggling. All of those narratives are designed to help understand the issues. Narrative is hugely important in effective communication."

When he's not arguing in death penalty cases, Stevenson teaches classes at the School of Law at NYU. Students, professors, and outsiders clamor for a seat because of his reputation as a "spellbinding" orator. Like many of the storytellers in this book, Stevenson picked up many of his public speaking skills from watching other gifted speakers. For Stevenson, the pastors he saw in church inspired his speaking style. One reporter who wrote a lengthy profile on Stevenson summed it up this way:

> It becomes clear during a series of conversations over several months that the roots of Stevenson's singular dedication—a term he might prefer to sacrifice—trace back to a childhood influenced by the African Methodist Episcopal church. The gospel of lost souls seeking redemption echoes in his memory. "I believe each person in our society is more than the worst thing they've ever done," he sermonizes in nearly every appearance, his voice intense yet controlled, his cadence that of a preacher in full command of a congregation. "I believe if you tell a lie, you're not just a liar. If you take something that doesn't belong to you, you're not just a thief. And I believe even if you kill someone, you are not just a killer. There is a basic human dignity that deserves to be protected."[4]

Inspiring preachers educate their audiences with a balance of facts and stories, stories making up a larger percentage of their content. As it turns out, inspiring business leaders do the same.

After I spoke with Bryan Stevenson I decided to analyze his now famous TED talk—which is very similar to the way he gives fund-raising presentations—and to categorize every line of content. I used Aristotle's three keys of persuasion: Pathos (emotion—stories), Logos (logic—analytical), and Ethos (evidence—credibility). For more than 2,000 years communication theorists assumed that "Logos" reigned supreme. They believed that people made decisions primarily based on the evidence: facts, reason, and logic. If that's true and you were trying to create a paradigm shift—a significant change in the way people see the world—you would be inclined to spend more time on Logos than Pathos.

In 1984 Dr. Walter Fisher proposed another theory, one that has since been confirmed by the advanced brain-scanning techniques mentioned in chapter 7. Fisher proposed that humans are "essentially storytellers," meaning we understand and interpret life experiences as ongoing narratives— stories that contain conflict, characters, and a clear beginning, middle, and conclusion. Fisher found that people relate better to stories than they do to mountains of data. Effective persuasion relies on telling a good story. If we can put our ideas into narrative form, it helps your audience understand the world better, giving them a common set of references and, ultimately, is more likely to encourage them to support your point of view.

Now let's go back to Bryan Stevenson, a masterful persuader. Although Stevenson has plenty of evidence to support his thesis, he understands that, as Fisher argues, humans are primarily storytellers. In Stevenson's TED talk, 65 percent of his content fell into the category of Pathos (triggering emotion through narrative). Stevenson told three personal stories in 18 minutes. Facts, figures, and statics (Logos) made up 25 percent of the content. Information intended to bolster his credibility (Ethos) supplied the remaining 10 percent of Stevenson's talk.

Stevenson's template works brilliantly. It breaks down as follows: In the first five minutes Stevenson establishes his theme—the power of identity— and tells his first story about the day his grandmother had him swear off alcohol. The story is followed by several paragraphs of data, supporting his thesis that while he was lucky, many other poor African American males are not. "This country is very different today than it was 40 years ago. In 1972, there were 300,000 people in jails and prisons. Today, there are 2.3 million. One out of three black men between the ages of 18 and 30 is in jail, in prison, on probation or parole."[5]

Stevenson then segues into his second story: the day he met Rosa Parks.

Ms. Parks turned to me and she said, "Now Bryan, tell me what the Equal Justice Initiative is. Tell me what you're trying to do." And I began giving her my rap. I said, "Well we're trying to challenge injustice. We're trying to help people who have been wrongly convicted. We're trying to confront bias and discrimination in the administration of criminal justice. We're trying to end life without parole sentences for children. We're trying to do something about the death penalty. We're trying to reduce the prison population. We're trying to end mass incarceration." I gave her my whole rap, and when I finished she looked at me and she said, "Mmm mmm mmm." She said, "That's going to make you tired, tired, tired." And that's when Ms. Carr [Ms. Park's friend] leaned forward, she put her finger in my face, [and] she said, "That's why you've got to be brave, brave, brave."

Stevenson provides more data to reinforce his theme, some evidence of the work he's done, and concludes with a third and final personal story, a powerful anecdote of the day he ran into a janitor on the way to a particularly contentious court appearance. The janitor took a seat behind Stevenson while he was making an impassioned argument to a judge:

During the break there was a deputy sheriff who was offended that the janitor had come into court. And this deputy jumped up and he ran over to this older black man. He said, "Jimmy, what are you doing in this courtroom?" And this older black man stood up and he looked at that deputy and he looked at me and he said, "I came into this courtroom to tell this young man, keep your eyes on the prize, hold on."

In 18 minutes Stevenson told three personal stories, provided relevant data points to support his argument, and moved members of his audience to tears. They had no choice but to stand up and cheer.

In 1993 Walter McMilliams walked out of an Alabama prison cell as a free man. A court of appeals overturned his conviction after the witnesses in his murder trial recanted their testimony after Stevenson had uncovered evidence that pointed to the man's innocence. The appeals court, however, was reluctant to address the case until Bryan Stevenson got the wheels of justice turning by granting an interview to *60 Minutes*. An observer who accompanied Stevenson recalls the scene: "Bryan was warm and affable as always, but he got right to the point. He told the story of his client's innocence and the prosecution's manipulation of the case through inaccuracies and racial taint. With Bryan weaving the story, it was spellbinding. After he finished, the producer said, 'If even half of what you are telling me turns out to be true, we'll be down in Alabama in a few days.'"[6] The newsmagazine aired a devastating piece. Stevenson's persuasive stories set the wheels of justice in motion.

"How much of your success do you owe to effective storytelling?"[7] I asked Stevenson.

Stevenson replied with the following:

> Almost all of it. There are so many presumptions that will condemn the clients I care about that it's all about overcoming the narratives that have evolved without much thinking. Almost all of what we're trying to do turns on effective communication. You need data, facts, analysis that will challenge people, but you also need narrative to get people comfortable enough with caring enough about the community that you are advocating for and willing to go with you on a journey. For concepts and ideas if you can engage people with their minds and their hearts you get a deeper investment than when you are trying just to engage the mind in some analytical exercise.

Many people find the task of educating audiences on complex topics—topics that face habitual resistance—to be overwhelming. Storytelling not only helps; it's essential. "A compelling story with an emotional trigger alters our brain chemistry, making us more trusting, understanding, and open to ideas,"[8] according to neuroscientist Paul Zak. Remember, data delivers information. Stories educate by adding soul to the data and, by doing so, forcing people to reconsider their closely held beliefs.

The Storyteller's Secret

Most speakers who must educate their audiences spend a majority of their presentations on what they think will win over their listeners: facts, figures, and data. They give very little thought to how stories move people. The world's most inspiring educators do just the opposite, devoting 65 percent or more of their content to stories that establish trust and build a deeper, emotional relationship with their audience. Once they've connected, they can educate.

11

Turning Sewage into Drinking Water

Teaching's hard! You need different skills: positive reinforcement, keeping students from getting bored, commanding their attention in a certain way.

—Bill Gates

On January 5, 2015, Bill Gates drank a glass of water and the media ate it up. Even the celebrity TV show, *TMZ,* normally more concerned with who the Hollywood star of the moment is dating, covered the event. Of course, the billionaire philanthropist didn't take a sip of just any water. That tall glass of water had been human waste five minutes earlier. The water had gone through a process that converted sewage to clean water.

Gates's water made such a splash that Jimmy Fallon joked about it in his monologue on *The Tonight Show* and, a few days later, invited Gates to be a guest on the show and to drink the water on television. The blogger Perez Hilton linked to the video on his popular site. News organizations around the world picked it up: CNN, NPR, *The Huffington Post,* BBC, and others. It all started from Bill Gates himself, who posted an article and video on his blog titled, "This Ingenious Machine Turns Feces into Drinking Water."

Gates pulls stunts like this every so often, but not because he's looking for attention. With a net worth of $50 billion he doesn't need the exposure. But he's learned that it can be a dramatically effective method for drawing attention to real solutions for very complex problems. More than 2.5 billion people have no access to safe sanitation, a problem that kills 700,000 children a year. These are the type of problems that keep Bill Gates up at night and he wants the rest of the world to think about it, too.

So why did Gates drink poop water? For the same reason he released mosquitoes in the middle of a PowerPoint presentation. Oh, you didn't hear about the mosquitoes?

In 2009 Bill Gates delivered a TED presentation on the toll malaria is taking around the world. Gates once said that sharks are considered deadly because they kill 10 humans a year. But sharks pale in comparison to the tiny mosquito, which claims 725,000 lives a year. Gates is serious about solving the crisis, but he can't have a serious discussion about the topic without grabbing our attention. About five minutes into his TED presentation Gates said, "Malaria, of course, is transmitted by mosquitoes. I brought some here so you can experience it."[1] And with that he walked to the front of the stage, opened a glass jar, and let the mosquitoes fly. "I'll let these roam around the auditorium. There's no reason why only poor people should have the experience."

Once again a Gates stunt had the media buzzing. Gates's presentation even made the *NBC Nightly News*. A PowerPoint presentation made the national news that night because Gates had committed a violation. He violated expectations, and in doing so, exceeded the expectations of his audience.

The Storyteller's Tools

The human brain is an energy hog. It consumes an inordinate amount of your body's resources. We develop daily rituals to save energy. If we had to relearn every step of brushing our teeth we wouldn't have energy to learn much else. The brain settles into comfort mode. Great storytellers make us uncomfortable. They catch our attention by breaking an expected pattern.

Dr. Judee Burgoon at the University of Arizona developed the "Expectancy Violations Theory" in the late 1970s. We expect people to behave in a certain way. If a person deviates from the expectation, a "violation" has occurred. Violations can be negative. For example, if someone seated next to you in a loud coffee shop is speaking on a cell phone, you'd think nothing of it. If that same person is talking on the phone in a quiet movie theater—just when the movie begins—you'd be very, very annoyed. You "expect" quiet in that setting. A violation is uncomfortable, but in some cases—like telling a great story—unsettling is quite positive.

Let's turn back to Bill Gates in his 2009 TED talk. You've seen a Power-Point presentation in the past (maybe more than you'd like) and you've developed an expectation of what it will be like. In a presentation on the causes of malaria, you expect slides with charts, tables, data, figures, and maybe a picture or two (a good storyteller will have more than a few pictures, but we'll get to that in later chapters). If the presentation contained each of those elements, it would "meet" your expectations. In other words, it would be average and forgettable. Bill Gates broke expectations and did it in such a big way it was impossible for the audience to ignore. In this age of instant and shareable content, Gates provided a Twitter-worthy performance.

Violating expectations is a "superior" communication strategy, according to Dr. Burgoon. She says the technique can enhance a speaker's "attractiveness, credibility, and persuasiveness." It works because the human brain cannot ignore novelty.

Dr. A. K. Pradeep, a neuromarketing specialist in Berkeley, California, once told me, "Our brains are trained to look for something brilliant and new. Something that stands out."[2] I'm not suggesting that you drink sewage water or release mosquitoes in your next sales presentation to stand out. I am suggesting that you violate expectations. Here are several examples of standing apart by standing out. You'll note that most of these examples are remarkably simple to execute. Great storytelling doesn't have to be complicated.

- I was working with a group of antiterrorism experts who update local officials on the safety of their city or state's infrastructure. In developing their presentation, they decided to show a photo of a broken lock on a power plant. I suggested taking it one step further—take out the real lock and put it on the table as the presentation continues. The lock was corroded, rusty, and broken. The audience members passed it around during the rest of the discussion. When attendees were surveyed after the presentation and asked what they had learned, state officials said, "We need to upgrade our infrastructure. Those locks left an impression on us." Notice that they didn't say, "Slide 22 was amazing." The slides were nicely designed, but "expected." The broken lock broke expectations.

- At the 2015 Consumer Electronics Show in Las Vegas (CES), Intel CEO Brian Krzanich unleashed the drones. In every CEO keynote at the famous electronics show, the audience expects to see new products and a demo of those products. Krzanich didn't disappoint. He introduced a new camera technology called RealSense 3D. He said the camera is so advanced it can be put in drones, giving the drones a sense of "sight," allowing them to be location-aware so they won't bump into things. Krzanich's presentation slides had a few photographs of the product, which met expectations. Krzanich took it one step further and invited "three friends" to join him on stage. Three drones appeared and literally flew around him on stage without crashing into one other. The camera made the robots aware of their surroundings. Krzanich continued to educate the audience on the implications of the technology while the drones buzzed around him. Intel's drones generated the biggest buzz of the entire conference. I later learned that the team responsible for crafting the presentation had read *The Presentation Secrets of Steve Jobs*. Jobs delivered wow moments in every product launch. It's a technique leaders can and should copy to bring their product stories to life.

- In 2009 Cisco CEO John Chambers introduced a new technology called Telepresence at a presentation in India. Telepresence is a set of high-definition cameras and monitors rigged to make it look like two people in different locations are actually in the same room together. Chambers explained that the Cisco vice president in charge of video, Marthin De Beer, had to stay back at the home office in San Jose, California. "Marthin, I wish you could be here,"[3] Chambers said. On cue, Marthin De Beer walked on stage to take his place next to John, or so it seemed. Cisco had set up a Telepresence monitor, which made De Beer look as though he were physically on stage. "I thought you were teaching classes in San Jose, Marthin. Where are you?" Chambers asked. "I am in California, John," De Beer said. "I'm 14,000 miles away." The two men then launched into the presentation and delivered an education on the future of virtual meetings, healthcare, and other areas where people need to collaborate face-to-face over long distances. John Chambers values the power of storytelling to such a high degree, Cisco surveys its customers and rates every executive's public presentations. Chambers openly shares his scores and demands to see the scores of others. At Cisco, storytelling starts at the top.

- In 2007 Steve Jobs introduced the first iPhone. The audience expected Apple to introduce three products because Jobs set the expectations himself at the start of his presentation. "We have three products . . . The first one is a widescreen iPod with touch controls. The second is a revolutionary mobile phone. And the third is a breakthrough Internet communications device."[4] Jobs paused and repeated the products again. "An iPod, a phone, and an Internet communicator." He paused and repeated the products again. "An iPod, a phone, are you getting it? These are not three separate devices. This is one device. And we are calling it iPhone." Steve Jobs set expectations, and within the next 30 seconds, broke those expectations. The 2007 launch of the iPhone is considered by many to be one of the greatest business presentations of all time.

- In my own keynote presentations on the subject of communication and storytelling, I refer to the Steve Jobs iPhone presentation to pull my own wow moment. I ask the audience for a show of hands: "Who has seen the 2007 iPhone presentation?" A few hands go up. "I bet I can predict which part of the presentation you remember the most," I say. "In fact I'm so confident about it I've already included it in my next slide. Can you tell me what left the biggest impression with you?" I ask some of the audience members. Nearly every person who has seen the presentation names the same portion—"The part where Steve Jobs said he had three products, but it turned out to be one." People are surprised when I show them that I accurately predicted what they'd say. It's not magic. I'm not psychic. I simply understand expectancy violation.

In a 1991 paper titled "The Narrative Construction of Reality,"[5] psychologist Jerome Bruner noted that a story is a sequence of events that occur in a certain order. For example, boy meets girl, they fall in love, get married, and live happily ever after. A "good story," however, offers "canon and breach." The "breach" is the page-turner, the unexpected twist that keeps you glued to the page or the screen. It's the breach that turns story into a compelling narrative that leaves an audience breathless.

The author Nicholas Sparks has sold 100 million books because he's a master of the breach. In *The Notebook,* a man reads a story to a woman in a nursing home. It's a classic story. Boy meets girl and they fall in love. But circumstances get in the way and they are no longer together. The girl's mother provides the first breach. Allie is a rich girl and her mother forbids her to see the boy, Noah, who works at the mill. A second breach—World War II—seems to put a permanent end to their love affair. But Noah returns from the war. Perhaps now they'll be together? Not quite. A third breach—Allie is engaged. Noah, however, has never forgotten her and spends years restoring a house hoping she'll return. Allie breaks off the engagement and returns to Noah. A happy ending, right? Not quite. Another breach—the woman in the nursing home is Allie and she's suffering from Alzheimer's. The story her husband reads daily by her bedside is their real-life love story. *The Notebook* is a roller-coaster ride because there are constant breaches of expectations. It's also a hit.

The greatest stories of our time—in movies, books, and yes, presentations—have canon and breach. Just when the audience thinks it knows what will happen next, a plot twist occurs. Business legends like Bill Gates have learned that it's not enough to tell a story. Average stories don't solve big problems. Hits do.

The Storyteller's Secret

One guideline that TED gives its speakers is to avoid "trotting out thy usual shtick." By violating expectations, storytellers who successfully educate their audiences give people something to talk about. They violate expectations in a positive way, crafting stories that are unexpected, shocking, or surprising.

12

What You Don't Understand Can (and Does) Hurt You

Stories are an essential part of how individuals understand and use evidence.

—Dr. Zachary F. Meisel

Adam found it nearly impossible to sit still, stay focused, or finish his schoolwork. He was hyperactive and impulsive. "I struggled with academics, even though I knew I was fully capable of performing well in school,"[1] Adam recalls. He was frustrated in school. In his early twenties, a doctor told Adam that he had ADHD (attention deficit hyperactivity disorder). The diagnosis explained his problems in school and his inability to finish anything he started.

As a young adult, Adam turned to music and found that he still had trouble focusing—not in class, but in the studio. "I had 30 ideas floating through my mind and just couldn't document them . . . when I can't pay attention, I really can't pay attention,"[2] Adam said. He went back to the doctor and learned that ADHD doesn't go away as a person grows out of childhood.

Adam decided to "own" his ADHD and sought treatment. With renewed focus Adam Levine threw himself into his music career and, together with his band Maroon 5, went on to win every major music recognition including Grammy, MTV, and Billboard music awards. Levine is estimated to earn more than $35 million a year, which includes the fee he receives as a coach on NBC's hit show *The Voice*.

Adam Levine is lucky. Eighty-five percent of adults who have ADHD don't even know it. Many are in prison. Many bounce from job to job. Many have experienced a string of failed relationships. ADHD is a grossly misunderstood medical condition. Some parents chalk up their child's inability to focus as a normal part of being a kid. Some parents think their child will grow out of it. Wrong and wrong. By openly sharing his story, Adam Levine helps thousands of people recognize the symptoms in themselves and encourages them to seek out an accurate diagnosis.

The condition of ADHD is actually well understood in the medical community. Outside of the medical community, however, it is surrounded by myth and misunderstanding. The problem lies in how the ADHD story is told.

Which of the following statements would you find to be more empowering?

"ADHD is a neurological disorder associated with a pattern of excessive inactivity in the frontal lobes of the brain. It is characterized by distractibility, hyperactivity, and impulsivity."

"ADHD is like having a Ferrari engine for a brain with bicycle brakes. Strengthen the brakes and you have a champion. People with ADHD are the inventors and the innovators, the movers and the doers, the dreamers who built America."[3]

Both statements are equally true. I think you'll agree that an adult who might have the condition or a parent who believes their child might have it will see ADHD far differently and be more inclined to treat it after hearing the second explanation. Dr. Ed Hallowell, a leading psychiatrist and a former faculty member of the Harvard Medical School, reserves the first explanation for people who have medical degrees and the second for everybody else.

The Storyteller's Tools

Hallowell's approachable explanation has made him a media darling. He has appeared on *60 Minutes, Good Morning America, The Oprah Winfrey Show, The Dr. Oz Show,* and nearly every other major media outlet. Hallowell sells millions of books and has appeared on television for 25 years because he makes complex subjects accessible. Hallowell credits having majored in

English for giving him the storytelling skills to explain complex science simply. "I didn't fit the mold of most medical students. They are science majors. I was an English major at Harvard before attending medical school at Tulane. Both sides of my brain were working,"[4] Hallowell once told me for an article I wrote for Forbes.com.

Hallowell comes armed to every television interview with the ultimate storyteller's weapon, a tool so potent it's nearly impossible to ignore.

Analogy: The storyteller's secret weapon

The ancient Greeks introduced analogy as a powerful means of persuasion. Today there's a new body of research looking at the power of analogy in product marketing, but for great storytellers, analogy has always been an essential part of their toolkit. An analogy is simply a comparison of how two things are alike. Analogy facilitates understanding because it makes abstract ideas more relatable. If a listener cannot relate to an idea, that person will find it difficult to remember the concept and unlikely to act on the information.

Hallowell uses analogies to bring clarity to complexity. "We need to use more analogies in this field,"[5] Hallowell says. "With ADHD, a list of symptoms doesn't show the power of the traits these people have—they are creative and imaginative. We're the people who colonized this country. Who would get on a boat in the 1600s and come over here? You'd have to be a visionary, a pioneer, a dreamer, and a risk-taker. That's why our gene pool is loaded with ADD. I see it as the American edge." In addition to the Ferrari Brain, Hallowell relies on several other analogies to explain ADHD to nonmedical audiences:

- "As ADD folks we have new ideas all the time. It's like a popcorn machine."
- "Take someone to a farm and leave them there for a week. If you come back a week later and they've turned the farm into amusement part, it's ADHD. If they're quietly relaxing on the porch, it was a severe case of modern life."
- "The mind of an ADD person is like a toddler on a picnic. It goes wherever the mind leads it without any regard for danger or authority. Sometimes it goes off and gets into trouble, other times it's discovering penicillin."

- "Telling someone with ADHD to try harder is like telling someone who's nearsighted to squint harder. It's not a matter of effort and will. It's a matter of how you're wired."

Analogies are the building blocks of an effective narrative intended to explain complex subjects. Analogies help us understand material we know little about because we can associate the content with something we do know something about.

Analogies are particularly critical in healthcare-related businesses. Adam Jackson is a successful entrepreneur who has started three venture-capital backed companies. He is the cofounder and CEO of Doctor on Demand, a service that puts you in touch with a doctor—face-to-face—through a computer, smartphone, or tablet. "Nothing is more important than storytelling,"[6] Jackson told me when we discussed the challenges of explaining the concept to the average consumer. Building an analogy from what is unknown—a digital interface with a physician—to what is known is an important component in the education process. Jackson uses the analogy of Urgent Care in his presentations.

"Doctor on Demand is like going to Urgent Care for a cold, flu, or sinus infection. You tell us what's wrong, we connect you to a board certified doctor licensed in your state, and you'll have a visit just like you were sitting in their office. In 10 or 15 minutes, we've just saved you a trip to Urgent Care or the long wait time to get in to your private care physician," Jackson explained.

Urgent Care is a category of medical clinic outside of the traditional emergency room. I've been to Urgent Care for a back sprain and my wife has been there for a cold. Many Americans are like us and are familiar with the service or they've experienced the pain of waiting for days or weeks to see their primary care doctor. Doctor on Demand is a new platform. If Jackson fails to make it relatable through analogy, he risks confusing his audience. Confusion makes education nearly impossible.

Personal Stories Grab Attention

When Ed Hallowell first appeared on the *Today* show a producer told him to remember that he's competing for the viewer's attention. How do you get viewers to pay attention when they are otherwise preoccupied with children, chores, or computer work? Hallowell has also learned that nothing is as attention-grabbing as revealing personal stories and experiences. Hallowell readily admits he has ADHD and dyslexia in every conversation and he doesn't wait to be asked: "I'm all about transparency and personalizing a discussion. You really grab people when you tell them about yourself, especially if it's something offbeat like 'I have ADD.' I tell stories to connect with my audience. When they leave my lecture I want them to take away the points, but I also want them to be hopeful and inspired. That happens through connection."[7]

According to an essay in *The Journal of the American Medical Association*, many medical experts "shun individual stories" in favor of the data used to bolster their argument. It's too bad because, as we have seen, stories are important tools for education, and what more important education is there than that related to our health? "Narratives—in the forms of storytelling, testimonials, and entertainment—have been shown to improve individual health behaviors in multiple settings,"[8] write Drs. Zachary F. Meisel and Jason Karlawish. "Moreover, evidence from social psychology research suggests that narratives, when compared with reporting statistical evidence alone, can have uniquely persuasive effects in overcoming preconceived beliefs and cognitive biases . . . Scientific reports are genuinely dispassionate, characterless, and ahistorical. But their translation and dissemination should not be." The doctors conclude that facts and figures are essential in healthcare debates, but aren't nearly enough to encourage people to change their behavior.

In the winter of 2015 a disease that had been nearly eradicated made a roaring comeback. The United States saw its worst measles outbreak in 20 years because thousands of parents had opted out of vaccinating their children. The measles vaccine was introduced in 1963; before that, 500,000 children got the measles every year, and hundreds of them died.

The situation so threatened the public health that the Centers for Disease Control and Prevention (CDC) and the White House didn't take any chances. Appearing on the *Today* show, President Barack Obama called the science "indisputable." According to Obama, "We've looked at this again and again. There is every reason to get vaccinated, but there aren't reasons to not . . . you should get your kids vaccinated."[9]

Obama urged parents to "look at the science, look at the facts." This well-intended statement likely did not have the result he hoped. Leaders often rely on emotionless facts to influence people who are emotional be-ings. The CDC director, Dr. Tom Frieden, appeared on CBS's *Face the Nation* to warn Americans that the country could see a "large outbreak" of measles. He, too, gave viewers plenty of facts, but no individual stories.

Despite the overwhelming evidence that vaccines protect children, two events caused some parents to be skeptical. First, a study published in a pres-tigious medical journal had linked childhood vaccinations to autism. The study had a big problem—it wasn't true. The doctor behind the study had fabricated the data and the journal in which it was published took the unpre-cedented step of apologizing and retracting the article. Dozens of studies followed, all finding no connection between vaccines and autism.

The fabricated story might have been all the evidence people needed to dismiss the false association between vaccines and autism. But something else happened that reignited the anti-vaccine movement, and it came in the form of story. An attractive celebrity—a former Playboy model—publicly dis-missed the evidence that vaccines are good and said she "knew" that the measles vaccine caused her son's autism. "My son is my science," she told a cheering studio audience.

If you've read this far, then you know exactly why the celebrity had an outsize influence on the narrative—personal stories are irresistible. Stories trump data. So what should the medical community have done to dispel the anti-vaccine myth? Tell stories of their own—stories of children who suffer from encephalitis or stories of families who lost their children to a disease that had all been eliminated from the United States. "When scien-tists encounter stories that promote unscientific approaches to health and healthcare, they should deploy an evidence-based counternarrative,"[10] ac-cording to Meisel and Karlawish. "Narratives have been shown to be most helpful for boosting clarity and believability of a health message if recipi-ents identify with characters from the stories."

What parents need to hear are counternarratives, the true and deeply disturbing stories behind the estimated 145,000 individuals around the world who lost their lives to measles last year.

A British site called the Vaccine Knowledge Project publishes informa-tion on infectious diseases by way of content "designed with a non-specialist audience in mind." The people behind the site know that "non-specialists" relate to stories, which is why the site is stuffed with heart-wrenching sto-ries of individuals who suffer from diseases such as measles.

Visitors of the site will learn the story of Sarah Clow. Clow was not vaccinated against measles as a child. The measles attacked her entire body, including her brain. She was in a coma for eight weeks and is now deaf and partially blind.

Visitors to the site will also learn the story of Sarah Walton, who caught the measles when she was 11 months old. Although she recovered, Sarah contracted a viral infection connected to her measles 24 years later. It destroyed her central nervous system. Sarah's mother, who is Sarah's care-giver, narrates the video by Sarah's bedside as Sarah lies on the bed, largely unresponsive with a feeding tube in her nose.

As an expert in the spread of diseases, Melinda Gates knows facts. She also knows how to deliver facts effectively by wrapping them in story. "Women in the developing world know the power of vaccines,"[11] she told *The Huffington Post* during the peak of the anti-vaccine controversy. "They will walk 10 kilometers in the heat with their child and line up to get a vaccine because they have seen death. We've forgotten what measles deaths look like . . . but in Africa, the women know death and they want their children to survive." Gates's interview on the subject went viral across social media because she had provided a powerful "counternarrative" to dispel inaccurate information.

Yes, many people had forgotten what the illness looked like. Stories of real people suffering real complications from not getting vaccinated served as a powerful reminder.

A financial adviser who ranked at the top of his field once told me that storytelling had a major impact on success, specifically because stories help clients see the ramifications of *not* taking action. For example, he paints a picture of what the world might look like should the client decline life insurance.

If something should happen to you and your family loses your income, your spouse might have to take a job she doesn't like. Your family might lose their home. Your kids would have to transfer to another school, and they might not be able to afford college . . . but let's say you make smart financial decisions. Should something happen to you, your family will be taken care of. Your spouse won't have to work if she doesn't want to. Your kids will be able to stay in their home and their school. And when they're in college they'll always think of you as the person who made it possible. Which legacy do you want to leave?

This salesman has generated more than $1 million in revenue for 32 straight years because he's learned that story is one of the most powerful educational tools available

Storytelling matters because what you don't understand can and often does hurt you. The next time you're attempting to make the complex understandable—whether you're in sales, healthcare, business, or teaching—think about Holloway's advice and use analogies and personal stories to replace abstractions and jargon. It might bring your topic into focus and, in some cases, save lives.

The Storyteller's Secret

Statistical evidence and industry jargon are the least effective means to educate a general audience on complex topics. Personal stories and analogies help people make sense of information and ideas they know little about.

13

The $98 Pants That Launched an Empire

> Story is everything, which means it's our job to tell better stories.
> — Kevin Spacey

A $98 pair of pants gave Sara the kick in the butt she needed to start her own business. For eight months the white pants hung in Sara's closet. Every time she tried them on she didn't like what she saw in the mirror. Traditional women's undergarments didn't seem to help. They were uncomfortable and unsightly. In desperation Sara took a pair of scissors and cut off the feet from a pair of panty hose. It solved her problem.

Sara wanted to turn her invention into a business. She was selling fax machines door-to-door at the time and had never taken a business class. She reached out to patent lawyers who charged $5,000. Since Sara only had $5,000 in her savings, she did her homework and patented the idea herself.

Most people told Sara her idea was insane, but their opinions didn't dissuade her. If one door closed, Sara looked for another. Sara's father had taught her about the power of failure. At the dinner table Sara's father would ask, "What did you fail at today?" He would be disappointed if she didn't have anything to say. Failure meant she was trying new things.

One day Sara placed a cold call to a buyer at Neiman Marcus who agreed to meet with her. Sara left her Atlanta apartment, which had doubled as her factory and global headquarters, carried a red backpack that held her samples, and boarded a plane to Dallas. The buyer gave Sara 10 minutes to make her pitch. Within a couple of minutes it became clear to Sara that the buyer was losing interest. Then the light switch flicked on. She would demo the product herself, explaining her product through her own story. She dragged the buyer into the bathroom, where she modeled the product, and sure enough, the buyer agreed to stock Sara's footless pantyhose in seven stores. Twelve years later Sara Blakely, the founder of Spanx, appeared on the cover of *Forbes* as the youngest self-made female billionaire in the world.

Sara Blakely's founder's story is one she tells often in television interviews, speeches, and on the Spanx website. The "About Sara" section of Spanx.com shows a photo of Sara in her original white pants that hung in her closet as she's holding the red backpack. The white pants and the red backpack both play a starring role in the product story.

The Storyteller's Tools

Sara Blakely sold 10 million products without spending a dime in advertising. Blakely leveraged the power of her personal story to make the product relatable and irresistible. In a CNN profile of Blakely, a customer said, "If a girlfriend tells you at a cocktail party or sitting at a restaurant about a product, you tend to become much more loyal and interested in it than if someone showed you a glossy picture in a magazine."[1]

Blakely has also learned the difference between a "story" and a "good" story. Here's a story: Sara invented a product, sold it to a department store, and made a fortune. The preceding sentence meets the definition of a story. It has a beginning, middle, and end. But it's not educational. It's doesn't draw you in. It's not relatable. And if it's none of those things, it certainly has no chance to inspire. Remember, the elements of a good story include struggle, conflict, and resolution. A good story also has specific details to help the listener see herself in the founder's story. A detail such as Sara's seat number on the airplane is irrelevant to the story. The fact that Sara's $98 pair of white pants hung in the closet for eight months because she didn't like the way they looked on her is something that many women can relate to. Sara didn't just bring her samples to Dallas, she carried them in a red backpack. Sara sold her products in red packages, a color that stood out among the other brands of pantyhose on the store shelves. The red backpack is an important symbol in the story. Sara didn't just pitch a buyer. She dragged a buyer at Neiman Marcus into the bathroom to demonstrate how the footless panty hose looked. Specifics add credibility to the story and transport the listener into the founder's world.

Jeffrey Zacks is the director of the Dynamic Cognition Laboratory at Washington University in St. Louis, Missouri. Using brain-imaging technology, he studies the blood flow in the brains of people as they read a book. His mission is to understand why people "get lost" in books. According to Zacks, our brains make vivid mental simulations of the sights, sounds, tastes, and movements we read or hear about. When we hear a speaker share a detailed sequence of events, the same regions of our brain are stimulated as if the experience were happening to us in real life.

Most new products today enter crowded categories. A vivid description of how that product came to exist is often the difference between a product that sits on a shelf and one that catches on. For example, Walmart .com carries about 4,000 headphones. A consumer can choose from in-ear, on-ear, or over-ear headphones. There are studio, sports, wireless, and DJ-quality headphones. There's noise canceling, noise isolating, and wireless headphones. The entrepreneurs at SOL REPUBLIC make a high-quality headphone. They know quality is not enough to capture the imagination of overwhelmed consumers, and so they differentiate their products through the story they share of the company's guiding philosophy.

SOL REPUBLIC cofounders Kevin Lee, Scott Hix, and Seth Combs share a vision of changing the way people listen to music by making great-sounding headphones at a more reasonable price than the high-end products on the market. In an interview, Combs explained the story of the company's founding:

> We sat at Crissy Field in San Francisco on the beach and we wrote a philosophy statement. Our first line is, "We are music lovers committed to changing the world one listener at a time." That was a key takeaway. Another takeaway is that if music sounds better it feels better. If we can get headphones out to everyone that sound good, they'll feel better and it's going to change the world. It was the passion that drove us. It led us to the name. SOL is an acronym that stands for soundtrack of life. Every great moment has a soundtrack that goes with it. From listening to your parents' wedding song, to your own wedding song, these are songs and moments that connect with you emotionally and you carry with you until your last breath. We're a new music lifestyle company that happens to make headphones.[2]

It's often instructive to listen to the response after a founder tells his story. In this case the interviewer, Brian Solis, said, "Anyone listening to that story is going to pick up that you care, that you're really passionate about this. I love what you did and I love that there's emotion behind your product."[3] Solis—a social media expert—said he's tired of soulless mission statements. Instead he, and many other consumers, are searching for products "that matter." Personal and vivid stories breathe life into products and ideas, whether it's an idea for a new headset or an undergarment.

Speaking at a business and marketing conference the actor Kevin Spacey recently offered the following advice: "Good content making is not a crapshoot. We do know how this works. And it has always been about the story. Audiences have spoken. They want stories. They're dying for it. They are rooting for us to give them something to talk about, to carry it with them on the bus and to the hairdresser, to tweet, blog, Facebook, make fan pages, silly gifs, engage with it with a passion and intimacy that a blockbuster movie can only dream of. All we have to do is give it to them. The prize fruit is shinier, juicier, than ever before."[4]

A good story can help explain an idea. A great story educates, entertains, inspires, and ultimately fires up our collective imagination. Tell great ones.

The Storyteller's Secret

Successful founders educate their customers with relatable stories of how they created the product to solve a problem, often one they themselves faced. They share those stories with specific, concrete, and relevant details to transport the listener into their world.

14

Japan Unleashes Its Best Storytellers to Win Olympic Gold

"On my desk in the Oval Office, I have a little sign that says: There is no limit to what a man can do or where he can go if he doesn't mind who gets the credit."

—Ronald Reagan

Mami Sato enjoyed an active lifestyle. Sato's days at Waseda University in central Tokyo were filled with classes, running, swimming, and cheerleading. One day the 19-year-old began to feel pain in her right ankle. The pain turned out to be cancer; within just weeks of the first symptom, she would lose her leg to the disease.

Sato was in deep despair, but she returned to college. At the university she was "saved by sport." She enjoyed setting goals and beating them. She said, "I developed new confidence. Most of all, I learned that what was important was what I had, not what I had lost."[1] Sato trained hard and earned a spot as an athlete at the Athens 2004 Paralympic Games, competing in the long jump event. She competed in Beijing in 2008 and once again in London in 2012. But it was during her preparation for the London Paralympic Games that her life would take another sudden turn.

At 2:46 p.m. on March 11, 2011, a 9.0 magnitude earthquake hit 230 miles northeast of Tokyo, 15 miles beneath the sea. One hour later waves up to 30 feet high rushed ashore the Japanese coast creating a wall of terror, killing more than 15,000 people and destroying the Fukushima nuclear power plant.

In less than seven minutes Sato's hometown, Kesennuma, north of Fukushima, was covered in water. Entire homes were swept away with families still inside. Tuna boats that were once in the bay were grounded in the middle of town. Puddles of water stood in spaces where homes once stood. Very little was left.

Six days went by until Sato learned of her family's fate: they had survived. Sato and a group of athletes collected messages and supplies to bring to the ravished town. More than 200 athletes made 1,000 visits to the area, bringing hope and inspiration to tens of thousands of children and adults. "Only then did I see the true power of sport . . . To create new dreams and smiles. To give hope. To bring people together," Sato said.

Sato shared her story in September 2013 as she stood at a podium to lead off Tokyo's presentation at the 125th session of the International Olympic Committee (IOC) in Buenos Aires, Argentina. Members of the IOC were watching the presentations to award one city the right to host the 2020 Summer Olympics. The other two finalists, Istanbul and Madrid, were said to have the upper hand.

In formal Japanese business presentations, the more senior executive or speaker has the opening role. In a traditional Japanese Olympic bid, a senior leader such as the prime minister would have been expected to speak first. But just 10 days before the finals, the team assembling the presentation realized that they needed to break the rules. They made the decision to kick off the presentation with an emotional story and concluded there would be no better storyteller/athlete than Mami Sato. They had one problem to overcome. Sato had never given a speech in English. "I had a lot of jitters. My legs were shaking in rehearsals,"[2] she later admitted. Sato was told that speaking fluent English was less important than delivering a passionate message and a personal story. "I was a runner. I was a swimmer. I was even a cheerleader," Sato told the Olympic committee about her life before the cancer. Once she returned to college and took up competitive sports, her attitude changed: "I found that I enjoyed setting a goal, and beating it. I developed new confidence. Most of all, I learned that what was important was what I had, not what I had lost. I felt privileged to have been touched by the power of sport."

When the IOC announced that Tokyo had won, hundreds of thousands of people took to the streets of cities and towns across Japan to celebrate. Sato had become a household name. "Sato Shines as Role Model," the *Japan Times* proclaimed. "Sato captured the eyes and ears of the audience by telling her own story," according to the article. The headline on London's

Guardian newspaper read: "Japanese bid's passion earns Tokyo the 2020 Olympic Games." According to the *Guardian,* "The emotional punch underpinning Tokyo's campaign was summed up by the Paralympic long jumper Sato, whose hometown was hit by the tsunami, and who powerfully described the power of sport to inspire."[3] Another article declared, "To succeed, Tokyo had to appeal to the hearts as well as to the heads of the voting IOC members. Tokyo pushed all the right buttons emotionally."[4]

Sato's personal story is only part of the story of how Japan won the right to host the 2020 Summer Olympic Games. The final presentation the Tokyo team delivered in Buenos Aires didn't just begin differently than the judges expected from a Japanese presentation, the entire 45-minute presentation was created for maximum emotional impact, and storytelling would play a starring role.

The Storyteller's Tools

The Japanese contingent all employed the storyteller's art. When Sato stepped off the podium, she introduced the next speaker, who introduced the next speaker, who introduced the next one. In all, eight speakers took their turn pitching the benefits of holding the Olympics in Tokyo. All of the speakers, including Prime Minister Shinzo Abe, shared stories of how sports changed their lives. Some speakers were assigned to tell the story of how citizens of Tokyo treat their guests. They did so because an undercurrent running through the judging process was the fact that the IOC wanted to avoid cities with safety risks and instability. The IOC judges said Tokyo made the case that the Olympics would remain in "a safe pair of hands." For example, in one memorable reference, presenter Christel Takigawa spoke of Tokyo's "selfless hospitality," and announced that every year Tokyo citizens find and return about $30 million that tourists had lost or misplaced. "If you lose something, you will most certainly get it back,"[5] she said.

According to the *Guardian,* "Previous Tokyo bids had been praised for their competence but criticized for lacking passion."[6] The IOC judges credited the Tokyo team for infusing their presentation with emotion and passion. Mami Sato's story set the pace for the rest of the presentation. Having a storyteller like Sato available is a plus, but only if she's allowed to tell her story. Emotional business presentations have drama, heroes, villains, and a collection of voices.

SAP Unleashes the Power of 65,000 Storytellers

When SAP chief executive Bill McDermott hired Julie Roehm to head the marketing department for the global technology giant, he wasn't looking for a traditional marketing director. McDermott hired Roehm as the senior vice president for global marketing, but gave her a title more descriptive of her role: "Chief Storyteller." Roehm told me that McDermott hired her to simplify the SAP story and to make the company's message human, authentic, and relevant to the lives of its customers. The CSO (chief storytelling officer) is a "thoroughly modern title" according to *Fast Company* magazine. As more leaders recognize the need for corporate storytelling, there's a corresponding rise in the number of executives who hold the title. The best CSOs recognize they're not alone in telling a brand story.

"It's false to say I'm the only storyteller,"[7] Roehm said. "We've created tools to allow everyone to be storytellers." SAP has more than 65,000 employees around the world and most of them have stories of how customers are using the company's software to run their businesses. It's impossible for one person in the marketing department to tell those stories. SAP creates "platforms" to let everyone in the organization be a storyteller because you never know when a story is going to happen.

For example, SAP created a smartphone app appropriately called "Share Your Story." The app is a video tool that enables anyone in the SAP universe—employees, customers, partners—to record a video testimonial (easy-to-answer questions serve as a guide) and submit the video clip. The marketing department captures the video, and then reviews, edits, and pushes it out across the company and on social media. "If only one team creates and shares stories, you'll miss a lot of opportunities in the social media age," Roehm says.

The ultimate goal is education. SAP's software can seem complex to new customers. Share Your Story makes it easier for SAP salespeople to educate customers by showing customer stories on any mobile device they happen to be carrying on a new business pitch. Since the videos are categorized, a sales professional can pull up a video that is relevant to the customer's issue.

SAP has the right idea. A *Harvard Business Review* study found that customers are often overloaded by too much information. The researchers found that, when selling complex products, it's more effective to tell vivid stories of other customers and their experiences with the product. Through its digital platforms SAP is unleashing the stories of 65,000 storytellers throughout the organization. Bill McDermott and Julie Roehm are senior leaders, but they recognize that education comes in the form of stories that are being created every day by members of the larger team.

Every brand can craft better stories. The secret is to tap the collective wisdom of all the brand's storytellers.

The Storyteller's Secret

Successful organizations and companies share the stage with their best storytellers. Brands are a collection of narratives. Unleash your best stories.

15

A Funny Look at the Most Popular TED Talk of All Time

> If they're laughing, they're listening.
> —Sir Ken Robinson

"Who calls you, *Sir* Ken Robinson?"
"My children. I insist on it." [1]

That's how Sir Ken Robinson, a prominent educator and TED star, the man who delivered the legendary TED talk "Do Schools Kill Creativity?," viewed more than 32 million times, opened an interview on National Public Radio. One of Robinson's endearing qualities is a disarming sense of humor. But like many of the storytellers in this book, his early years were marked by pain and struggle, tension and triumph—the stuff stories are made of.

Born in Liverpool in 1950, Robinson was one of seven children. His father played semi-professional soccer and had dreams of his son following in his footsteps, and perhaps taking the family soccer legacy to the next level. The father's hopes were dashed when Robinson contracted polio at the age of four, causing partial paralysis in one leg.

Undeterred, Robinson would seek success on the field of academics. He poured himself into his studies and, in 1968, attended Bretton Hall College as an English and drama major. In 1981 Robinson completed a PhD at the University of London with a specialization in theater and drama in education. A list of credentials doesn't make a storyteller, but in Robinson's case his focus on drama explains part of the reason his TED talk would become a viral sensation—indeed the most popular TED talk of all time.

Robinson was a notable voice in creativity, education, and human potential long before his now famous TED talk. Queen Elizabeth had knighted him in 2003 for his contributions to the field of creativity and the arts, but it was his 18-minute TED talk that catapulted him to the world stage.

The subject of Robinson's talk was education, specifically, and why our educational system fails to nurture creativity. While this is certainly a topic of wide popular interest, this alone does not explain how an educator's 18-minute discussion has been viewed more times than any other talk in TED's 30-year history. So what does explain it? Robinson himself may have provided the answer. "If they're laughing, they're listening,"[2] Robinson said.

The Storyteller's Tools

Ken Robinson tells compelling stories that reinforce his theme that the educational system needs to be retooled. As an educator, Robinson knows nobody will stick around for his stories if they've mentally checked out.

"The brain doesn't pay attention to boring things,"[3] writes University of Washington molecular biologist John Medina. Robinson is anything but boring. In his TED talk, the laughs start early. Here are several portions of Robinson's presentation that elicit the biggest laughs in the first 5 minutes.

If you're at a dinner party, and you say you work in education—Actually, you're not often at dinner parties, frankly. [Laughter.] If you work in education, you're not asked. [Laughter.] And you're never asked back, curiously. That's strange to me. But if you are, and you say to somebody, you know, they say, "What do you do?" and you say you work in education, you can see the blood run from their face. They're like, "Oh my God," you know, "Why me?" [Laughter.] "My one night out all week."[4] [Laughter.]

I heard a great story recently—I love telling it—of a little girl who was in a drawing lesson. She was six, and she was at the back, drawing, and the teacher said this girl hardly ever paid attention, and in this drawing lesson, she did. The teacher was fascinated. She went over to her, and she said, "What are you drawing?" And the girl said, "I'm drawing a picture of God." And the teacher said, "But nobody knows

what God looks like." And the girl said, "They will, in a minute."
[Laughter.]

When my son was four in England—Actually, he was four everywhere,
to be honest. [Laughter.] If we're being strict about it, wherever he
went, he was four that year. He was in the Nativity play. Do you
remember the story? [Laughter.] No, it was big, it was a big story. Mel
Gibson did the sequel, you may have seen it. [Laughter.] "Nativity II."
But James got the part of Joseph, which we were thrilled about. We
considered this to be one of the lead parts. We had the place crammed
full of agents in T-shirts: "James Robinson IS Joseph!" [Laughter.]

In the first five minutes Robinson elicited about 10 laughs from the audience. At 2 laughs per minute, that makes Robinson's talk funnier than the
movie *Anchorman* (1.6 laughs per minute) and on par with *The Hangover* (2.5
laughs per minute).

You might have noticed that some of Robinson's humor is self-
deprecating. Although you have to be careful about poking too much fun
at yourself and risk losing credibility, social psychologists have found that a
little self-mockery can score big points with an audience. When a reporter
brought up Robinson's millions of views he responded, "Mind you my son
showed me a video on YouTube recently, which is 90 seconds long. It's of
two kittens that look like they are having a conversation. And that's been
downloaded 20 million times. So I am not getting carried away. Kittens
still win."[5] Modesty is endearing. Combine humility with humor and you've
got presentation gold.

Humor Is an Emotionally Charged Event

Humor is what John Medina calls an "emotionally charged event," much
like joy, fear, or surprise. "When the brain detects an emotionally charged
event, the amygdala releases dopamine into the system. Because dopamine
greatly aids memory and information processing, you could say the Post-it
note reads, 'Remember this!' Getting the brain to put a chemical Post-it note
on a given piece of information means that information is going to be more
robustly processed. It's what every teacher, parent, and ad executive wants."[6]

Humor enhances learning in any language. In a study of international students from 10 countries, the researchers found that the students learned best when the lecturers grabbed their attention with humor. Study participant Xu Yang from China said, "I like funny lecturers. He or she can make lectures interesting and not too boring. Some lecturers are boring, that's the problem."[7] According to the study, "A further significant insight offered by the study is those students' perceptions of 'good' lecturers. It is common sense that good lecturers are lecturers who are knowledgeable. However, the students in this study revealed more than that. They believed that 'good' lecturers are lecturers that go beyond the subject matter, and who are humorous."

Listeners want to be engaged *and* entertained and that hasn't changed for thousands of years. In the scientific paper "Embers of Society," anthropologist Dr. Polly Wiessner found that good storytellers were cherished for their verbal skills, including humor: "Stories provided a win–win situation: those who thoroughly engaged others were likely to gain recognition as their stories traveled. Those who listened were entertained while collecting the experiences of others with no direct cost."[8]

You Don't Need to Tell a Joke to Get a Laugh

People want to learn and laugh. Good storytellers teach and have fun. When Jon Stewart stepped down as host of Comedy Central's *The Daily Show* after 16 years, it was big news because Stewart had become a significant source of information for members of the Millennial generation. Many Americans in the age range of 18 to 34 cited *The Daily Show* as their primary source of news. Stewart often beat the established nightly news programs in the ratings among that age group, as well. The success of *The Daily Show* proved that the secret to high ratings is a charismatic host who combines educational content with humor.

You may be saying to yourself: *That's fine, but I'm not funny, and so this advice is of no use to me.* But the funny thing about humor is that you don't need to tell a joke to get a laugh—you just have to be able to recognize a funny situation. Great storytellers ditch the urge to be clever and just tell people about an experience or event that elicited a smile. If something made them chuckle, there's a good chance their audience will, too.

Apple executive Craig Federighi is getting a lot of stage time these days. His boss, Apple CEO Tim Cook, once called the senior vice president of software engineering "Superman" because he commanded up to 70 percent of a new product launch. When Federighi takes the stage he often steals the show. It's easy to see why. Right out of the gate Federighi injects humor into his presentations. Federighi kicked off a discussion of the new Apple operating system, "Yosemite," by poking fun at the "crack product marketing team" that develops names. "We shoved them in their VW mini bus and set them out on the road. They ventured south and discovered OS X Oxnard . . . before boldly venturing north, landing at OS X 'weed.' Strangely, this had large pockets of support within the product marketing organization,"[9] Federighi said as 6,000 attendees laughed and cheered at the marijuana reference. Throughout the presentation Federighi pulled a Ken Robinson, poking good-natured fun at himself, especially his mane of salt-and-pepper hair, which he jokingly refers to as "hair force one."

When Federighi was demonstrating new phone features of the iOS devices he was interrupted by a call from his mother (all of this is planned and rehearsed, of course). "She surely wants to grill me about the newest fourth tier LVM compiler, but this is not the right time," as he hung up on her. The audience playfully groaned when Federighi hung up on his mother. "I'm sorry," Federighi responded. "She's a wonderful, wonderful woman, but this is my space," he said with a smile.

The Serious Reason to Use Humor

"The end of laughter is followed by the height of listening," according to sales coach Jeffrey Gitomer. It's important to note that storytellers like Craig Federighi or Ken Robinson use humor not for the laugh itself, but for what follows: to grab attention and tee-up the key story that supports their product or idea. For example, once the laughs subsided in Robinson's TED talk, he told the story of Gillian Lynne. Here's a lightly edited excerpt from Robinson's presentation:

> Gillian Lynne. Have you heard of her? Some have. She's a choreographer, and everybody knows her work. She did *Cats* and *Phantom of the Opera*. She's wonderful . . . Gillian and I had lunch one day and I said, "How did you get to be a dancer?" It was interesting. When she was at school, she was really hopeless. And the school, in the 30s, wrote to her parents and said, "We think Gillian has a learning

disorder." She couldn't concentrate; she was fidgeting. I think now they'd say she had ADHD. Wouldn't you? But this was the 1930s, and ADHD hadn't been invented at this point. It wasn't an available condition. [Laughter.] People weren't aware they could have that. [Laughter.] Anyway, she went to see this specialist . . . In the end, the doctor went and sat next to Gillian, and said, "I've listened to all these things your mother's told me, I need to speak to her privately. Wait here. We'll be back; we won't be very long," and they went and left her. But as they went out of the room, he turned on the radio that was sitting on his desk. And when they got out, he said to her mother, "Just stand and watch her." And the minute they left the room, she was on her feet, moving to the music. And they watched for a few minutes and he turned to her mother and said, "Mrs. Lynne, Gillian isn't sick; she's a dancer. Take her to a dance school."[10]

Robinson wrote a book called *The Element,* about following your life's true mission, where "natural aptitude meets personal passion."[11] Robinson says there's a serious reason for finding one's element: "Very many people lack purpose in their lives. The evidence of this is everywhere: in the sheer numbers of people who are not interested in the work they do; in the growing numbers of students who feel alienated by the education system; and in the rising use everywhere of antidepressants, alcohol, and painkillers."

Nobody's going to listen to a story if they're not paying attention and if they're not paying attention, they won't learn. Robinson's serious themes would struggle to find a large audience if it hadn't been for his humorous take on everyday situations.

The Storyteller's Secret

Effective educators serve up serious stories with a side of funny.

16

Dirt, Cigars, and Sweaty Socks Put a Marketer on the Map

Quality storytelling always wins. *Always*.
—Gary Vaynerchuk

Nazi Germany invaded Belarus in 1941. More than 1 million Jews were killed in the occupation, about 90 percent of the Jewish population. The Soviet Red Army drove out the Germans in 1944; the USSR would occupy the country for the next 47 years, and life for its residents, particularly for the country's remaining Jews, was difficult to say the least. When, in 1978, Jews were given special permission to leave the country, a man named Sasha seized the opportunity to move his family to Queens, New York. "America was a place where you could build a life for yourself according to your own rules, and you didn't have to wait six hours in line to buy a loaf of bread, either,"[1] according to his son, Gary Vaynerchuk.

Gary was three years old when his family began a new life in America. The American economy was tanking in those days, and Gary watched his dad work as a stock clerk in a liquor store to make ends meet. Gary remembers the tight times, but he doesn't recall his parents complaining. Ever. "My parents were hungry—hungry to provide for their family, and hungry to win,"[2] says Gary. Although Gary adopted his family's work ethic to become a successful entrepreneur and to help his father run a successful wine store, Gary's storytelling skill launched his personal brand on social media.

Armed with passion, knowledge, and a Jets helmet that doubled as a spit bucket, "Gary Vee" launched Wine Library TV in 2006. It was the first video wine blog and one of the first video blogs in any field. Using a simple Flip video camera Gary recorded himself talking about wine and posted the videos to a platform that had started exactly one year earlier, YouTube.

Vaynerchuk's first episode, on February 21, had a simple set: a circular office desk, three bottles of wine, wineglasses, and a spit bucket. A video edit occurs about 4 minutes into the 12-minute episode. Vaynerchuk explains that the camera wasn't working correctly and he had to run out to Best Buy to purchase a new one. Vaynerchuk was transparent from the very beginning. "Watch me for two seconds and you know exactly who I am and what I stand for. Authenticity is key,"[3] he says. By the time Vaynerchuk ended the show on the one-thousandth episode, he had established himself as one of the preeminent storytellers on social media. But make no mistake: Wine Library TV was not created for the sole purpose of selling wine over the Internet. Vaynerchuk says he started it to build equity in his personal brand. Storytelling would play a key role in advancing his personal brand. And not just any story, but a story only Vaynerchuk could tell in his unique and authentic style.

The Storyteller's Tools

In Vaynerchuk's very first episode it was clear that he had a deep knowledge of the world of wine and could hold his own with the connoisseurs of the industry. While he was swirling a 2001 Vérité La Muse he said, "The nose is remarkable. It's 85 percent Merlot, a little bit of Cab Franc, about 13 percent, classic Pomerol-style. When I smell this, it reminds me of a VCC [Vieux Château Certan]. I'm not going to push the Petrus envelope, but it's way up there, let's put it that way."[4] Nobody talks that way about a glass of wine unless they really know their stuff. Vaynerchuk was no pretender.

Although 97 percent of all wines sold in the United States are under $10 a bottle, most wine critics and reviewers use terms only wine aficionados can understand. Vaynerchuk did something different. Although he was clearly proficient in the language of wine royalty, he typically spoke in the language of the commoner. Vaynerchuk made wine approachable. The experts, he said:

> Swirl and smell and slurp and spit and then spout the same classic terminology every time, how the bouquet was rose petals or the finish was silk. I would stick my nose in my glass suck in a mouthful of air and wine, and the only thing running through my head would be, "Man, this really tastes like Big League Chew" or, "If this isn't a Whatchamacallit

bar, I don't know what is." It's not that I didn't appreciate the complexity of an excellent vintage . . . I just didn't see why I had to use the same forty-five-cent words to describe my experience when drinking it.[5]

Conan Eats Dirt, Cigars, Wet Rocks, and Sweaty Socks

It didn't take long for Vaynerchuk's authentic storytelling style to attract fans and generate buzz. In 2007 comedian and talk show host Conan O'Brien invited Gary to appear on his show, to teach the viewers on how to train their palate for wine tasting. The next 10 minutes were social media gold.

Conan acknowledged that many people think of wine critics as snobs. "It's very intimidating. When I'm in a restaurant and they ask me about wine, I feel like I need to know a lot. Like I'm not educated enough. I think a lot of us feel inferior,"[6] Conan said.

The first wine that Vaynerchuk featured was a New Zealand Sauvignon Blanc, which is often described as having notes of grapefruit and grass. He squeezed a grapefruit into a dish of grass and ate it. Conan did the same. The next wine was a Sancerre. To help understand "minerality," Vaynerchuk gave Conan a wet rock to lick. Next came the red wines. Since red wines are often described as characteristic of the soil from which the grapes are grown as well as fruit and tobacco, he mixed dirt, cherries, and a cigar into a dish and ate a handful. Conan's jokes and expressions during the segment brought the house down.

For the last wine, a French Burgundy, Vaynerchuk wanted Conan to try a "sweaty sock." Gary reached down, took off his shoes, and held up a sock. He smelled it and said, "This is really the essence of Burgundy." Since French Burgundy is also said to have a hint of asparagus, he wrapped the sock around a piece of asparagus and offered it to Conan. "No! No! I'm not going to eat your sock," said Conan. "I'll eat my own," he said with perfect comedic timing. The video of the wine-tasting segment went viral and a social media star was born.

Know Your Stuff, but Be True to Your Brand

Vaynerchuk is widely considered a social media powerhouse, but he defines himself as a "storytelling entrepreneur" because he understands that social impact is the direct result of creating content people will want to see and read. "I'm only interested in one thing, the one thing that binds us all together. No matter what your profession is, no matter what you do, our job is to tell our story and that is never going to change,"[7] says Vaynerchuk. "The way you make great money, the way you make great impact, the way you make great change is through great storytelling. It's always been that way and will always be that way."

Vaynerchuk has parlayed his content into a powerful personal brand that extends to books, keynote speeches, and a digital consulting agency that employs nearly 200 people. Vaynerchuck acknowledges he rubs some people the wrong way. For example, his speeches are laced with profanity. The descriptions of his presentations on YouTube often come with a warning that the material contains curse words. Some may find the language acceptable; others do not. The point is that Vaynerchuk stayed true to his personality from day one and in today's social media environment, authenticity is rewarded. "Your brand will be unique and interesting because you are unique and interesting,"[8] says Vaynerchuk. "Don't put on an act to try to imitate me or anyone else who's had some success with social marketing. You will lose because people can sniff out a poser from a mile away." Storytelling is not a press release, Vaynerchuk reminds us. "You need to be authentic from the heart, not a cold-minded press release that means nothing to anybody," Vaynerchuk once admonished. The opposite of the press release is being "in the trenches," sharing your personal story and your customers' stories on every available platform and doing so from the heart.

Vaynerchuk convincingly argues that brands are built by embracing their DNA, their unique identity. "It doesn't matter what you're selling, identify what makes you unique and interesting and have the courage to be authentic across all of the social media platforms from which you share your story. Be yourself, put out awesome content, and people will be interested in what you have to say."[9]

While many marketers create one story and push it out across several social platforms (Facebook, Twitter, Instagram, etc.), Vaynerchuk recommends that marketers stay true to the brand while tailoring the story to meet the unique demands of specific social media venues and audiences. "The far majority of people—business companies, organizations, media companies, all across the board—are storytelling like it's 2007."[10] For example, Vaynerchuk likens sites like Twitter, Facebook, Vine, and Instagram to creating a "gateway drug to awareness." These sites were never intended to host comprehensive long-form content, but rather to seed your interest with just enough information to grab your attention and serve as a gateway to your full material.

The Storyteller's Secret

Successful brands—individuals and companies—see themselves as storytellers first. They go to where their audiences are living their lives and, once there, create authentic, personal, and passionate stories that are tailored to fit the way their audiences consume content.

17

A Burger with a Side of Story

People will forget what you said, people will forget what you did, but people will never forget how you made them feel.

—Maya Angelou

Danny never wanted to be a lawyer, so how did he find himself having dinner with his uncle Richard and aunt Virginia just 12 hours before taking the law school entrance exam? Something didn't feel right.

"I can't believe I'm doing this LSAT thing tomorrow, I don't even want to be a lawyer,"[1] Danny confided.

"Why don't you just do what you've been thinking about your whole life?" Richard asked.

"What's that?"

"All you've ever talked about is food. Open a restaurant," Richard suggested.

Uncle Richard was right. Food and restaurants had consumed Danny's attention since he was a little boy. While most people vividly remember the sights and sounds from trips they took when they were young, few people can recall the exact dishes they ate at those destinations. Danny was different. "When I was four I fell in love with stone crab at the Lagoon restaurant in Miami Beach. Over the next years I remember savoring variations of key lime pie in Key West, trying Dungeness crab and saline abalone at San Francisco's Fisherman's Wharf; and having a lobster roll in Ogunquit, Maine . . . I tasted a baguette with saucisson and pungent moutarde in Paris's Jardin des Tuileries."[2]

Yes, Danny was different but he didn't know it until his uncle brought it to his attention over dinner in 1983. Danny took the LSAT the next morning, but never applied to law school. Instead, he left a $125,000 job as a commissioned salesman to make $250 a week as an assistant manager in a restaurant. Danny's salary plummeted, but he was on a high. Danny looks back at his uncle's suggestion as "the greatest gift" he ever received. Danny had found his calling.

For two years Danny studied everything about the restaurant industry. He describes a return trip from Rome as a "scribble fest." An eight-hour plane trip wasn't enough time to write down all of the ideas he was bringing home. Danny said the feeling was like "an intense desire, a burning sense of urgency." Danny didn't go looking for a career. It grabbed him by the shoulder and wouldn't let go.

Three years after that fateful dinner, Danny Meyer opened his first restaurant in New York City, Union Square Cafe. It would sit atop the Zagat restaurant guide food rankings for many years. More followed: Gramercy Tavern, Blue Smoke, The Modern, Maialino. Meyer's Union Square Hospitality Group now owns and manages some of the most acclaimed restaurants in town. In 2001, Meyer tried something a little different. He opened a stand in Madison Square Park selling hot dogs. It lost $5,000 in its first year. It lost $7,500 in its second year, before breaking even in its third year. In the fourth year Meyer turned the cart into a 20-by-20-foot kiosk and added burgers, shakes, and sundaes to the menu. Shake Shack was born. Fourteen years later Shake Shack had more than 60 locations around the world including London, Moscow, Dubai, and Tokyo. On January 30, 2014, Shake Shack went public. Shares doubled on their first day of trading, valuing the company at $1.6 billion.

From the opening day of his first restaurant, Meyer knew that patrons wanted good food at a fair price, but they'd return because of how they were made to feel. Hospitality is king. The emotional experience guests have at one of Meyer's restaurants means everything to him. According to Meyer, a company's culture sets the foundation for its success and a great culture is built on its stories.

The Storyteller's Tools

"Culture is a way to describe how we do things around here,"[3] says Danny Meyer. "If you can use stories to provide examples, you get closer to perpetuating and advancing the culture." Meyer tells stories, lots of them. He tells stories in television interviews. He tells stories in keynote speeches. And, most importantly, he tells stories to educate cooks, chefs, sommeliers, and servers in the art of customer service.

Stories educate employees on the fine art of customer service because they bring abstract concepts to life. For example, Meyer is an entrepreneur and he wants his staff to think like entrepreneurs on the restaurant floor. An entrepreneur often spends a little more upfront for the potential of a bigger reward down the line. Meyer makes the concept tangible with the following story.

My wife and I were having dinner at Eleven Madison Park, a restaurant I used to own. We could see and hear what was going on at the next table. It was very clear that a young woman had just moved to New York from somewhere in the Midwest. She had brought her parents to dinner at this expensive restaurant and it was clear that they didn't think it was a good idea that their daughter had just moved to the city. It was also clear that she wanted to show her parents that New Yorkers were, in fact, very nice and it was a great place for her to live. The restaurant's job was to help the daughter achieve her mission, which was to help her make the parents feel more comfortable about her decision. Things are going pretty well until the dessert menu is being handed out. The father looks at the menu and says, "Are you kidding? $42 for one glass of dessert wine?" The father starts laughing and says, "That's what I'm talking about here in New York. Everything is so expensive." The wine was Chateau D'Yquem. It's actually a fair price at $42 a glass. The waiter overhears the entire conversation and, five minutes later, shows up at the table with three glasses and a bottle of Chateau D'Yquem. The waiter says, "We are so grateful that you came tonight. I heard you talking about the Chateau D'Yquem. This is one of the rarest and best dessert wines in the entire world and we would love to offer you each a taste with our compliments." He pours out the equivalent of a third of a glass for everybody so it probably cost us $42—the perceived value—and he gave it as a gift. I'm high-fiving my wife because it's the greatest thing I've ever seen. What a brilliant moment of entrepreneurship. The server sized up the situation and decided that giving the equivalent of a $42 gift to these people at this

table at this moment—and doing it with love and generosity—will
probably return $4,200 in word of mouth. The parents will feel great
and the daughter will feel great about taking her parents here.[4]

The Mind Is Wired for Stories, Not Abstractions

For Meyer, entrepreneurship is using your head and your heart in a way
that makes guests feel great about their experience. Meyer's criteria for hiring is to look for people with a "high HQ," a high hospitality quotient. He
defines ideal candidates as 51-percenters. He looks for candidates who have
49 percent technical proficiency and 51 percent emotional skills. Technical
skills like how to set a table are teachable. But how do you motivate people to
create emotional experiences? For example, if Meyer simply tells his staff
that they are empowered to do what's in the best interest of the customer,
the concept will not have the same impact as the story he tells. The human
brain doesn't handle abstractions well. It's wired for story. "Over time we
can almost always train for technical prowess. We can teach people how
to deliver bread or olives, take orders for drinks or present menus; how to
describe specials . . . training for emotional skills is next to impossible,"[5]
according to Meyer.

A writer for *Delta Sky* magazine interviewed Danny Meyer on the
subject of building a winning culture. Meyer told one story that so perfectly
captured what he was trying to attain the writer couldn't help but to
include it in the magazine article. The writer said the story even made an
impact on him. It went like this. Meyer had taken a business trip to Florida. When he got to his hotel room, he just wanted to kick back, order a
cheeseburger, and watch his beloved Cardinals (Meyer grew up in St. Louis,
Missouri) take on the San Francisco Giants in a play-off game. The writer
picks up the story.

When he discovered that the hotel didn't carry Fox Sports 1 in the
room and the game was blacked out on his iPad, he went down to
the bar. The TV was tuned into the Jets-Patriots pre-game show, but
nobody was in the bar, and the waiter switched the channel over to
the baseball game for him. "Later, the bar started to fill up a bit, and
the television magically switched over to the Jets game." When the
waiter came over to check on him, he noticed somebody had changed

the channel. "Not a big deal," Meyer told him. "I'll just take my cheeseburger over to the other lobby bar, nobody is over there." But the waiter insisted. "No, that's not right. You were here first. Let me take care of this for you." The waiter returned with the remote control, switched the channel back to the baseball game, removed the batteries from the remote and handed them to Danny. "I'm getting shivers just telling you this . . . The burger was OK—not great—but I'll never forget that he handed me the batteries."[6]

The writer said the story gave him shivers, too. He understood that Meyer has forged a career on recreating these scenes for his own guests: "Danny Meyer knows what looks good in the movie in his head." Storytelling brings the movie to life.

Stories as Flight Simulators for Real-World Scenarios

"Storytelling supports our culture,"[7] Meyer told me. "My hope is that through storytelling I'm able to name some things that you already knew in your heart, but had not named." Through stories Meyer unlocks hospitality concepts for his staff. This allows them to repeat and perfect the concept, teach it to others, and in the process cement it as part of the team's culture.

It's nearly impossible for a restaurateur to train dozens, hundreds, or in Meyer's case thousands, of employees in every potential scenario. Before pilots take to the sky they spend hours in a flight simulator. Stories act as a flight simulator for real-world scenarios.

Psychology professor Keith Oatley and his research team at the University of Toronto have found that detailed stories stimulate the same neurological regions of the brain that would be activated if we were encountering the situation in real life. The more detailed the description, the more vivid and evocative the story, the more deeply it sears itself into the listener's brain. It helps that Meyer's stories are vivid and emotional. The closer he can bring his listeners to the restaurant floor, the more impactful the story becomes and has a greater chance of leading to desired behaviors Meyer wants to see in his staff.

For example, another powerful hospitality concept that Meyer created is *"ABCD"* which stands for Always Be Connecting Dots. In an industry that many people see as a basic transaction—I give you money, you give me food—Meyer encourages his staff to connect information that can turn a guest's experience into a richer, more memorable event. It sounds good on paper, but it's still an abstract concept. Meyer's stories bring it to life.

Meyer tells the story of the night a political convention was being held in town and 11 members of the press showed up for dinner. One of those guests was then-NBC news anchor Tom Brokaw. Meyer saw 11 opportunities to connect dots and to amplify word of mouth. As Meyer was leaving at 1:00 a.m., the group was still there. He casually said, "If you folks stay long enough we'll have to serve you scrambled eggs for dessert."[8] One guest turned to Meyer and said, "I bet you've never had 'eggs daffodil,' that's the real thing." On his way out Meyer instructed the staff to search for "eggs daffodil" and, if they had the ingredients, to put a bowl of it on the table. Chef Kerry Heffernan found a vague description online, enough to create an inspired recipe. At 2:00 a.m. the group was "blown away" when the wait staff served eggs daffodil in a copper pot. It was so delicious the chef added it to the restaurant's brunch menu. Two years later Meyer ran into Tom Brokaw. Brokaw said he had told at least 12 people the story of the eggs daffodil.

That single act of listening to his customer and using the information learned to make their experience memorable had a clear impact on those 11 people and the people they told about the experience. But Danny Meyer's real genius is in how he uses stories like that to educate and motivate his staff and to impart to them the culture of hospitality that has made his restaurants so successful. Storytelling is a force replicator; it takes that single act and turns it into a regular happening at his restaurant.

Restaurants, like many companies in the field of hospitality, cannot survive without repeat visitors. The more dots a restaurant connects through Google, Open Table, or other means of gathering information about a guest's preferences, the better positioned it is to make a powerful first impression, second impression, third, and so on. Storytelling gives those dots their soul.

The Storyteller's Secret

Business, like life, is all about how you make people feel. Stories help people feel more deeply and help to internalize the behaviors your team is expected to model.

Storytellers Who Simplify

PART III

Storytellers Who Simplify

18

If Something Can't Be Explained on the Back of an Envelope, It's Rubbish

Great leaders are almost always great simplifiers.

—Colin Powell

Richard dropped out of school at the age of 15. Richard has dyslexia and had trouble reading. Although an estimated 4 to 8 percent of schoolchildren have the condition, Richard's teachers and peers didn't understand dyslexia at the time he went to school.

"I was trouble—and always in trouble,"[1] Richard recalls. "By age eight I still couldn't read . . . Dyslexia wasn't deemed a problem in those days, or put more accurately, it was a problem only if you were dyslexic yourself. Since nobody had ever heard of dyslexia, being unable to read, write, or spell just meant to the rest of the class and the teachers that you were either stupid or lazy. And at prep school you were beaten for both."

Like other storytellers in this book Richard turned his weakness into a strength and reframed his life's narrative. After all, the world is filled with famous dyslexics: Thomas Edison, Alexander Graham Bell, Albert Einstein, and Walt Disney to name just a few. Leonardo da Vinci, the great painter, had both dyslexia and ADHD, a trait Richard is nearly certain he has, too. Richard was well aware of these individuals and the power of the mind to shape his future. What he may not have realized at the age of 15 when he dropped out of school was that dyslexia would give him an uncommon advantage.

"The reason that I think people who are dyslexic seem to exceed quite well in life, having had hell at school, is that you do simplify things,"[2] Richard once told CNN's Anderson Cooper.

Sir Richard Branson did do quite well. The billionaire founder of Virgin Group inspires employees and customers with his vision of customer service and philanthropy. Simple storytelling has always been a core component to his success, beginning with his very first venture.

While attending a boarding school in Buckingham, England, the young Richard Branson had an idea. He wanted to launch a magazine that challenged the status quo. The magazine, called *Student,* would spearhead campaigns against bullying and corporal punishment. Branson had a problem, though. He had to persuade advertisers and distributors to back a magazine that had yet to publish a single issue. When the school's headmaster refused to give Branson a phone in his room, Branson used a pay phone to place calls to potential sponsors. "In order to avoid the operator coming back on the line to cut me off," Branson said, "I learned how to pack all this into five minutes."[3]

He discovered by necessity that persuasive storytelling must be confident, clear, and, above all, concise and simple. "Complexity is your enemy. Any fool can make something complicated. It's hard to make something simple,"[4] according to Branson.

"I can't speak for other people but dyslexia shaped my—and Virgin's—communication style,"[5] Branson once told me. "From the beginning, Virgin used clear, ordinary language. If I could quickly understand a campaign concept, it was good to go. If something can't be explained on the back of an envelope, it's rubbish."

The Storyteller's Tools

If something can't be explained on the back of an envelope, it's rubbish. In a short sentence of just 13 words Branson identified one of the key components of a compelling business story—brevity. Branson's advice reminds me of a tip I heard from one of Google's early investors at Sequoia Capital: "If an entrepreneur cannot explain his idea in 10 words or less, I'm not interested and I'm not investing. Period." Clearly, Branson agrees.

Branson values a short story and if it can fit on a beer coaster, even better. Brett Godfrey is a former Virgin Group financial manager who turned a trip to a London pub into an $80 million payday. Godfrey drew up what became the business plan for Virgin Blue (now Virgin Australia) on the back of coasters he had placed his beer on. Branson listened to the "beer mat" pitch and threw his support behind Godfrey's ideas. In 2003, Virgin Blue went public and challenged Ansett and Qantas's stranglehold on the Australian airline industry. The IPO turned Godfrey and his 35 million shares into one of Australia's most successful and admired entrepreneurs. Today Virgin Australia, the company that started on a beer mat, is now the country's second biggest airline.

Investors like Richard Branson want to see the big picture before they dive into the details of a business idea. Just as every story needs a headline and every book needs a title, a good storyteller will start with the one big idea before expanding on the details.

In a business pitch or presentation, the headline is the one sentence that's going to grab your listener's attention and put the narrative into context. It's the one thing your listener needs to know. For the best examples of how to write a headline, look no further than Twitter and its 140-character limit. "In anything I write I now make a conscious effort to condense the point I want to make into a Twitter-like format,"[6] says Branson. "Even if I only manage to get it down to a couple of hundred characters, I can still count on getting my message across much more effectively than if it were ten times the length."

Steve Jobs is the entrepreneur Branson says he most admired. It's easy to see why. Steve Jobs was a master of simplicity and turned the business presentation into an art form. Whenever Jobs introduced a product, he would describe it with one perfectly crafted sentence, or headline, that always fit well within the 140-character Twitter limit. Jobs repeated the headline so often in his presentations and marketing material that consumers and journalists would become marketing extensions of the product, circulating the message in conversations and articles. In 2008 Jobs introduced Apple's first ultraportable notebook, the Macbook Air. "In a sentence," he said, "It's the world's thinnest notebook." In just 29 characters—the world's thinnest notebook—Jobs's message spoke volumes while easily fitting in a Twitter post.

Or another example: in 2001 Steve Jobs knew all too well that 5 gigabytes of storage would be meaningless to his customers. Instead Jobs crafted one sentence that told a complete story. At the product launch for Apple's first MP3 player—the iPod—Jobs told his audience that 5 gigabytes was "the equivalent of 1,000 songs." That was only part of the story. An MP3 music player that stored 1,000 songs wasn't unique at the time, but nobody had been able to do it in so compact a form, so Jobs added one sentence that made all the difference. The iPod, he said, is "1,000 songs in your pocket." In one sentence that easily would have fit in a Twitter post, Jobs spoke volumes and told his consumers nearly everything they needed to know about the new product. In one sentence people knew what they were getting. In one sentence Jobs launched one of the most iconic product taglines in business history.

Creating what I call a "Twitter-friendly headline" requires work because you're hiding complexity. "Simple can be harder than complex,"[7] Steve Jobs once said. "You have to work hard to get your thinking clean to make it simple. But it's worth it in the end because once you get there, you can move mountains."

Richard Branson believes that stories can move mountains, but a speaker must scale the mountain in short bursts of relevant information. Each piece builds on the one before. Just as you can't climb a mountain by starting at the summit, you can't sell an idea by dumping all of the information on your listener. Consider the Twitter-friendly headline as base camp. It sets the foundation for the rest of the conversation. A longer e-mail might be base camp one, a 10-minute presentation might serve as base camp two, and so on, until finally you reach the mountaintop and you've taken your listener along for the journey. Once you've reached the summit your vision will be much clearer and both you and your audience can enjoy the view.

The Storyteller's Secret

Great stories start with great headlines that capture the one key message behind an idea. According to Richard Branson, "The power of stories is their ability to not only inform and challenge but also inspire and create change in the world."[8] Branson's storytelling advice is as simple as it is concise: "Say what you mean and mean what you say and preferably in as few well-chosen words as possible."

19

The Evangelizer in Chief

I have just three things to teach: simplicity, patience, compassion.

—Lao Tzu

A sales slip saved young Mario Bergoglio's life. His parents had booked passage on a ship that would take them from Italy to Argentina, where the family hoped to make a new life. Though they were very poor, they had scratched together enough money to secure spots in steerage on the ship *Principessa Mafalda*. The ship left its port in Genoa in October 1927, but it would never reach its final destination. After a propeller ripped a hole in the ship's hull, it sank off the coast of Brazil. Five hundred people drowned, including nearly everyone in steerage.

Only a twist of fate kept Mario from boarding that ship. Mario's father had sold the family business, but the sales slip was late to arrive, and they couldn't board without it. At the last minute, the family was forced to cancel the trip and rebook seats on another ship the following month.

Mario's son Jorge frequently tells the story of his family's roots, often connecting it to the larger plight of immigrants. Jorge has become one of the most influential storytellers on the planet today. More than 3 million people packed a beach in Rio to watch Jorge Mario Bergoglio—Pope Francis—speak on World Youth Day in 2013. But that was just a precursor of even larger audiences: A record *6 million* people flocked to see him at Manila's Rizal Park during his visit to the Philippines in January 2015. In the United States millions of Americans lined the streets of Washington, D.C. New York City, and Philadelphia to catch a glimpse of the pope during his historic six-day trip in September.

While Pope Francis is revered for his acts of compassion and humility, his stories connect for another reason: their simplicity. Pope Francis religiously follows one of the cardinal rules of storytelling—the rule of three.

The Storyteller's Tools

In his first homily as the newly elected pontiff, Francis summed up his faith in three bullet points: journeying, building, and professing. It wouldn't be the first or the last time he relied on a three-part narrative structure. He had learned the technique years earlier and uses it in nearly every conversation, speech, or sermon. "First of all, I will talk about three things: one, two, three, like old-timer Jesuits used to do, right? One, two, three!"[1] Francis once told an audience as they laughed and cheered.

Pope Francis credits his Jesuit training for teaching him the rule of three, but the technique is one of the oldest and most powerful guidelines in storytelling. Francis uses the template beautifully as a framework to simplify his message.

In Manila, Pope Francis blended vivid metaphor with the rule of three (I bolded the key words for emphasis): "God created the world as a beautiful garden . . . man has disfigured that natural beauty with social structures that perpetuate **poverty**, **ignorance**, and **corruption**."[2]

On Christmas Eve 2014, Francis said, "We have **passed** through the darkness which envelops the earth, **guided** by the flame of faith which illuminates our steps, and **enlivened** by the hope of finding the great light."[3]

On Ash Wednesday 2015, at the Basilica of Santa Sabina, Pope Francis heralded the period of Lent, or fasting, by highlighting components of the Lenten journey.

> Today's Gospel indicates the elements of this spiritual journey: **prayer, fasting and almsgiving**. The first element is prayer. Prayer is the strength of the Christian and of every person who believes . . . The second key element of the Lenten journey is fasting. Fasting involves choosing a sober lifestyle; a way of life that does not waste, a way of life that does not throw away . . . [Francis sometimes even uses the rule of three within the rule of three!]. The third element is almsgiving. It points to giving freely, for in almsgiving one gives something to someone from whom one does not expect to receive anything in return.[4]

In the previous excerpt Pope Francis uses an effective method for delivering a message or idea. He first introduces the list (prayer, fasting, almsgiving), and provides details of each item in the next paragraphs. It's an easy and proven method of simplifying a message.

The Three-Act Structure of Great Stories

The rule of three is a fundamental building block of communication. Decades ago researchers found that the human mind is only capable of remembering three to seven items in short-term or "working" memory. A phone number in the United States is seven digits because researchers found that seven is the upper limit of numbers people can retain. But how do most of us remember a phone number? We chunk the digits into smaller groups of three and four.

Why do we find "three" inherently satisfying? People think in patterns and three is the lowest number of units that can establish a pattern or progression. For example, movie directors say, "lights, camera, action." Sprinters are conditioned to listen to the command, "Ready, set, go." What should you do if you caught fire? Hopefully you'd remember to "stop, drop, and roll." If you had to recall 18 steps, you'd be severely injured before you completed the progression. The examples are endless because the directions are effective and they're effective because they're simple to remember.

The rule of three makes any story more effective because audiences are more likely to recall the content. Great writers follow the rule. Thomas Jefferson changed the course of civilization with three "unalienable rights": life, liberty, happiness. Our favorite children's fables are grouped in threes: the three little pigs, the three bears, the three Musketeers, the ghosts of Christmas past, present, and future, etc.

Aspiring screenwriters who take classes in the art of emotional storytelling learn the Three-Act Story Structure. In a two-hour movie, Act I is about 30 minutes. It establishes the genre (action, romance, comedy) through an attention-grabbing scene called the hook. We are also introduced to the protagonist and antagonist (hero and villain). Act II is longer, about 60 minutes. In Act II the characters are developed and hurdles (conflict/tension) are introduced that create obstacles for the hero. The tougher the obstacles are to overcome, the more satisfying the final resolution. In Act III, about 30 minutes, the fun really happens as the movie climaxes in a showdown between hero and villain.

While all storytellers love the rule of three, for business storytelling, the three-act structure is particularly critical to making your case simply and persuasively. Your customer doesn't want to know all 200 features of your product; explain three features they will care the most about. Your client doesn't want to hear 52 marketing ideas; offer your three best ones. Your investor doesn't need to know 23 reasons to invest in your company; list the top 3 reasons they'll be rewarded.

The rule of three is one of the habits shared by nearly every storyteller featured in this book. Steve Jobs told "three stories" in his famous 2005 Stanford Commencement address. Bryan Stevenson told three stories to receive the longest standing ovation in TED history. Sheryl Sandberg launched the Lean In movement with three messages for women in the workplace. Although these people are all rule breakers to some extent, challenging the status quo, the rule of three is one rule they all follow.

The Storyteller's Secret

Beginning with Aristotle and continuing through to Pope Francis today, the world's greatest storytellers stick to the rule of three because it accomplishes, well, three things:

1) It offers a simple template to structure your story.
2) It simplifies your story so your audience can remember its key messages.
3) It leads to the ultimate goal of persuasion—action!

20

A Film Mogul's Granddaughter Cooks Up
Her Own Recipe for Success

The audience wants to be attracted not by the critics, but by a great
story.

Dino De Laurentiis

I n 1994 a young woman graduated from UCLA and stumbled upon the
ingredient for a happy and wildly successful life. She enrolled in a Paris
culinary school. The girl's parents considered her career path to be an odd
choice. The entire family was in the movie business and they expected the
girl to follow the same recipe.

The girl had been born in Rome, the place where her grandfather had
produced some of the most iconic movies of the period. In 1976 the family
relocated to the United States, where her grandfather set up his own studio. In all Dino De Laurentiis would produce 150 movies over a 70-year
career with hits such as *Serpico* and *Conan the Barbarian* among them. While
she may not have chosen his career path, the young woman did look up to
her famous grandfather: Upon the famous movie producer's death in 2010,
she would say: "My grandfather was a true inspiration. He was my champion."[1]

And he was. The woman's career choice may have puzzled her parents,
but it didn't confuse her grandfather, Dino. He was the son of a pasta maker
and loved Italian cooking. He was a storyteller on the big screen, while his
granddaughter, Giada De Laurentiis, made food her storytelling palette. "I
come from a big Italian family and if there's one thing they love more than
food, it's storytelling,"[2] Giada once said. "I loved listening to my grandfather's elaborate tales of all the places he had been and all the food he had

tasted along the way, and I couldn't wait to explore and see and take in all those amazing places he talked about."

Giada's movie mogul grandfather understood the elements of a good story, chief among them the need to simplify content. "If you get a book which is 600 pages, you have to reduce it to a script of 100 pages. In two hours of film, you cannot possibly include all the characters,"[3] he said. For Giada, simplifying stories was in her family's DNA, so she set out to demystify the story of Italian cooking. Today Giada has five shows on the Food Network and has published seven books, nearly all of which have become number one *New York Times* bestsellers.

When Giada began hosting *Everyday Italian* on the Food Network critics blasted her for trying to make dishes accessible to the everyday home cook. "Proper" Italian meals like pasta must be made from scratch, the critics argued. Giada countered that few people have the time to make their own pasta, but they could make delicious meals with simple ingredients. "I didn't want to talk like a chef," she said. "I didn't want to make complicated dishes. I wanted to make it my own. I wanted to share my Italian roots and I wanted people to enjoy it. I put my chef's jacket in the closet and created easy recipes. If I had not done it my way, I wouldn't be here."[4]

Giada had graduated from UCLA with a degree in anthropology, but she found her true calling—teaching people simple techniques to make delicious Italian food at home. On her first television shows, however, her road to stardom seemed to have hit a snag. She wasn't comfortable in front of the camera. "When I did *Everyday Italian* for the first time, it was a rough show. I was awkward and uncomfortable in front of the camera and I had tons and tons of anxiety,"[5] Giada recalls. "It manifested itself in a nasty stomachache all the time and a major case of insomnia. It was very humbling."

Humility is a trait that most successful storytellers share. Storytelling requires constant and never-ending trial and error. It requires practice, hours and hours of it. And practice is exactly what Giada did to improve her performance.

The Storyteller's Tools

"I was honest with myself and my shortcomings,"[6] Giada once said. "That's when my little brother helped me out. He followed me around with a camera all the time. I talked to the camera and eventually the camera kind of became a real person and a real friend. At the end of every day my brother and I would review my performance, which was nerve-racking. Slowly and surely I became better. What began as a rough start became more successful."

Storytelling, by definition, requires a performance. A strong narrative isn't enough. Giada's comfort in front of the camera would eventually lead to an Emmy award and her own restaurant on the Las Vegas strip. Giada has several qualities that can help anyone improve their performance in front of a camera, whether the video is for a television show, a YouTube channel, a company blog, or a Kickstarter campaign.

Passion

It's nearly impossible to be a successful storyteller without passion. Passion leads to energy and without energy, enthusiasm, and excitement it becomes very difficult to hold an audience's attention. Giada exudes enthusiasm in front of the camera because she's doing what she loves. Giada knew that the film industry wasn't her calling. She wanted to share her passion for food, even though she didn't know what a career in food would look like. "But," she said, "I knew I loved hanging out in the kitchen with my family, cooking with my family, laughing, telling stories, the smell of the food, and I loved eating! I knew I had to do it and that was enough for me."[7] Authentic passion comes across on video. Don't press RECORD without it.

Smiles

You'd think smiling is easy. When we're happy we smile. Why, then, do most business professionals look like they're miserable when recording a video? Smiles are rare on professional business videos, but ubiquitous on the faces of celebrated television personalities. Giada is known for her radiant smile. Remember that storytelling is all about emotion and smiling has been associated with the strongest emotional reaction. According to a Forbes article on the untapped power of smiling: "Smiling stimulates our brain's reward mechanisms in a way that even chocolate, a well-regarded pleasure inducer, cannot match."[8]

Neuroscientists are also finding that people can tell the difference between a real smile and a fake smile, which is why emotional storytelling always comes back to passion. If you're genuinely excited about a topic, it will show and your enthusiasm will rub off on the viewer.

Conversation

We've all heard people who sound "stilted," "stiff," or "wooden." These are all words to describe the same thing—someone who doesn't sound natural. When a person reads from a teleprompter or directly from notes, it slows down their rate of speech, which is unnatural. Web video is an informal platform that rewards a more natural, conversational delivery. People want to do business with someone they like, someone who sounds like they're talking to friends over dinner.

Conversational speakers use short, simple words and they keep their videos short. When Bill Gates introduced Satya Nadella as Microsoft's new CEO, he made the announcement in a simple YouTube video that lasted just 1 minute and 45 seconds. A short video of under two minutes is ideal for an audience with a dwindling attention span. The sheer amount of noise on social media demands a performance that gets right to the point. Lloyds TSB, a London-based insurance firm, once launched a study to learn why household accidents were climbing. The researchers discovered that people who didn't pay attention to a task were more likely to get hurt. That makes sense, but the researchers went one step further to study just how long people could maintain their attention. In a study of 1,000 people, the study found that the average adult attention span had declined from 12 minutes in 1998 to 5 minutes in 2008. And what happened in 2008? The explosion in social media platforms that challenge our attention spans: Vine (featuring 6-second videos), Twitter, Instagram, and Snapchat, among others. Many business-related social media sites are finding the ideal length of time for a video to be anywhere from 60 to 90 seconds.

Business leaders are increasingly relying on video to disseminate their transformational stories across the organization. But those videos mean nothing if your audience doesn't watch the video or internalize its message. Taking a cue from popular television personalities like Giada will make your videos engaging and, ultimately, more impactful. It's a recipe worth copying.

The Storyteller's Secret

Storytellers who capture the public's heart are passionate about their message and they share that content in simple, approachable language. Video has become an essential component of delivering a story. Successful storytellers embrace the medium in a personable, friendly style that makes the viewer feel as though they're having a one-on-one conversation with the speaker.

21

The Storytelling Astronaut Wows a TED Audience

The more visual the input becomes, the more likely it is to be recognized—and recalled.

—Dr. John Medina

Neil Armstrong and Buzz Aldrin took their first steps on the surface of the moon on July 20, 1969. Meanwhile 238,000 miles below, watching the event on television in a small cottage on Stag Island, Ontario, a nine-year-old boy was inspired to become an astronaut. Chris Hadfield dreamed of going to space. "I just thought they were the coolest guys ever,"[1] he remembers. He walked outside to look at the moon and said, "I don't know how but that's what I really want to do." Hadfield's dream had to overcome one seemingly insurmountable obstacle—Canada didn't have a space program. The dream seemed impossible, but so had walking on the moon before John F. Kennedy, another great storyteller, first inspired a nation to shoot for the stars.

Hadfield had boundless imagination, fierce ambition, uncompromising dedication, and the storyteller's gift for articulating ideas confidently and persuasively, a skill he used to make his childhood dream a reality. Hadfield recalled winning a public speaking contest in the eighth grade: "I don't remember the teacher's name, but someone taught me how to construct a talk and to convey my ideas so others would get something useful out of the ideas and remember what I said."[2]

When the newly formed Canadian Space Agency began soliciting for candidates in 1992, Hadfield threw his name in along with 5,329 applicants. He received positive news five months later. He had *almost* made it into the program. Hadfield had been chosen as one of 500 people to advance to the next round. After three more rounds of psychological evaluations and interviews, Hadfield made it to the top 20. The final candidates were sent to Ottawa for a week and that's where Hadfield's storytelling skill made a difference. Each of the candidates was required to participate in a mock press conference. The Canadian Space Agency was not well funded so astronauts, as the chief ambassadors for the program, had to be exceptional storytellers to sell the program to the public.

At 1:00 p.m. on a Saturday in 1992, the phone rang in Hadfield's kitchen. He received the news he had dreamed about since looking up at the moon as a nine-year-old—he'd been chosen to be an astronaut.

Hadfield served as the commander of the International Space Station. He became Canada's most decorated astronaut and the first Canadian to walk in space. In 2013 Hadfield became a social media sensation by picking up his guitar and singing David Bowie's "Space Oddity" while floating weightless in a space capsule. He posted the video on Twitter and had attracted 1 million followers to his Twitter profile by the time he returned to Earth.

Hadfield came on my radar in March 2014 when he received a rare standing ovation at TED for his riveting presentation titled, "What I Learned from Going Blind in Space," which told the story of the time Hadfield's eyes slammed shut and stopped working in the middle of a space walk. Even though the spaceship was traveling around the world at five miles per second, Hadfield didn't panic because he had been trained to prepare for nearly every situation that might occur. He offered a lesson in how to overcome one's fears. Hadfield's presentation was an astonishing display of visual storytelling.

Hadfield's PowerPoint deck contained 35 slides, all photos and no text. "I'm a big believer in the power of a compelling visual,"[3] Hadfield told me. "A really good visual isn't just beautiful; it makes you think. You draw conclusions from the depth of the information that's in it." For example, when Hadfield describes what the world looks like from the space shuttle it's nearly impossible for us to picture it ourselves. The close-up images of continents and waterways are like paintings that would look at home in a museum. Hadfield uses analogy to describe the scenes: "Like a self-propelled art gallery of fantastic, constantly changing beauty that is the world itself . . . it's roaring silently with color and texture." Analogy helps make the complex relatable, but a simple photograph stamps the analogy in the mind's eye.

As an ambassador for the Canadian space program, Hadfield had given weekly presentations for 25 years before he reached the TED stage. In those years he learned that the presentation itself doesn't tell the story. He is the storyteller; the slideshow complements the story and brings the narrative to life. He says, "When I go into an art gallery I'm always drawn to the information. Who the artist was and when they painted it. Where did they paint it? The back story brings soul to the image. Otherwise it's just a pretty picture. The story that goes with it is what really matters."

The Storyteller's Tools

Hadfield relies on two powerful storytelling techniques to transport his audience to the seat next to him in the spaceship: the use of pictures and analogies.

Using pictures to tell stories is a technique well established in the neuroscience literature in a concept called picture superiority. Researchers have found that if you simply hear information, you will recall about 10 percent of the content. If you hear the information *and* see a picture, it's likely that you will retain 65 percent of the content.

Hadfield's 16-minute presentation contained 35 photos and two videos. For example, while he was talking about being inspired to be an astronaut at an early age, he showed a slide of a photo of a nine-year-old Hadfield in a cardboard box cut out to resemble a rocket. The picture itself doesn't tell the story. Without Hadfield's narration, it would just be a cute picture of a little boy. In another example, Hadfield describes what it feels like to land with a thud in the middle of Kazakhstan. The accompanying slide shows Russian space officials helping Hadfield out of the landing craft.

In one section of Hadfield's now famous TED presentation he brings up the common fear of spiders and suggests how to overcome the fear. Since most of us have a natural aversion to spiders, it makes sense to show a photo of dangerous spiders like the brown recluse and the black widow. Hadfield could tell the story without the photos, but because we have a deep emotional reaction to spiders, the photos help to reinforce Hadfield's theme that knowledge and preparation will help you overcome your fears. Hadfield makes the point that there are some 50,000 types of spiders, of which only about a dozen are venomous; it's unlikely that you'll run into those dangerous ones. "So the next time you walk into a spider web, you don't need to panic. The danger is entirely different than the fear," he advises.

One image—for example, a photograph of a human face—activates up to 30 million neurons in the visual cortex, according to neuroscientist Uri Hasson. The Princeton researcher says a large number of activated neurons enhance the "signal to noise ratio."[4] In science and engineering, the signal to noise ratio is a measure of signal strength relative to background noise. Communication and presentation designers use the phrase to explain why some slides are easier to remember. PowerPoint slides that have a lot of "noise" are complicated and cluttered with extraneous text, charts, or numbers that are nonessential to the one idea the speaker is trying to get across. Hasson's research finds that by lowering the noise—the nonessential elements— and strengthening the signal in the form of pictures, recall and recognition are enhanced. An impactful presentation keeps the noise down and the signal up.

The Picture Superiority Effect (PSE) explains why the photos in Hadfield's presentation are more impactful and easier to recall than if he had created slide after slide of nothing but words. "Human PSE is truly Olympian,"[5] writes molecular biologist John Medina. "Tests performed years ago showed that people could remember more than 2,500 pictures with at least 90 percent accuracy several days post-exposure, even though subjects saw each picture for about 10 seconds. Accuracy rates a year later still hovered around 63 percent. In one paper—adorably titled 'Remember Dick and Jane?'—picture recognition information was reliably retrieved several decades later."

Successful educators have learned that a combination of pictures and words facilitates learning much more than words could do on their own.

The $875 Million PowerPoint

Hadfield is selling ideas, but even company pitches benefit from visual storytelling. For example, one company transformed its PowerPoint from words to pictures and won an $875 million contract as its reward. The company is in the business of industrial construction equipment. Everything about the industry is big. Some cranes weigh as much as 15 million pounds, the equivalent of nearly 80 space shuttles. The cranes stand as high as 600 feet, four times taller than the Statue of Liberty. In America alone there are

2 million miles of pipelines that feed our energy needs. Many pipelines are hundreds of miles long, delivering trillions of cubic feet of natural gas and hundreds of billions of tons of liquid petroleum every year. The financials are also big. It's not uncommon to find industrial construction contracts worth tens of billions of dollars.

There was, at one time, a company, a small player in this big field, that wanted to be as big as the equipment they sold. But although its leaders had aspirations to grow substantially, one thing held them back—their presentations were dull and uninspiring. And it wasn't that they were dull people. Rather, they had fallen prey to a common malady of businesses large and small: They were using wordy PowerPoint slides to deliver facts and figures. They had plenty of data that measured how many miles of electrical wiring they had installed, how many coils they were fabricating for steam furnaces, or how many turbines they had built. The problem was that the company's competitors also had similar data—in many cases, even bigger and more impressive data points.

The company's marketing officer had an idea that would help the company's message stand out. Instead of using PowerPoint slides to deliver chart after chart of data, he would tell a story around the data and use PowerPoint slides to illustrate the story with photos. Once the transformation took place, business began flowing once again, and in bigger ways than anyone in the company had predicted.

The marketing director replaced 72 slides of charts and text with 30 photo-rich slides. For example, many of the slides in the original presentation contained 200 words or more (these aren't slides, but documents masquerading as PowerPoint slides). Many of the slides in the new deck contained fewer than 10 words alongside a photograph. The data didn't go away, but it was packaged in story form. For example, one slide showed one number (240,000) over a photo of the moon. "We've installed over 240,000 miles of pipe. That's enough pipe to route heating oil from here to the moon," the marketing director would narrate over the slide.

Some senior leaders in the company were skeptical. They didn't believe that a PowerPoint with fewer words and more pictures could be effective. But since the company was struggling to attract new business after the 2008 recession, they didn't have much to lose. The marketing director received the go-ahead to deliver the presentation in a series of public presentations intended to woo new clients.

What happened next took the senior leaders by surprise—but it shouldn't be remarkable for those who understand the power of visual storytelling. A leader from a large oil firm asked the company to bid on a project. They did, and eventually won the $875 million contract. It was the largest contract in company history.

After the contract was signed the marketing director asked the head of the oil firm why his company had chosen the small construction company. "Your presentation was so different it made me see the possibilities," the oil executive responded. "That kind of thinking is where I want to invest."

A concise deck, simpler slides, and more pictures told the company's story far more persuasively than a long, convoluted, wordy PowerPoint could ever do. PowerPoint is not the enemy. A lack of creativity is the culprit. When PowerPoint is used to illustrate a story, it can and does change minds.

When a Picture Isn't Enough

Now we know that a photo will enhance your story, but pictures aren't nearly enough. Painting pictures in the mind's eye is also a component of successful storytelling. Astronaut Chris Hadfield doesn't earn standing ovations simply because he shows pretty space pictures. Just as Ed Hallowell does in explaining ADHD to his audiences, Hadfield skillfully uses descriptive analogies to create mental pictures of his experiences. Most of us will never set foot on another planet or ride a rocket into space. How it is possible to experience what it feels like? Analogies are the closest we'll get and Hadfield is a master at creating them. Here is Hadfield's description of liftoff:

> It is incredibly powerful to be on board one of these things. You are in the grip of something that is vastly more powerful than yourself. It's shaking you so hard you can't focus on the instruments in front of you. It's like you're in the jaws of some enormous dog and there's a foot in the small of your back pushing you into space, accelerating wildly straight up, shouldering your way through the air, and you're in a very complex place—paying attention, watching the vehicle go through each one of its wickets with a steadily increasing smile on your face. After two minutes, those solid rockets explode off and then you just have the liquid engines, the hydrogen and oxygen, and it's as if you're

in a dragster with your foot to the floor and accelerating like you've never accelerated. You get lighter and lighter, the force gets on us heavier and heavier. It feels like someone's pouring cement on you or something. Until finally, after about eight minutes and 40 seconds or so, we are finally at exactly the right altitude, exactly the right speed, the right direction, the engine shut off, and we're weightless. And we're alive.[6]

The jaws of a dog, the foot in the small of your back, the dragster, the concrete—all analogies that help us infer what the experience feels like. Analogies help us connect abstractions to stored knowledge. The analogies stamp the content into our brains.

An increasing body of evidence is emerging in the neuroscience literature to support the power of storytelling and, as we've discussed in chapter 12, the effectiveness of using analogies to bring those stories to life. Stories work because they activate many parts of our brain and metaphor and analogies are critical devices to make it happen.

In 2006 Spanish researchers published a paper in the journal *NeuroImage* titled "Reading *cinnamon* activates olfactory brain regions." The scientists were the first to reveal that simply reading metaphorical language activated areas of the brain associated with sights and smells. For example, when the subjects read words such as "cinnamon," "perfume," or "coffee," scientists could see regions associated with smell—the primary olfactory cortex—light up on the MRI machine. When the subjects read words that did not evoke smells—words like "chair" or "key"—the brain regions remained inactive. The conclusion: "Reading words with strong olfactory associations in their meaning activates olfactory regions of the brain."[7]

Hadfield's photos on his PowerPoint slides stimulate the visual cortex while his analogies stimulate other parts of the brain such as the somatosensory cortex, associated with touch.

"Analogy is the only we way we learn about anything of which we can have no direct experience, whether it's the behavior of subatomic particles or the content of other people's experience,"[8] writes James Geary in *I Is an Other*. Analogies simplify complex topics and introduce us to new, unique experiences that we otherwise would have no way of understanding.

Hadfield spent a quarter of a century in the Canadian space program, serving as one of its ambassadors, giving public presentations nearly every week. He learned that there's no point in delivering a presentation or speaking to an audience if they fail to get anything out of it. Hadfield's pictures and analogies bring the story of space down to Earth.

The Storyteller's Secret

Great storytellers use pictures—sometimes real, sometimes by analogy—to create a vivid portrait of an experience or event.

22

"Dude's Selling a Battery" and Still Inspires

The people who are crazy enough to think they can change the world, are the ones who do.

—Steve Jobs

While storytellers like Chris Hadfield dreamed of traveling to space, Elon wanted to build the spaceship to get them there. Story played an important role in Elon's childhood in South Africa. "He seemed to have a book in his hands at all times," wrote his biographer. When school let out at 2:00 p.m., he would go to the bookstore and stay until 6:00 p.m. *The Lord of the Rings* and *The Hitchhiker's Guide to the Galaxy* were among his favorites.

Young Elon loved reading stories and hearing them. He remembers listening, transfixed, to the stories of his grandfather, Joshua Haldeman, who had "a lust for adventure." Haldeman would pack his family into a single-engine airplane and travel from their home in Pretoria, South Africa, on trips that would traverse 22,000 miles across Europe. "My grandmother told these tales of how they almost died several times along their journeys,"[1] Elon recalls.

Today Tesla and SpaceX CEO Elon Musk believes those stories of his grandfather's exploits help to explain his insatiable desire for excitement, adventure, and his "unusual tolerance for risk." Musk is one the most influential innovators of our time, pioneering advances in electric cars, space travel, and sustainable energy.

On April 30, 2015, Musk introduced the Tesla Powerwall, a home battery that captures and stores sunlight from solar panels and converts it to energy. Although it's designed for the average consumer, the technology that makes it work is highly complex. According to the website, "The Tesla

Powerwall is a wall mounted, rechargeable lithium ion battery with liquid thermal control. It delivers a 5.8 amp nominal current and 8.6 amps at peak output. Powerwall is available in 10kWh, optimized for backup applications or 7kWh optimized for daily use applications."[2] And that's the easy material. The technical specs are understandable only to the most advanced scientists and physicists.

Elon Musk is one of the smartest inventors on the planet, but when he explains technology to consumers he uses language even a sixth-grader can read.

The Storyteller's Tools

Peter Kincaid codeveloped the Flesch-Kincaid readability test in 1975 for the U.S. Navy. The U.S. Defense Department began using it to assess the reading difficulty of training manuals. Today educators rely on the score to gauge the appropriate reading level for books used in the classroom. The Flesch-Kincaid grade level test measures word length, sentence length, and other factors to assign a grade level—the number of years of education generally required for a person to understand a specific text. For example, articles in the *Harvard Business Review* return a grade level of 17 or higher. Articles in the *New York Times* are written for ninth grade or higher, while, according to the tool, "Text to be read by the general public should aim for a grade level of around 8."

Let's take a closer look at the key phrases in Elon Musk's Powerwall presentation. Musk understands story and he knows that all great stories, as we've discussed, have a hero and a villain. Musk introduces the villain and the hero as a problem and a solution. And he uses simple words and sentence structure to do it. Musk's first slide shows a picture of smokestacks spewing emissions into the air. Musk says:

> Welcome everyone to the announcement of Tesla Energy. What I'm going to talk about tonight is a fundamental transformation of how the world works, about how energy is delivered across Earth. This is how it is today. It's pretty bad. It sucks. I just want to be clear because sometimes people are confused about it. This is real. This is actually how most power is generated, with fossil fuels.[3]

The previous paragraph returns a Flesch-Kincaid grade level of 6.3, meaning that the average sixth-grader should be able to read it and generally understand it. Surely the solution must be more complicated, right? Well, let's see. According to Musk the solution starts by looking up:

> The solution is in two parts. Part one, the sun. We have this handy fusion reactor in the sky called the sun. You don't have to do anything. It just works. It shows up every day and produces ridiculous amounts of power.

The previous paragraph returns a Flesch-Kincaid readability score of just 2.9. While the average third-grader doesn't understand a "fusion reactor," they should be able to read it. The sentences are short and most of the words are made up of just one syllable. I was skeptical when I first saw a grade level of 2.9, but I had access to my own personal experiment. My youngest daughter had just completed the second grade. I recorded her reading the paragraph on her first try. She read it almost perfectly, stumbling on just two words: reactor and ridiculous. My eldest daughter—who had just completed the third grade—read it perfectly and understood all of it, including the word "fusion."

Once Musk introduces the sun as the hero of his narrative, he introduces another challenge—existing batteries. Once again he uses simple language to describe the problem:

> The issue with existing batteries is that they suck. They're really horrible. They're expensive. They're unreliable. They're sort of stinky, ugly, bad in every way, and very expensive.

And once again, the Flesch-Kincaid tool returns a grade level of 6.1 for the preceding paragraph, meaning that a person doesn't even need a high school education to understand it.

A blogger for *The Verge* covering the Elon Musk presentation wrote an article titled, "Watch Elon Musk Announce Tesla Energy in the Best Tech Keynote I've Ever Seen."[4] In the article T. C. Sottek wrote, "Dude's selling a battery and he still managed to be inspiring." Yes, the "dude" is selling a battery, but batteries don't inspire. Stories do.

Musk's keynotes are being compared to another technology innovator and storyteller, Steve Jobs. Jobs, too, understood the need to introduce villains and heroes (problem/solution) in product narratives and he did so in words so simple a grade-school student could understand it.

In a 10-minute presentation on April 28, 2003, Steve Jobs reinvented the music industry and persuaded millions of music lovers to pay 99 cents for a song. The iTunes music store completely changed how people acquire and enjoy music. For 99 cents per song users could choose from 200,000 tracks. More than 1 million songs were sold in the first week. Today, the Apple iTunes music store is the largest music retailer on the planet.

Steve Jobs revolutionized the music industry by doing something quite extraordinary: He persuaded millions of music lovers that it was a good idea to pay for something many of them were getting for free on peer-to-peer file-sharing programs, and he did so using the classic narrative technique of introducing a villain and a hero. The villain appeared first—a problem in need of a solution. The hero followed—an Apple product.

Jobs began with a brief discussion of Napster and Kazaa, sites that offered "near instant gratification"[5] and, from the user's perspective, free downloads. On the next slide he listed the "dark side." They were:

- Unreliable downloads
- Unreliable quality ["A lot of these songs are encoded by seven-year-olds and they don't do a great job."]
- No previews
- No album cover art
- It's stealing ["It's best not to mess with karma."]

Jobs continued to paint a picture of the villain, using Kazaa as the antagonist in the narrative. He demonstrated how a typical user might have to guess at among the 50 or 60 files of the same song and choose which one to download. He said, "The download is slow as molasses and craps out half way through." Finally, he said, you've downloaded the song only to discover it was encoded poorly and the last few seconds had been cut off. After 15 minutes, the user gets a clean version of the song. Jobs brilliantly put this time into perspective:

What that means is you'll spend an hour at that rate and you'll get four songs; four songs that cost under four bucks from Apple and you calculate that you are working for under minimum wage.

Jobs challenged the notion that consumers would balk at paying 99 cents a song:

> How much is 99 cents? How many of you had a Starbucks latte this morning? Three bucks. That's three songs. How many lattes got sold across the U.S. this morning? A lot. Ninety-nine cents is pretty affordable.

Finally, Jobs listed the benefits (the hero) of downloading songs on the new iTunes music store. His slide revealed the following text:

- Fast, reliable downloads
- Pristine encoding
- Previews of every song
- Album cover art
- Good Karma

In 10 minutes Jobs had completely transformed the mind-set of those who didn't believe in paying 99 cents, let alone any price, for the songs they were already downloading. He also convinced skeptical analysts that the service would provide a strong enough benefit to encourage music lovers to spend 99 cents a song and make money for Apple. Remarkably, the text from Steve Jobs's introduction of iTunes—when run through the Flesch-Kincaid grade level tool—returns a grade of 4, meaning a fourth-grader could follow along and understand the problems and solution Steve Jobs had explained.

The next time you face a skeptical audience, paint a picture of the villain before you introduce your product or service—the conquering hero. The villain/hero narrative simplifies the problem your idea solves and, if you use simple words, you might be surprised at just how quickly your idea catches on.

"Simple can be harder than complex,"[6] Steve Jobs once said. "You have to work hard to get your thinking clean to make it simple. But it's worth it in the end because once you get there, you can move mountains." Steve Jobs, Elon Musk, and other inventors of our time do move mountains and they often carry their message with simple stories, simply told.

The Storyteller's Secret

You may have the greatest product in the world, the greatest ideas, but if people can't understand the problems they solve, they'll never buy into it. Storytellers introduce heroes and villains to simplify the story, and they craft the message in words that are so simple an elementary school student can understand it.

23

An Entrepreneur Makes *Shark Tank* History

Storytelling is everything. Show me an MBA and your sales numbers, that's fine. But tell me a great story about how you got started and your vision, and we'll talk.

— Barbara Corcoran, *Shark Tank*

like many children his age, six-year-old Charles Michael Yim decided to open a lemonade stand on the curb outside of his family's house. Yim would continue to display a knack for entrepreneurship. In middle school Yim's friend gave him a free basketball trading card. Yim traded the card for three others, flipped those over, and soon he had amassed 1,000 trading cards without spending a dime. And the cards had real value: one happened to be Michael Jordan's rookie trading card. Showing an early penchant for a dramatic performance, he brought the cards to a store that allowed kids to trade cards. Yim came armed with a story and a hook. He put the cards in brown bags and charged $4 for each bag. The hook? One of the bags contained a valuable card worth much more than $4. Finding that other kids responded to the possibility of winning a golden ticket, he did the same with other sought-after cards and, by the time he finished middle school, had made $5,000.

Fast-forward to September 2013. Now 30 years old, we find that Yim still has a flair for the dramatic, though now the stakes are a bit higher. He's asking for an investment of $250,000 on ABC's *Shark Tank,* an *American Idol*–style show for entrepreneurs. His pitch revealed several important components of effective storytelling:

Hello, Sharks. My name is Charles Michael Yim and I am the founder and CEO of Breathometer. Just imagine you're at a dinner party, or at a tailgate [points to Mark Cuban, owner of a sports team], or at a bar with some friends having some champagne [points to a small table on his right with five glasses of champagne]. Would anyone care for a glass? [Yim hands a glass to each judge. They toast and enjoy the drink as the pitch continues.] You know how it goes. You eat some food, have some drinks. Before you know it, the night's over and it's time to go home. The most important question is, are you safe to drive? Who would want to carry around one of these bulky old Breathalyzers? [Yim holds up a large Breathalyzer unit you'd see police officers use to test drivers.] That's why I created Breathometer. It's the first smartphone Breathalyzer. It's so small, it can fit in your pocket. [Yim does his best Steve Jobs, but instead of pulling out an iPod from his jeans, he takes out a small smartphone adapter.] Let me show you how it works. Simply retract the audio jack, plug it into a smartphone, activate the app. [Yim breathes into the device.] Within a matter of seconds, you'll be able to know what your breath alcohol level is. Better yet, it will tell you how long it will take to sober up, and if need be you can even hail a cab with the push of a button. Please join me on this mission to help people make smarter, safer decisions one breath at a time.[1]

For the first time in the show's history, all five sharks invested in the company, to the tune of $1 million. Mark Cuban invested $500,000 in the company and the remaining four sharks combined contributed another $500,000.

The Storyteller's Tools

Yim has refined the Breathometer story over thousands of pitches and conversations. He, too, has learned that simplicity is key to telling a compelling story. He says, "It doesn't matter how advanced, how scientific your company is. If the average consumer or investor is trying to understand your business, you need to boil it down to the most basic fundamentals for anyone to understand."[2]

Yim's product is a breath analysis platform, but you may have noticed in the *Shark Tank* pitch that he never uses jargon nor does he use a technical definition. According to Wikipedia, breath analysis is "a method for gaining non-invasive information on the clinical state of an individual by monitoring volatile organic compounds present in the exhaled breath." Instead Yim relies on narrative, transporting his audience to a bar where they've had a few drinks with friends.

In February 2015 Yim was handed another golden opportunity to make the pitch of a lifetime and, once again, he came out on top.

Yim was one of three entrepreneurs who were invited to pitch their startups to billionaire Sir Richard Branson at Branson's home on Necker Island. This was part of the Extreme Tech Challenge—an event mentioned earlier in the Introduction, in which a group of innovative entrepreneurs pool their talents and resources to advance startups that have the potential to improve the world.

In spite of Yim's *Shark Tank* success, the road to Necker had been a long one. Out of 2,000 original entries, 10 finalists were invited to pitch their startups in person at the Consumer Electronics Show in January 2015. The top 3 were selected to take the trip to Necker to pitch Branson and a panel of judges. Yim won Branson's heart and his wallet.

"Whether it's *Shark Tank,* Richard Branson, or any other meeting, I need to be able to clearly articulate, communicate exactly what you're trying to build whether it's a product or service. The value proposition must be clear. If it's not crystal clear, you'll lose people in the first five minutes,"[3] Yim explains.

Breathometer's first product detects alcohol on a person's breath. Yim's vision is much bigger than simply detecting whether someone has had too much to drink. A person's breath contains about 300 biomarkers, molecules that can identify the existence of a disease like cancer or diabetes. Since most of Yim's audiences are not experts in disease detection, he has to paint the picture one step at a time. He says, "Every consumer can understand that they can read alcohol from breath. I take that well-understood notion and say, 'There are 299 other things we can read off your breath, too. Yes, we do alcohol but we can do so much more. Lung cancer detection, pneumonia, bacterial infection, fat burning.' I try to keep it as simple as that."

In 10 minutes and 10 slides, Yim tells a compelling story that's impossible for most investors to resist. Yim represents the young guns in business today: men and women in their twenties and thirties who are tired of dry, boring, unemotional presentations. They realize the power of story will help them get their ideas across. Yim tells a product story successfully because he breaks down the narrative into smaller, digestible chunks. It's much like fitting a ship in a bottle. How do you put a ship in a bottle? The ships—usually models of ancient sailing ships—are built before they're fit into the bottle. Think of the bottle as a person's mental capacity and the ship as a story. The bottle's capacity doesn't change. It's the ship that must be made to fit.

Most of us who see a ship in a bottle are left in awe. We're amazed that it can happen. What we don't see is the hours of detailed craftsmanship that went into building it. The hull itself is bigger than the opening so it's not made from one piece of wood. It's built in parts, the upper and lower half of the hull. Next come the keel and the rudder. Masts and booms are also constructed. The artists use a sketchpad to draw a rendering of the ship and then layer the pieces of wood and toothpicks on the drawing. The ship is constructed outside of the bottle and is carefully collapsed and fed through the opening little by little. Once inside it's expanded to fill the space. Small details of the ship are then fed in piece by piece and reassembled.

The ship is your story. There are many parts to the story—masts, booms, sails, hull, bowsprit. The entrance to the bottle—the tiny opening—is the "working memory" or short-term brain capacity of your listener. The entire ship can't fit through at once, so you feed the story to your listener in its component parts. Once complete, the listener can see the narrative from start to finish and understand how the parts fit together. The story can set sail and open up new worlds for you and the audience.

The Underbelly of a Great Commercial

Yim successfully grabs an audience's attention—as he did on *Shark Tank*—in just 60 seconds. The best Super Bowl spots do the same. "People are attracted to stories because we're social creatures and we relate to other people,"[4] says Johns Hopkins researcher Keith Quesenberry. In *The Journal of Marketing Theory and Practice,* Quesenberry studied 108 Super Bowl commercials and accurately predicted which spot would score highest among consumers.

Quesenberry predicted that a Budweiser commercial would score the highest ratings among consumers because it was like a "mini-movie" which told a complete story in 60 seconds. The ad was called "Puppy Love."

The commercial starts with a setting of a small house with a white picket fence and a sign that reads, "Warm Springs Puppy Adoption." An adorable puppy—a yellow Labrador—climbs out from beneath the fence to visit his friend, a Clydesdale horse in the adjoining barn. On the day the puppy gets adopted the horse chases the car down as the puppy is seen barking at the horse from the backseat. The horse jumps the fence and is joined by the other Clydesdale horses to stop the car. The two friends are reunited at the end and play together in the pasture. The YouTube video of this spot received nearly 60 million views.

Remarkably Quesenberry made his prediction two days before Super Bowl XLVIII on February 2, 2014. The "underbelly" of a great commercial, according to Quesenberry, is not whether it has animals or sexy models. A great commercial tells a story.

Quesenberry predicted that commercials that squeezed an entire story in 60 seconds would turn out to be the winner and the Budweiser commercial came the closest to doing it. He was right. The $4 million ad earned the top spot in *USA Today*'s Ad Meter, a gauge of viewer engagement.

Yim and other entrepreneurs who achieved an extraordinary degree of success do so because 1) they build products that solve real-world problems and 2) they've learned to craft a compelling narrative lasting as little as 60 seconds. They also remind us that no generation has a monopoly on storytellers. Entrepreneurs in their twenties and thirties are often dynamic storytellers because they're driven by mission, passion, and purpose. They've also grown up in the era of YouTube, Twitter, and Facebook—telling a succinct, simple story comes second nature. Great storytellers come in all ages.

The Storyteller's Secret

Storytellers who simplify complexity speak succinctly. They practice their pitch until they can tell a compelling story in as little as 60 seconds.

PART IV

Storytellers Who Motivate

24

Find Your Fight

You can't connect the dots looking forward. You can only connect them looking backward.

—Steve Jobs

"My parents divorced when I was eighteen months old," Darren says. "My mother didn't want me so she gave me up to my father. My dad was only twenty-four at the time so he didn't really know what to do with me, either."[1]

Today Darren Hardy is one of the great storytellers of his generation. He generates more than $1.5 million a year in speaker's fees and, as publisher of *Success* magazine, is one of the world's foremost experts in the study of human achievement. It will not surprise you, by this time in the book, that there is a link between his inauspicious beginnings and his great success.

Hardy's feeling of abandonment is the reason why he's "vigorously self-reliant, self-motivated, goal oriented, and results-driven." Many people have suffered through similar issues as children and continue to cart those wounds with them through adulthood. Hardy chose to turn adversity into an advantage. "My dysfunctional childhood is the reason why I'm the functional achiever that I am today," Hardy says.

Today Hardy readily shares the stories of his childhood with his audiences. He compares his father to Gunnery Sergeant Hartman in Stanley Kubrick's movie *Full Metal Jacket*. "Stop crying or I'll give you something to cry about," Hardy recalls his dad saying.

Hardy didn't always shine a spotlight on his childhood. "I'm not a natural storyteller. I had to work at it,"[2] Hardy told me. Only after years of studying communication and persuasion did Hardy realize he had to revisit his childhood and give it a starring role in his public presentations. "People don't want to hear about your successes until they know you understand their failures. By talking about your own failures and struggles, you make an emotional connection with your audience. You become accessible and relatable. Once you make an emotional connection you can take them where you want them to go."

The Storyteller's Tools

Hardy believes that the human brain evolved to provide the tools to survive. "It also hides a great secret to achievement—motivation. You can hack your ancient brain and use it to give you 'superhuman' powers,"[3] says Hardy. All you have to do is "find your fight."

Everyone needs a worthy adversary, according to Hardy: "David had Goliath. Luke had Darth. Apple had IBM, then Microsoft . . . A good enemy gives you a reason to get fired up. A nemesis pushes you to reach deep and use your skills, talents, and abilities to their fullest. Having to fight challenges your character and resolve. A fight will lead you to push harder, go farther, and hang on longer than you ever would otherwise."[4]

The fight. The nemesis. The villain. Every great story has one, and every great life story has one, too. Inspiring leaders revel in their failures and embrace their struggles. The question is: *Why?* Why must tension and triumph be present in all great stories? Why must we, as humans, experience struggle to build a strong central character in our own life narrative? Just as pressure gives the diamond, the pearl, and the grape their value, great storytellers turn their struggle into strength, conflict into confidence, and tension into triumph. As it turns out, we tell stories not only as a survival instinct but to leave a legacy for the next generation.

The theme of struggle and redemption is as old as civilization itself. "The cathartic or transformative consequences of human suffering are themes in Greek tragedy. Literature throughout the world for a few thousand years, in all its various forms, has attempted to come to grips with the possibilities for meaning and change emerging from the struggle with tragedy, suffering, and loss,"[5] write Dr. Richard Tedeschi and Dr. Lawrence Calhoun.

Tedeschi and Calhoun are psychology professors at the University of

North Carolina, Charlotte. They are pioneers in the field of "Posttraumatic Growth." The researchers study how traumatic experiences (e.g., illness, loss of a loved one, abuse) lead many people to reframe those events and to find meaning and purpose in their lives *because* of the event. They turn trauma to their advantage and become better people—and better storytellers.

In Calhoun and Tedeschi's posttraumatic growth model, a person experiences a "seismic event" that disrupts their internal narrative, the story they expected their life to take. The event leads to "rumination," where they turn things over in their minds to make sense of the event. Rumination is followed by "self-disclosure," where they become comfortable writing and talking about the event. They are also eager to share how the event changed them for the better.

Human Beings Are Storytellers by Nature

Our brains love and need a good rags-to-riches story. In 1993 Dr. Dan Mc-Adams, professor of human development at Northwestern University, published *The Stories We Live By*. Based on 10 years of research, he explores how our personal myths—internal narratives—form our identity. "The human mind is first and foremost a vehicle for storytelling. We are born with a narrating mind,"[6] writes McAdams.

McAdams identified several components of storytelling that even internal narratives must share: characters (hero/villain), conflict, and yes, even a happy ending. When something traumatic happens in our lives, our brains kick into storytelling mode, crafting a narrative where we—the heroes—emerge "happier, better adjusted, more enlightened, or improved in some way."

There's a good reason why humans are hardwired to share stories and to enjoy listening to stories. We need to. Stories not only ensure our survival as a species, they help us on a personal level to make sense of the negative events all of us inevitably experience. Turning negatives into positives is so important to our survival and happiness we even play the role of screenwriters in our life narrative, revising, retooling, and reworking the script. Every story—even the stories we tell ourselves—requires a hero, a struggle, and a happy ending.

Heroes Challenge Us to Reframe Our Internal Narrative

Our internal narrative shapes our destiny. A good story, as we've discussed, requires a struggle and a villain to overcome. When Hardy was in the eleventh grade a teacher told him, "Success just isn't in your DNA." With that statement Hardy's teacher unwittingly cast herself as a villain in Hardy's life narrative. If McAdams's theory is correct, Hardy should revisit his life story and craft an internal narrative that would give the event purpose and meaning, and he would do it in the years of "middle adulthood." And that's exactly what Hardy does in his book *The Entrepreneur Roller Coaster,* written at the age of 44.

"No. My DNA wasn't special,"[7] writes Hardy. "You are the creator of your destiny. The mindset of 'they were born to be successful, and I am not' is a trick of the imagination. It's a trap of the worst kind, and the only way to escape it is by creating a 'success-destiny' mindset."

Hardy reinforces his narrative with stories of heroes who didn't have the right education, the right connections, and who could have been counted out early as not having the DNA for success: "Richard Branson has dyslexia and had poor academic performance as a student. Steve Jobs was born to two college students who didn't want to raise him and gave him up for adoption. Mark Cuban was born to an automobile upholsterer. He started as a bartender, then got a job in software sales from which he was fired."[8]

The list goes on. Hardy reminds his readers that "Suze Orman's dad was a chicken farmer. Retired General Colin Powell was a solid C student. Howard Schultz, the CEO of Starbucks, was born in a housing authority in the Bronx . . . Barbara Corcoran started as a waitress and admits to being fired from more jobs than most people hold in a lifetime. Pete Cashmore, the CEO of Mashable, was sickly as a child and finished high school two years late due to medical complications. He never went to college." What do each of these inspiring leaders and storytellers have in common? They rewrote their own internal narratives and found great success.

"The biographies of all heroes contain common elements. Becoming one is the most important,"[9] writes Chris Matthews in *Jack Kennedy, Elusive Hero.* Matthews reminds his readers that young John F. Kennedy was a sickly child and bedridden for much of his youth. And what did he do while setting school records for being in the infirmary? He read voraciously. He read the stories of heroes in the pages of books by Sir Walter Scott and the tales of King Arthur. He read, and dreamed of playing the hero in the story of his life. When the time came to take the stage, Jack was ready.

At 2:30 a.m. on the night of August 2, 1943, Kennedy, the skipper of a PT boat on patrol in World War II, got the chance to play the hero in his own life story. An enemy destroyer rammed the boat and split it in half. Two members of the 13-man crew were killed. One man was terribly injured and would certainly die if left on his own to swim to safety. Kennedy took a strap of the man's life jacket, put it between his teeth, and swam four hours to a tiny uninhabited island that was only 70 yards wide. "With the physical courage of which he'd shown himself to be capable, Jack Kennedy had turned his years of frailty and private suffering into a personal and public confidence that would take him forward,"[10] writes Matthews. Stories of heroes and heroic actions challenge us to remake our own internal narratives.

In March 2015, Disney released a live action remake of *Cinderella*. It would lead the box office in its first week and became one of the top-grossing films ever to be released in March. Some executives even within Disney said they were surprised at the outcome because, as one distribution chief said, "people already know what the story is." My two girls were in that camp, but knowing the story didn't stop them from bringing Daddy to watch the film, twice.

It's hard for anyone to ignore a Cinderella story. The movie begins with "Ella" living a charmed life. Conflict is introduced when Ella's father dies and she's forced to live with her wicked stepmother and her devious daughters, who give her the name "Cinder" Ella because, as a servant doing the household chores, her face is covered in ash. Although success doesn't seem to be in her DNA, Ella meets her prince, loses her prince, and ultimately finds her prince and lives happily ever after. In one of the last scenes of the movie Ella embraces her name for the first time and calls herself "Cinderella." She has reframed her personal narrative to give those ashes a new meaning. The story is timeless because it perfectly matches the way our brains are built to consume and enjoy content. As Emory University neuroscientist Gregory Berns points out in his book *Satisfaction,* "The road to satisfying experiences must necessarily pass through the terrain of discomfort."

Our personal narratives—and the characters in those stories—form our identities. The reason why rags-to-riches stories will never get old is our brains are wired to love them. We derive meaning from our lives in the form of story. We create internal narratives to shape our identity and to give our lives purpose and meaning so we can leave a legacy. Storytelling is not something we do. Storytelling makes us who we are.

The Storyteller's Secret

Inspiring storytellers reframe their personal narratives to give their lives purpose and meaning. In doing so they motivate the rest of us to dream bigger and to accomplish everything we're capable of achieving.

25

The Hospital Steve Jobs Would Have Built

I can hardly imagine medicine without medical stories.
—Dr. Oliver Sacks

I f the Apple Store were a hospital, it would look like the Walnut Hill Medical Center in the heart of Dallas. In April 2014 the media reported on the opening of a new eight-story, 16-bed acute care hospital in North Dallas. The media accounts also made note of the fact that Walnut Hill has a 10-bed emergency room and four cardiac care suites.

The "facts" make Walnut Hill sound like just about every other hospital. The facts don't tell the story. The facts don't explain why it's harder to get a job at the hospital than it is to be accepted to Harvard. The facts don't explain why the hospital is different from nearly every hospital you've ever seen, attracting visitors from as far away as China who want to learn its secrets. The facts don't explain how the hospital is reimagining healthcare. Facts need storytellers to breathe life into them. At Walnut Hill, a Dallas cardiologist serves as the hospital's chief storyteller.

Every two weeks Dr. Rich Guerra kicks off an orientation for new employees. Guerra's presentation is intended to motivate the men and women who have chosen to devote their full-time work to this particular hospital. "Today I want to share the story of how we got here and why we do what we do,"[1] Guerra begins.

For the next 60 minutes Guerra takes his audience on a narrative journey that pulls the curtains back on the hospital's vision and how its employees can work together to reinvent and reimagine the hospital experience.

Patients who enter Walnut Hill instantly discover that it's unlike any hospital they've entered. A valet takes the car and warmly greets the patient, providing clear information on where to go next. Since the valet is the first and last person the patient sees, the valets are specially trained in customer service skills. In fact, regardless of position, everyone at the hospital is trained in hospitality practices.

The Storyteller's Tools

The first 15 minutes of Guerra's presentation isn't about the hospital. He tells stories about the Apple Store, The Ritz-Carlton, Zappos, Disney, Starbucks, and Virgin. By doing so he helps his audience understand how these brands reinvented their categories and, by using similar hospitality techniques, Walnut Hill will reinvent healthcare. Guerra explains that Disney's mission isn't to build theme parks. It's to "create happiness." The Ritz-Carlton isn't in the business of providing beds for heads, but it's in the business of fulfilling the expressed and unexpressed wishes of their guests. Starbucks isn't in the business of coffee as much as it's in the business to inspire and nurture the human spirit. "Let's think about what we do in medicine. We're there at the beginning of life. We're there at the very end. We're about enriching lives. It's the core of everything we do," explains Guerra.

Once Guerra's audiences learn about the brands that inspired Walnut Hill, they are more likely to understand the reason behind strategies like the "15–5" rule: At 15 feet from a patient or a visitor, an employee should make eye contact. At 5 feet the employee should greet and say hello to the patient or, if the patient looks confused, ask if he or she needs help. Guerra explains that the hospital adopted the strategy from studying hospitality techniques at hotel chains like the JW Marriott.

Most people have sat through orientation at a school or a business. In most cases they are handed a packet of information and encouraged to read it. If the purpose, however, is to motivate people to perform specific activities in their day-to-day roles, packets are far less effective than stories. Guerra's orientation presentation at Walnut Hill is similar to Disney's "Traditions" program that all new employees—cast members—are required to attend before working at Disney's theme parks. As one training facilitator noted, the goal of Traditions is not to put people in Disney. It's to put Disney in people. And it does so by tapping existing cast members who consider it an honor to share their stories during orientation. "Don't underestimate the power of a good orientation program to create a portrait of the organization and its culture,"[2] according to the Disney Institute. "While the history, mission, and values of your business may be as familiar as a favorite childhood story to you, chances are good that your new employees have never heard them."

We're Not Smashing Rocks, We're Building a Cathedral

At Walnut Hill every employee is given a name badge with his or her photo. On the back of the badge they find six steps of service defined in the acronym W-E-C-A-R-E. Each employee is trained to follow the six steps in every interaction: beginning with a **W**arm welcome; **E**mpathize, **C**ommunicate, and Connect; **A**ddress concerns; **R**esolve and reassure; **E**nd with a fond farewell. The steps of service are directly inspired by The Ritz-Carlton and the Apple Store, both of which have successfully adopted similar steps to elevate the customer experience.

If new employees were simply handed a document or a badge with steps of service and asked to follow them, the strategy would surely fail to have its intended effect. People follow guidelines to keep their jobs, but people will go above and beyond expectations when their work has meaning. And as Dr. Guerra has learned, stories carry meaning. Stories evoke emotions that make people feel more deeply, making them more likely to internalize the habits and practices that will move the brand forward. Guerra expertly blends stories of real employees delivering exceptional service along with fables like the following:

Imagine living in medieval times and you're traveling through the countryside. There's all sorts of dust, noise, and activity. You come across a man with a sledgehammer and he's smashing rocks.

"What's going on here?" you ask.

The man responds, "What does it look like I'm doing? I'm breaking rocks."

You continue on your way and find another man who's got a sledgehammer and he's breaking up rocks.

"What's going on here?" you ask.

The man responds, "I'm making a living."

You walk further down the road and you see a man doing the same thing. He's got a sledgehammer and is smashing rocks.

"What's going on here?" you ask.

"I'm building a cathedral."

This man does not see what he's doing as trivial. He is a part of
something bigger. We don't want people who are here to break rocks.
And if you're here to make a living, this place probably isn't the best
fit for you. If you're here to do something great, this is the place to be.

Make note of two elements of Guerra's story. First, it's short. Guerra tells
the story of the man and the sledgehammer in under 60 seconds. Second,
he quickly ties the story back to the role of the audience in creating patient
experiences.

In a paper titled "An Integrative Review of Storytelling," Professor
Robert Gill makes the case that leaders who tell corporate stories strengthen
employee engagement, which improves a company's external reputation.
Employees who internalize the company's vision through stories become
"reputation champions." According to Gill, "Stories enable staff to identify
with the narrator on a personal level, and through their interpretation take
a form of ownership over how the brand is represented . . . Stories can be used
in organizations as a means to motivate people and create a message memorable enough for people to take cause and action."[3]

Walnut Hill's staff have certainly become reputation champions. Word
of mouth began to spread less than one year after the hospital opened its
doors. Walnut Hill received 9,000 applications in its first year. Only 3.2 percent of applicants were selected to work there, making Walnut Hill Medical Center harder to get into than Harvard.

The Story of a Lifetime Pumps Life into 200 Employees

Howard Leonhardt is a pioneer in the treatment of cardiovascular disease.
He invented the endovascular stent graft system for treating aortic aneurysm
repair, a medical device that has saved hundreds of thousands of lives. Although Leonhardt was an inventor, he learned quickly that he had to build
his storytelling skills if he hoped to succeed. "If you're in the biotech business, by default you're in the capital raising business,"[4] Leonhardt says. "The
CEO of a biotech company spends 50 percent of time raising capital. Storytelling is a core competency," Leonhardt told me.

In the spring of 1997 Leonhardt's company had grown to about 200
employees when he received an unusual call at home. Leonhardt picks up
the story in the present tense.

It's 3:00 a.m. and my home phone rings in Ft. Lauderdale, Florida. I answer and it's Dr. Barry Katzen, the director of the Miami cardiovascular institute. We had been doing research together on the TALENT stent graph. "Howard, I'm sorry to be calling at this ungodly hour but we have a situation. We have a patient who has a ruptured thoracic aneurism. They don't want to cut open his chest and break his ribs to get to his heart because they think by the time they do all of that he'll be too weak to survive. Luckily, it's only a small tear. He's only gurgling a little blood with each beat of his heart into his chest. They want to use one of your stent graphs instead of performing open-chest surgery."

I assume they need it in Miami. So I tell him I'll go get it and drive it down.

"Well that's the second part," Barry tells me. "This patient is in Vienna, Austria. We checked and there's a 6:00 a.m. flight out of Miami direct to Vienna and they think they can keep him alive until you get there."

I drive down to our facility, pick out a bunch of sizes from our inventory, stuff them in my suitcase, and make it to the airport by 5:00 a.m. I get to Vienna, grab a taxi, and rush to University of Vienna hospital.

In the next scene of the story, Leonhardt describes the situation he and the medical team faced when he arrived in Vienna.

When I got there the medical team said, "What took you so long?" We try to run the catheter up the groin to get to the aneurism and, after all that, he has a tortuous anatomy. We can't get to the aneurism because there's a bend in the femoral artery.

We figure out a way to insert the stent. We finally release the stent graph above the aneurism and isolate the bubble out. We sealed it off. No more gurgling into chest. The man's blood pressure comes back up and he's fine.

If the story had ended there, it would have offered Leonhardt's staff a good reminder of the value of their work. What happened next gave Leonhardt a story his staff would always remember.

Dr. Mandel takes me to the waiting room and there are two ladies standing there. The wife of the man we saved and his daughter. They seem worried. Dr. Mandel begins to speak to them in German: "I want to introduce you to Dr. Leonhardt. He's the inventor of the device that saved your husband's life and he traveled here from Miami. We feel that your husband wouldn't be here if Dr. Leonhardt had not done so."

The two ladies look up and say two simple words. In a soft, sweet way they said, "Thank you." I looked into the eyes of the daughter. She was sixteen. I thought, she's going to graduate from high school, get married, have kids. If we wouldn't have succeeded, that father would have missed all those things and she would have missed having her father.

When Leonhardt returned to Florida, he shut down the plant temporarily and called all 200 employees to the production area. He shared the story with them—it was perhaps the best opportunity he'd ever have to drive home that their jobs are about more than just making something: They are in the business of saving lives, of giving people more time with their families. There's a face and a story behind every life they save.

"When you experience something like that, it's hard to go to another line of work. When you feel the immense importance of the work that you do, it's hard to do anything else," says Leonhardt. "Even though medicine is all about facts and data, the driving force of what engages people (employees, investors, customers) is the human story behind what we're doing. Again and again we have found that crafting it into human terms is the most effective way to engage those three groups."

Stories Give Science Its Soul

Oliver Sacks was one of the great medical minds of our time. You might remember the movie that made him famous—*Awakenings* starring Robin Williams as the doctor who discovered L-dopa, a form of dopamine, as a therapy for patients who had been stuck in a catatonic state for decades. The movie was based on Oliver Sacks's book of the same name. Sacks described *Awakenings* not as a medical book, but a book of 20 biographies. We might also say a book of 20 stories.

Sacks grew up in a family of physicians. The talk around the dinner table every night took the form of stories—stories of real doctors and real patients. Those stories, which "fascinated and frightened" the young Sacks, led him to pursue a career in medicine. "The hunger for narrative and stories has been very strong for me and it's a necessity for everyone,"[5] Sacks once said. In medical school Sacks's professors saw cases; Sacks saw people and wanted to know their stories. "I retain very little memory of the medical lectures there, but on the other hand I remember all the patients I saw," he says.

Sacks became a vocal proponent of narrative medicine. His famous book, *The Man Who Mistook His Wife for a Hat and Other Clinical Tales,* is a series of stories from Sacks's work as a neurosurgeon.

"Each of us is a biography, a story,"[6] Sacks writes. "Biologically, physiologically, we are not so different from each other; historically, as narratives—we are each of us unique." Sacks argues that empirical science "takes no account of the soul."

When a medical story does have soul it can warm a person's heart and if the heart belongs to billionaire Mark Cuban, a story can have a profound impact.

At the 2015 South by Southwest (SXSW) festival in Austin, Texas, a unique pitch competition was held to feature companies advancing pediatric medicine. Kezia Fitzgerald was one of the contestants and had three minutes to deliver a presentation to Mark Cuban and a panel of judges.

Fitzgerald decided that if she only had three minutes to pitch her product, she'd better reach the judges' hearts and there would be no better way to do it than to share her own story.

As her husband advanced the slides (a series of photographs) Fitzgerald told the story of the day she was diagnosed with cancer in 2011.[7] Four months later her infant daughter, Saoirse, developed cancer as well, a stage-four neuroblastoma. Saoirse had a central line inserted that delivered constant medicine directly in her bloodstream. At 11 months old Saoirse's first response was to pick at and chew her line. If the line gets caught on something, comes out, or breaks it needs to be replaced with emergency surgery. Tape was the only solution the Fitzgeralds were offered, and it didn't work well. The couple developed a cloth sleeve and wrap made of cotton and spandex. It keeps children from picking at central lines. It's a simple solution that results in fewer irritations, fewer infections, better sleep, and lets children be free to be kids. The Fitzgeralds started CareAline to make the sleeve available to patients around the world.

Cuban was immersed in the story. His first question, "How is your daughter today?" Cuban's head visibly dropped when Fitzgerald said that her daughter had died. Without asking for any equity in return, Cuban offered to buy 1,000 sleeves, brand them with the Dallas Mavericks logo (the basketball team Cuban owns), and introduce the products to Dallas hospitals. Fitzgerald told me that she began the pitch with her personal story, not because she wanted the judges to feel sorry for her but because it was the only way she knew how to demonstrate her passion for the product. She said, "It's not just another product to market to the medical community. It's a true necessity. It's a way to keep our daughter's name and legacy alive."[8]

Fitzgerald does not have an MBA or a career in marketing. She went to art school and became a photographer. But the picture she painted that day won first place in the pitch competition, earned Mark Cuban's support, and paved the way to help children and adults undergoing cancer treatment.

Stories bring soul to the human condition. In healthcare, storytelling leads to more effective diagnosis and treatment. In organizations of any kind, storytelling creates brand champions who are motivated to deliver exceptional service and exceptional treatment to every customer and every patient.

The Storyteller's Secret

Successful leaders motivate their teams with stories that paint the picture behind the organization's mission, purpose, and vision. People don't care about how they're supposed to do their jobs until they understand why they're doing it.

26

A Hotel Mogul Turns 12,000 Employees into Customer Service Heroes

Storytelling has changed my business and changed my life.

—Steve Wynn

Steve and his wife married when they were young. They were broke and didn't have enough money for a honeymoon. When Steve was presented with the opportunity to oversee a small business transaction in Las Vegas, he decided to give his wife the trip she deserved. Little did he know that the short adventure would transform the very city they were visiting.

The couple decided to enjoy Thanksgiving of 1965 in Palm Springs before heading to Vegas. They had chosen to have dinner at a restaurant called Ruby's Dunes. By chance and a stroke of luck Frank Sinatra was dining at the next table and walked over to say hello to the businessman who had invited Steve to develop a new hotel on the Vegas strip. "What hotel are you staying at in Las Vegas?"[1] the famous crooner asked the young couple. "We're staying at the Dunes," Steve responded. "No you won't. You'll stay at the Sands as my guest," Sinatra offered. He also invited the couple to a show. When Steve and his wife, Elaine, arrived at the nightclub in Vegas, they were escorted to the front row to watch the biggest act in America: The Rat Pack. Joining Sinatra on stage were Sammy Davis Jr., Dean Martin, Peter Lawford, and Joey Bishop. The couple sat next to the biggest Hollywood stars at the time: Lucille Ball, Elizabeth Taylor, Gregory Peck, Roger Moore. The act was like one big party because the performers knew just about everyone in the audience. As Sinatra was working the room he spotted Steve and said, "How do you like the seat, kid?"

Steve had no intention of staying in Las Vegas. The 23-year-old simply wanted to take his wife on a vacation. But the experience so moved him that he decided he would stay and over the next 50 years Steve Wynn would transform Las Vegas from a seedy backwater town with a few motels and small casinos in the middle of the desert to the gambling and resort mecca it is today. Wynn built the Mirage in 1989. With a price tag of $600 million it was the most expensive hotel of its time; he subsequently topped it with Bellagio. Today, Wynn is the founder and chairman of Wynn Resorts, overseeing hotels that bear his name in Las Vegas and Macau, China.

You'd think that a hotel mogul worth $4 billion would know everything about the hospitality business. Wynn does know a lot, but admits he only recently discovered the secret that "changed my business and my life." Wynn calls the secret his "competitive edge." The secret is storytelling.

The Storyteller's Tools

To understand how storytelling transformed Wynn's hospitality business, you need to understand what Wynn calls the strongest force in the universe— self-esteem. "If you can make someone else feel good about themselves, they will love you for it. They will be loyal to you. If you get someone to feel better about themselves, you've hit the jackpot. That's a dead-on bull's-eye in human relations,"[2] says Wynn.

Steve Wynn discovered a technique that I've been recommending since I wrote my sixth book, *The Apple Experience*. I called it "wow stories." Here's how it works at Wynn Resorts. It had been standard practice at Wynn's properties that every department supervisor called a meeting before every shift. For example, the restaurant managers would meet with waiters, the chefs with the line cooks, the housekeeping supervisors with the maids, etc. At first the meetings were strictly tactical, a means of sharing information for employees to do their job that day. Several years ago, though, Wynn started something new and astonishingly effective—astonishing because it's simple, free, and works like magic. The supervisor simply asks this question of the team:

Does anybody have a story about a great customer experience they'd like to share?

In one of the first storytelling meetings, a bellman told the following story.

A couple had checked into the hotel. The bellman asked them if he had all the bags on the cart. The woman panicked as she realized that she had left the bag with their medicines on a table in the front hallway of their house. Her husband was diabetic and needed insulin. She also required prescription medicines. The bellman asked where they lived.

"Pacific Palisades in Los Angeles,"[3] the woman responded.

"Is anyone at the house?" the bellman asked.

"The housekeeper will be there today."

"My brother lives in Encino. It's not too far from your house. If someone's home he can pick up the medicine bag," the bellman offered.

"But we need the medicine by tomorrow morning at 7:00 a.m.," the woman said.

"Don't worry, you'll have it. Now go enjoy a nice dinner and good night's sleep."

The bellman had just started his late afternoon shift. He called his brother to make the arrangements and asked his supervisor if he could drive to his brother's house in Encino. The bellman retrieved the bag of medicine and returned to Las Vegas at 4:00 a.m. The couple had their medication at 7:00 a.m. when they awoke.

"Do you think the hotel will ever be the same for that couple again?"[4] Steve Wynn says. "Forget the crystal chandeliers, the onyx, the marble, the hand-woven carpets—it means nothing. They're going to tell their friends about what an incredible place the hotel is."

I've Got 12,000 Employees Looking for a Story

Within minutes of the bellman telling his story, the marketing team at the hotel recorded it and posted the video on the company's intranet. They made a large poster with employee's face and story on it and posted it in the staff room. What happened next is easy to predict, but profound in its implications. Employees started looking for their own stories to tell. Why? Because of "the most powerful force in the universe"—self-esteem. They wanted to be recognized in front of their peers.

"Now I've got 12,000 employees looking for a story, someone to help,"[5] says Wynn. A dealer on break might notice someone who looks lost and walk that person to the right place. "It might take him five minutes, but he's got a story," says Wynn. "He's going up on the Internet tomorrow. He's going to be a hero . . . It's the power that makes a guy like me sleep good at night."

Wynn can sleep comfortably because he has confidence that thousands of employees around the world will be taking the steps necessary to create exceptional customer experiences. They want to be the hero of their own story.

Wow Stories Lead to Better Customer Experiences

A company doesn't have to be in the hospitality industry to benefit from sharing wow stories among the staff. I introduced the technique to a franchise called FRSTeam, which has about 50 locations in the United States and is in the business of fabric restoration. When a person's house is damaged by a fire or flood, the insurance carrier uses FRSTeam to clean and restore damaged clothes, upholstery, and other items.

FRSTeam implemented wow stories among its delivery drivers, who are the customer-facing employees of the organization and in the best position to create wow moments. The stories caught on quickly as drivers tried to top each other in customer satisfaction. The drivers began asking customers a key question: *What item means the most to you?* Supervisors empowered the drivers to turn those objects into wow stories. For example, one customer told the driver that they were distraught over a family photograph that had been damaged in the fire. FRSTeam doesn't restore photos, but the driver, on his own time, used Photoshop to restore the picture. He framed it and returned it to the family. Another customer told a driver that an old barn on her property had a sentimental value to her. Once again, the barn itself had nothing to do with the damaged items the driver was there to pick up. The driver took a picture of the barn and had a friend who makes ornaments put the picture on a Christmas tree ornament. In yet another story, a driver went out of his way to return a cleaned and restored teddy bear to the homeowner on the same day he picked it up so the homeowner's child didn't miss a night without her stuffed animal. The results were anything but child's play. The franchise's customer service scores skyrocketed as it began implementing wow stories. The poet Maya Angelou famously said people will forget what you said and what you did, but they'll never forget how you made them feel. These drivers made homeowners feel cared for.

According to Steve Wynn, when employees believe they are being treated fairly for a job, money doesn't become the number one issue for them. They want to be happy. They want to feel as though their role has meaning. They want to be celebrated. Storytelling does just that. Raise a person's self-esteem and, according to Steve Wynn, you'll have "plugged into the ultimate energy available on the planet."

The Storyteller's Secret

Successful leaders use storytelling to build great cultures. Culture is created by loyal, frontline employees who are passionate about delivering an exceptional experience to every customer, every time. Getting employees to see themselves as the hero of their own customer story is the magic to creating an unbeatable culture.

27

A Revolutionary Idea That Took Off on the Back of a Napkin

If something can't be explained on the back of an envelope, it's rubbish.

—Richard Branson

The St. Anthony Hotel in San Antonio, Texas, has a long and storied history. President Lyndon B. Johnson spent his honeymoon there, and the first movie to win the Academy Award for Best Picture, *Wings,* was filmed on the property. But its most famous story, perhaps, involved neither presidents nor Hollywood. It happened in the hotel's restaurant, the St. Anthony Club.

One day in 1966, two men met for drinks at the hotel's bar. One was a Texas businessman; the other a chain-smoking, whiskey-swigging lawyer. Herb Kelleher and Rollin King had been kicking around a business plan, which they now sketched out on the back of a cocktail napkin. First, one of the men drew a triangle in the center of the napkin. At the top of the triangle, they wrote "Dallas," on the bottom left, "San Antonio," and on the bottom right, "Houston." Their vision was simple—to create a small, local airline connecting three Texas cities.

That business plan, sketched on the back of a St. Anthony Hotel cocktail napkin, would transform the lives of millions of Americans. One year later March 15, 1967, their vision came to life as Southwest Airlines.

Today, the original napkin sits under glass in the Dallas headquarters of Southwest Airlines. The company has come a long way. Southwest is the world's largest airline, employing 46,000 people, carrying more than 100 million passengers a year, and generating billions of dollars of quarterly profit in an industry where profits are hard to find.

Southwest democratized the skies. In the 1960s, 80 percent of Americans had never flown on an airplane. Only wealthy businesspeople could afford a ticket. As airfares dropped thanks to the Southwest model, more and more people took flight. Today, a full 90 percent of Americans have flown in an airplane and Americans make 700 million plane trips each year. If you also consider the fact that pilots have never been better trained and that flying has never been safer, the golden age of travel isn't yesterday; it's today. And much of the credit goes to Herb Kelleher, Rollin King, and the business plan that fit on a napkin.

The Storyteller's Tools

Many businesses have tried to figure out the secret to Southwest's success. "We used to have a corporate day. Companies would come in from around the world and they were interested in how we hired, trained, that sort of thing,"[1] according to Kelleher. "Then we'd say, 'Treat your people well and they'll treat you well,' and then they'd go home disappointed. It was too simple."

Culture matters at Southwest. "If you ain't got culture, you ain't got s***,"[2] Kelleher once said in his trademark salty language. "Competitors can buy tangible assets, but they can't buy culture." Kelleher made what he called "an audacious commitment" to put employees first, customers second, and shareholders third. To this day employees can recite Kelleher's core mantra—if employees took care of him, he would take care of them.

Unlike most leaders who give lip service to the importance of culture, Kelleher talked about it incessantly. In many of his public presentations to shareholders and employees, culture was all he talked about it. As a storyteller, Kelleher understood that culture is not something that a committee brainstorms once and moves on. Instead culture is a story that must be shared every day.

In one interview the reporter asked Kelleher why it was so hard for competing airlines to copy Southwest's success. Kelleher explained the difference with the following story:

> I think the difficulty for them is the cultural aspect of it. That cannot
> be duplicated. One of the things that demonstrates the power of
> people is when the United Shuttle took out after us in Oakland. They

had all the advantages. I mean, they had first-class seats for those who don't want to fly anything but first class. They had a global frequent flyer program, which we did not have. They probably spent $25 million or $30 million on their advertising campaign. I probably have something like a thousand letters at my office that tell you why they finally receded from Oakland. Those letters say, "Herb, I tried them, but I just like your people more, so I'm back." Don't ever doubt, in the customer service business, the importance of people and their attitudes.[3]

As Southwest grew larger many experts assumed it would become more difficult to maintain the company's friendly, empowered, and productive employee base. Kelleher disagreed. "Our mission statement is eternal. Our mission statement deals solely with people. That never changes—in any way, shape, or form,"[4] Kelleher explained.

Stories Turn Employees into Crusaders

Culture stories are more impactful when they are shared among employees. One of Kelleher's storytelling tools was to perform simple gestures that would ripple across the organization.

One of the things that we do is continue to emphasize that we value our people as people, not just as workers. Any event that you have in your life that is celebratory in nature or brings grief, you hear from Southwest Airlines. If you lose a relative, you hear from us. If you're out sick with a serious illness, you hear from us, and I mean by telephone, by letter, by remembrances from us. If you have a baby, you hear from us. What we're trying to say to our people is, "Hey, wait a second, we value you as a total person, not just between eight and five."[5]

When an employee gets a handwritten note or a call from the boss, that person tells another, who tells another, who tells another. Stories perpetuate themselves and bolster a company's culture. I spoke to a Southwest pilot who repeats a story he heard 10 years earlier—the time Kelleher found out that an employee's son had been killed in a car crash. The employee was in Baltimore and his family was in Dallas. Kelleher had a plane that was about to be taken out of service for routine maintenance rerouted to land in Baltimore, pick up the employee, and get him back to his family immediately. "Stories like that make me proud to work for this company," the pilot said.

Public Stories Rally People Around a Common Purpose

After building one of America's most admired companies, Kelleher stepped down in 2007. The pilots, flight attendants, and ramp crews who remember Kelleher's stories are among the most loyal employees you will find at any company, in any industry, in any country. But what about the thousands of employees hired every year that don't have the benefit of hearing the founder's stories directly? A paycheck is usually enough to get most people to work on time, but only an inspiring purpose beyond a paycheck will encourage people to go the extra mile. According to Southwest CEO Gary Kelly, a company's purpose should answer the question, "Why do we exist?"

Kelly adds, "We exist to connect people to what's important in their lives through friendly, reliable, and low-cost air travel."[6]

Only storytelling can rally passionate people around a common purpose. Each week Kelly gives a "shout out"—public praise—to employees who have gone above and beyond to show great customer service. Each month the Southwest *Spirit* magazine features the story of an employee who has gone above and beyond. Southwest highlights positive behaviors through a variety of recognition programs and awards. Finally, internal corporate videos are filled with real examples and stories to help employees visualize what each step of the purpose looks and feels like.

Friendly
In one video, Jessica, a Southwest customer, talks about the day she and her family saw her husband off for a six-month deployment in Kuwait. Kelli, a customer service agent, saw the family and asked if they all wanted to go to the gate. "It bought us thirty more minutes to spend time together,"[7] Jessica said. Yet another employee asked if the family would like to go on the plane. The man's children were able to give him one last hug as passengers cheered.

Reliable

Reliability stories at Southwest often focus on business travel (Southwest is the top-rated airline among business travelers). In one video a business-woman says, "They board the fastest, they get my bags off the fastest, which is efficient. I know exactly when I will land every week and I can easily schedule my meetings because I know they'll be on-time."[8]

Low Cost

In one video, Vicki, a passenger and a soon-to-be grandmother, received a call from her pregnant daughter who had been diagnosed with a serious medical condition. Vicki was a teacher and didn't have much money, but Southwest's low rates allowed her to take five round-trips from Orlando, Florida, to Birmingham, Alabama, during the pregnancy until the grand-child was born. "I realized what a significant role Southwest had played in the whole story,"[9] Vicki said. Another video shows a mother's emotional reaction as she sees her daughter show up unexpectedly at her doorstep dur-ing the holidays. The daughter didn't have enough money to fly home, but one night she received a "ding alert" (notices of limited-time fare deals). The low price allowed her to book a flight for the next day and to give her mom "the best gift she could receive."

Although anyone can view these videos on YouTube, they were not nec-essarily intended for the public. They are meant to motivate and educate Southwest's internal audience, to remind them why their jobs matter to mil-lions of people. "Because of you, me and my family have a memory for a lifetime," Jessica says into the camera. "Because of you, I was able to be at my daughter's side during a difficult pregnancy," says Vicki.

Herb Kelleher said the core of the company's success is the most diffi-cult thing for a competitor to imitate. "They can buy all the physical things. The things you can't buy are dedication, devotion, loyalty—the feeling that you are participating in a crusade,"[10] Kelleher said.

Do your employees feel as though they are participating in a crusade? Do they have a sense of purpose beyond receiving a paycheck twice a month? "It's not one of the enduring mysteries of all time,"[11] Kelleher once said. "A motivated employee treats the customer well. A customer is happy so they'll keep coming back, which pleases the shareholder. It's just the way it works."

The Storyteller's Secret

Successful leaders build an award-winning culture with stories that bring the company's purpose to life. Publicly sharing those stories triggers a crusade.

28

When Amy Lost Her Legs, She Found Her Voice

> Show me a hero and I'll write you a tragedy.
> —F. Scott Fitzgerald

Amy thought she had the flu. Her body ached and she had a slight fever. Amy was only 19 years old, in good health, and could tear up a mountain on her snowboard. She went home to rest, but got sicker and sicker. Luckily her younger cousin had just gotten her driver's license and rushed Amy to the hospital.

Amy's entire body was crashing. Her kidneys were shutting down. "Massive kidney failure" she heard the doctor say. Amy had entered severe septic shock. At one point Amy was sure she'd felt her last heartbeat. Just before doctors put Amy into a medically induced coma, she remembers seeing her feet. They were discolored and had turned from purple to violet. A body in septic shock pulls blood from its extremities to feed failing organs. Amy was dying.

Miraculously, the doctors were able to perform emergency surgery and saved Amy's life. Her legs, however, had to be amputated below the knee a few weeks later.

After a very long recovery Amy Purdy doesn't look like she's lost a step in life. She continued to compete and won a bronze medal in adaptive snowboarding at the 2014 Paralympic Games. Purdy won the hearts of millions of viewers when she reached the finals of ABC's popular show, *Dancing with the Stars*. Millions of others were exposed to Amy's story when they watched her deeply emotional TEDx talk, "Living Beyond Limits." Amy's storytelling skills even landed her on the stage next to Oprah Winfrey on Oprah's eight-city "The Life You Want Weekend" stadium tour.

Although Purdy's story has inspired millions, most people don't realize how close Purdy came to shutting the door entirely on her public speaking career because she didn't believe she had a story worth telling. Once Amy embraced her story, an entirely new world opened up for her.

"You'd think my darkest days were when I lost my legs,"[1] Amy told me. "Instead my darkest days were when I went home and had to walk in these metal legs for the first time. I had to rethink the rest of my life. I felt so out of control. I was at the bottom of the barrel. I was sick and tired of being sick and tired. That's when this question popped into my head: *If my life were a book and I was the author, how would I want the story to go?* I knew what I didn't want. I didn't want people to feel sorry for me. I didn't want people to see me as disabled. I wanted to live a life of adventure and stories. The question allowed me to daydream; daydream about traveling the world, daydream about snowboarding, daydream about all the things I wanted to do and completely believing that it was possible."

When Amy Purdy lost her legs, she found her voice.

The Storyteller's Tools

Like many of today's great storytellers, Amy Purdy was a bundle of nerves in her first appearances before an audience. In Purdy's book, *On My Own Two Feet,* she describes what happened when a woman's conference invited her to be a keynote speaker and offered to pay $8,000. "I was in panic mode. I stopped eating. I could barely sleep."[2] She drove herself sick with worry because she couldn't figure out how to boil down 30 years of life into 30 minutes. Unable to overcome her panic, she finally backed out. "The first and last time I've ever walked away from a big commitment," according to Purdy.

Purdy decided to take the pressure off by teaming up with a friend who also had an inspiring story to share. Together, they spoke at high schools to improve their public-speaking skills. "I started to get fascinated with the craft of storytelling,"[3] Purdy says. "What I found was that you don't always have to have the most amazing story. It's learning to share the story that you have that counts."

Purdy told me that she leaned on her training as an athlete to transform herself into a confident storyteller. She watched great speakers, accepted as many opportunities as possible, and visualized her success.

"It has been an evolution. I've experienced success on stage and failure, where I stood on stage for 45 minutes and wanted to die as I tried to figure out what I wanted to say next,"[4] Purdy said. "I knew I wanted to share my story to help other people . . . I got invited to my old high school and I shared my stories with all the classes. I remember I was so nervous and didn't know where to start, but I knew I had information they could take away."

In 2011, a TEDx conference invited Purdy to give "the speech of her lifetime." In Purdy's book she dedicates three chapters, more than 30 pages, to the events that resulted in the amputation of both legs below the knees. For the TEDx audience she'd have to do it in 18 minutes in front of a live audience of 1,500 people.

In spite of her growing confidence in smaller venues, Purdy acknowledges that she was "completely freaked out" about giving the TEDx talk. Her hands shook as she opened, and her voice cracked. Yet the story flowed—from a raw and emotional place. When she finished, there wasn't a dry eye in the house. She said, "I'd delivered a speech made perfect by its imperfections."[5]

Purdy's Story in Three Compelling Acts

Purdy's presentation was perfect. If you'll recall, a narrative with a beginning, middle, and end qualifies as a story. Amy Purdy's "story" might go like this: A 19-year-old girl falls ill. She's brought to the hospital with meningitis. She loses her legs, but survives. The preceding sentence meets the definition of story, but it's not going to win any awards, go viral on TED, or catch Oprah Winfrey's attention. It's also not going to inspire anyone to dream bigger.

Now let's turn to the three-act structure Purdy used in her now famous TED talk. It closely resembles the structure of a successful screenplay. Act I introduces the protagonist—the hero—and establishes the setting in which the character is living her everyday life. Above all, the first act must create empathy for the hero. We identify with characters we care about. The first act also establishes the turning point. It ends with the introduction of the conflict—if you've seen the movie *Titanic,* it's the iceberg moment.

Purdy's Act I:
Growing up in the hot Last Vegas desert, all I wanted was to be free.
I would daydream about traveling the world, living in a place where it

snowed, and I would picture all of the stories that I would go on to tell. At the age of 19, the day after I graduated high school, I moved to a place where it snowed and I became a massage therapist . . . For the first time in my life, I felt free, independent and completely in control of my life until my life took a detour.[6]

Act II heightens the tension and turns up the obstacles the hero must overcome. A solid second act takes dramatic turns, often more than one. *Titanic* hit an iceberg in Act I. Sinking is an even bigger problem.

Purdy's Act II:

I went home from work early one day with what I thought was the flu, and less than 24 hours later I was in the hospital on life support with less than a two percent chance of living. It wasn't until days later as I lay in a coma that the doctors diagnosed me with bacterial meningitis, a vaccine-preventable blood infection. [Purdy introduces another obstacle, and another, and another as she loses her spleen, part of her kidneys, and the hearing in her left ear, and both of her legs below the knee. Just as the audience thinks the worst is over, Purdy adds yet another dramatic turn]. *I thought the worst was over until weeks later when I saw my new legs for the first time. The calves were bulky blocks of metal with pipes bolted together for the ankles and a yellow rubber foot with a raised rubber line from the toe to the ankle to look like a vein. I didn't know what to expect, but I wasn't expecting that . . . I was absolutely physically and emotionally broken.*

At this point the audience is broken, too. We've established empathy with the hero and we've been through hell with her. Well, at least the worst is over. Or is it?

Four months later I was back up on a snowboard, although things didn't go quite as expected: My knees and my ankles wouldn't bend and at one point I traumatized all the skiers on the chair lift when I fell and my legs, still attached to my snowboard—went flying down the mountain, and I was on top of the mountain still. I was so shocked, I was just as shocked as everybody else, and I was so discouraged, but I knew that if I could find the right pair of feet that I would be able to do this again. And this is when I learned that our borders and our

obstacles can only do two things: one, stop us in our tracks or two,
force us to get creative.

In Act III, the conflict reaches its peak and everything seems hopeless. Our hero must dig deep within her soul to find the emotional strength to fix the problem and rise above the seemingly insurmountable odds. This is the climax—*Titanic* cracks in two pieces and sinks to the bottom of the ocean. The character of Rose survives and goes on to live a long life. But Rose is forever changed by her brief love affair with Jack and always keeps a piece of him in her heart.

Purdy's Act III:

My legs haven't disabled me, if anything they've enabled me. They've forced me to rely on my imagination and to believe in the possibilities . . . So the thought that I would like to challenge you with today is that maybe instead of looking at our challenges and our limitations as something negative or bad, we can begin to look at them as blessings, magnificent gifts that can be used to ignite our imaginations and help us go further than we ever knew we could go.

It's nearly impossible to resist the urge to stand up and cheer for Purdy because, as we now know, our brains are wired to respond to such a story.

Purdy believes that storytellers who have experienced struggle feel more deeply because they've experienced the depth of life and its highest peaks. "My biggest struggles have led to my biggest accomplishments,"[7] Purdy says.

Behind every hero there's a story of struggle and sacrifice, a story of dreams dashed and dreams found. If your life were a book and you were the author, how would you want your story to go? All of us have a story worth telling, but all too often we're reluctant or afraid to share our stories. Amy Purdy, the woman who backed away from her first speaking request and nearly backed out of TED, has now become a sought-after and popular motivational speaker because she learned to embrace her story. "When you go into speaking, you think you have to have grand ideas,"[8] says Purdy. "But really, it's the simplest of ideas that we all relate to that has the most impact."

The Storyteller's Secret

Motivational storytellers ignite the dreams of others with stories of hardship, heartache, and overcoming seemingly insurmountable odds. Tension and triumph are integral to the story. They wear struggle as a badge of honor, inspiring their listeners to tell their own stories and to treat life as a book in which the individual is the author of his or her own destiny.

29

From Hooters to the C-Suite—A Former Waitress Shares Her Recipe for Success

*I was always running from where I came from, but as I get older I
realize it is the very thing that makes me unique.*

—Kat Cole

Kat's mother endured her alcoholic husband for years before finally con-
cluding that the only way to keep herself, Kat, and her two younger
daughters safe was to move away. The move did not automatically make
things easier; for the next three years, Kat's mother fed the family on $10 a
week, mostly in the form of frozen lasagna and canned meat.

When Kat was in high school, her mother was supporting the family
on one income as an administrative assistant. Kat wanted to help support
the family and eagerly sought a job "as early as the law would permit." At
the age of 17 Kat took a part-time job. After school, she changed into orange hot pants and a tight tank top and served chicken wings at a Florida
Hooters restaurant. The job wasn't glamorous, but it taught her to run a
kitchen and manage a staff. The job was important, because in addition to
helping her mom, Kat was working to save enough money to become the
first person in her family to attend college. And sure enough, she had, prior
to her graduation from high school, saved enough to enroll at the University
of North Florida, where she planned to get an engineering degree. She had
made remarkable progress in a very short time, and it appeared that things
would go smoothly until the day of the kitchen mutiny.

One day, in the middle of her shift, she heard a sudden buzz of conversation from the kitchen, followed by the sudden swing of the door as the
entire kitchen staff walked off the job. She would later learn that they'd had

a dispute with the manager. They bolted midshift, leaving Kat and the other waitresses wondering how the patrons would get their food, not to mention how they would get their tips. Kat managed to bring home the bacon that day because she had cooked it. "I jumped into the kitchen and made chicken wings. By the way, frying chicken wings with little orange shorts and panty hose on is a really bad idea,"[1] Kat recalls. Kat took charge, rallying the manager and the remaining staff, and succeeded in averting a restaurant disaster. In that moment Kat discovered her gift. "On paper I was a train wreck," she said. "Single parent household, alcoholic father, worked for Hooters. If you just look at that on paper it does not appear to be a very compelling resume. But in real life, if I am put in charge of your business, I am a sure bet."

Kat was such a sure bet that her boss trusted her to train the staff of a new Hooters franchise in Australia. But she faced several obstacles. She had never been on a plane, didn't have a passport, and had never traveled out of the country. Most importantly, she lacked confidence—what was so clear to her boss was not yet clear to her. For answers, she turned to the most inspiring leader she knew—her mom, explaining her desire to take on the job as well as her paralyzing fear of failure. Kat's mother grabbed her by the shoulders and said, "You can do anything and I'm expecting you to do everything."[2] Kat made it to Australia.

Kat no longer runs that Hooters in Australia, though she made a success of it. Kat Cole is now president of Cinnabon, a $1 billion franchise with 1,100 stores in 56 countries. What's more, she was named Cinnabon's president at the age of 32 and joined the ranks of the most successful young American business leaders. Cole has achieved remarkable career success, but an important part of her story is reminding her audiences that "My story is only interesting if you understand where I came from."

The Storyteller's Tools

Stories do more than entertain us. They guide us. They inspire us to live a life with "no borders and no boundaries," the motto that guides Kat Cole. We all have profound crises of confidence, or even fail at some point in our careers. Successful leaders fight through the crises and failures, and focus on results. If those results are unacceptable, they try again and again until they're satisfied with the outcome. Further, leaders transform themselves into inspiring storytellers when they muster the courage to share the sometimes difficult lessons they've learned.

Cole Finds Common Ground by Telling Her Personal Story

Cole openly shares her origin story with nearly everyone she meets. Early in her career she discovered that honesty and authenticity offered a fast track to building trust and credibility. When Cole was assigned the role of opening the first Hooters franchise in Australia, she was given three weeks to train a new owner, motivate its new staff, and open the restaurant. To make matters more difficult, Cole was the youngest person in the room, making it that much harder to establish credibility and trust. "To equalize the differences I had to find common ground,"[3] Cole told me. "I'm a crazy learner. I observe people. I watched people respond. The more I gave, the more they gave. When you smile, and give and share, those things expedite the building of trust. And you cannot work on a team and accomplish a lot in a short amount of time without trust. When you don't know each other, find a way to fast track it."

Cole learned such a valuable lesson about building trust that she continues to share her origin story in nearly every setting—keynote speeches, media interviews, employee meetings. In fact, moments before I spoke to Cole, she had been on the phone with a new franchise owner, sharing her origin story with him.

"Why did you feel it necessary to talk about your background?" I asked.

"You can't assume people will trust you because they've read about you or because you run a successful company. People are naturally skeptical. If you lower your guard, and be kind, and share your own mistakes, faults, and your story in a way that says 'I am like you, more than you probably realize,' there is so much more that you can get done together."

Four words explain Cole's ability to build strong business partnerships based on trust: *I am like you*. People want to do business with people they like and who they trust. Cole's transparency makes her refreshing, likable, and trustworthy. "People care and are motivated by being inspired and knowing they are working with, buying from, or working for really good people,"[4] says Cole. "People vote with their wallets when they know there is a good family, a good person, or a good company behind a product. Employees stay through the tough times when they know they are working for good people."

Recall the classic storytelling narrative of tension and triumph. Cole's stories of struggle and redemption always end with a lesson she's learned and how it positively impacted her career.

For example, in a presentation to Atlanta-area business leaders Cole reminded the audience that Cinnabon started as one store in a mall in Seattle, Washington. It began with one product—a high calorie, "disturbingly delicious" cinnamon roll. From those humble beginnings Cinnabon grew into a global franchise through broadening its product offerings and establishing innovative partnerships. Cole ties the Cinnabon origin story back to her life's struggle and extracts lessons that all businesses or professionals can adopt to find success.

> There's always a core. A core to each of us, where we came from. Our roots, our background. We all have the potential to grow into something very different. Having the courage to expand from our core, but the discipline to keep it aligned with our brand, has allowed the business to continue to grow despite massive economic headwinds and a huge increase in competition. The only brands and businesses that will survive in the next five, ten, twenty years are not brands and businesses that have a particular product. They are the brands and businesses that have the discipline and the core competency of being flexible, of being able to partner, of being able to understand that just because they've been on one path for the last two years, or five years, or ten years, that does not mean that it is the path that will take us to continued success in the future.[5]

Cole sees her leadership role as being "a constant ambassador" for the brand. An "ambassador" is a messenger. The message you deliver to partners, stakeholders, employees, and team members will fail to elicit the desired action if the source (you) is considered untrustworthy. Origin stories create trust, strengthen relationships, and build credibility for the messenger, the brand ambassador.

Cole works in the food service industry, a trade traditionally made up of young workers. Millennials now make up the majority of employees in the workplace. Their career goals are very different than those of previous generations. Unlike Baby Boomers or Gen Xers, Millennials don't see "climbing the career ladder" as the ultimate goal. They want more than a paycheck. They want mentorship and meaning. Survey after survey shows young workers don't feel an attachment to their employers as their parents did. They dislike structured hierarchies and wish to be part of communities with shared interests and passions. They don't want to be managed; they want to be inspired. Leaders like Kat Cole motivate young workers because those employees can see themselves in her identity story.

Today's audiences are increasingly sophisticated and very, very good at spotting a fake. Speakers who don't "keep it real" risk losing the credibility they need to affect behaviors and to make an impact. "It is important that a leader be a good storyteller, but equally crucial that the leader embody that story in his or her life,"[6] writes leadership author Howard Gardner. According to Gardner leaders must fashion "stories of identity" if they hope to change hearts and minds. The story of identity is the origin story: the story of where a person came from and the lessons they learned from struggle or failure.

"I was deathly afraid of being defined by where I came from,"[7] says Kat Cole. "My mom, every year on my birthday, sends me a card that says, 'Don't you dare forget where you came from, but don't you dare let it define you.' I have grown a deep level of appreciation to protect those roots."

The Storyteller's Secret

Inspiring leaders embrace their past and have the courage to share the lessons they've learned. Appreciate your roots, protect those roots, and share the stories that strengthened you.

30

Trading Wall Street Riches for the Promise of a Pencil

The real voyage of discovery consists not in seeking new land-
scapes, but in having new eyes.

—Marcel Proust

On his twenty-fifth birthday Adam decided to create a life story worth
telling. He left a lucrative career in private equity to start a nonprofit
organization with an initial investment of just $25. The motivation for this
action had come four years earlier, when he'd spent time in India as part of
a Semester at Sea program. It was there that his eyes were opened to poverty, pain, and suffering on a scale he had never imagined. He met a young
boy "covered in dirt from head to toe, begging for money and food."[1]

"If you could have anything in the world, what would you want most?"
Adam asked.

"A pencil," the boy replied.

Adam was surprised. He had expected the boy to ask for a toy or an
iPod. He reached into his backpack, pulled out a No. 2 pencil, and watched
"as a wave of possibility" washed over the boy's face. "For me that pencil
was a writing utensil, but for him it was a key . . . that single stick of wood
and graphite could enable him to explore worlds within that he would never
otherwise access."[2]

Adam returned to the United States with his eyes wide open, but those
around him still had a narrow vision of what a life of meaning looked
like. Adam had completed a triple major at Brown University. His parents,
professors, and friends said he'd be crazy to give up on a Wall Street career
nearly guaranteed to bring in millions of dollars over his lifetime. And so
Adam did what was expected.

One day he made the following notation in a notebook, "I wish I was more interested in this work, but it's just not for me. Find your passion, and you'll find your strength."[3]

Adam finally found the courage to follow his passion and, in doing so, found his strength. On October 1, 2008, Adam Braun's nonprofit, Pencils of Promise, was born. Five years after starting the organization with $25, Braun's organization has opened more than 200 schools, serving more than 30,000 students in impoverished areas around the world. Every 90 hours Pencils of Promise breaks ground on a new school. "I was just a regular guy with $25 who wanted to prove that regardless of age, status, or location, every person has the capacity to change the world,"[4] Braun says. "Every person has a revolution beating within his or her chest."

I spoke to Braun upon the publication of his book, *The Promise of a Pencil*. Although Braun was only 30 years old at the time, I found him to be one of the most gifted storytellers of his generation. Braun has a keen sense of storytelling, sharpened after making thousands of fund-raising pitches. He asks for feedback, constantly analyzes the reaction of his audience, and has learned that the path to a person's head runs through the heart. For example, Braun acknowledges that it's not "rational" for people to write a check to support a child on the other side of the world, a child the donor will probably never meet. But making the audience—the donor—the hero of a story in which they play a role in changing the world, triggers the desired action of persuading people to open their wallets.

"The ability to captivate another individual through storytelling is essential to the early stage growth of a company,"[5] Braun told me. "I spent a lot of time refining how I presented our work through thousands of conversations. I learned the parts of our story that got people's eyes to light up and their heads to nod. I also learned when they started to fidget or their eyes glazed over. Through persistent communication we refined the language through which we describe the organization. It still remains the most critical part of driving the growth of the organization."

The Storyteller's Tools

Pencils of Promise needed wealthy donors to write big checks. The challenge, of course, was to persuade people to contribute money to faceless and nameless children on the other side of the world. The solution was to put a face and a name to those children so the donors could "meet" them and get to know them as individuals. And nothing comes closer to a real face-to-face meeting than video.

Three little girls that Braun met in the small village of Pha Theung, Laos, would provide the wow moment that Braun's pitch presentation required. In March 2009 Braun was scouting the location for the organization's first preschool. Most families in the village lived in bamboo huts on less than $2 a day. Braun stumbled upon three little girls in one of the huts, playing with letters on a chalkboard. They wanted to learn but had no teachers and no classroom. Their names were Nuth, Nith, and Tamund.

Braun took out a simple Canon point-and-shoot and recorded a short video. In the video Braun can be heard off-camera asking, *"Jao seu nyang?"* (What's your name?) The girls answer, smile, and giggle to each other. Braun pans the camera around to show the existing three-room primary school and the empty site that he hoped would be the first Pencils of Promise school. "You're going to be our first preschool students," Braun tells the girls as they giggle and smile.

Braun posted the video on Facebook and received an "overwhelming" response. Braun now inserts the 40-second video into his PowerPoint presentations, which is always a hit with the audience. "There's an authenticity to the footage because it's not super high quality and it's in the first person. You feel as though you are witnessing a special moment. The video is less than one minute long and it's a powerful element for drawing out an emotional response," says Braun.

Once the video clip ends in Braun's presentation, he advances to a slide that shows a photograph taken four months after he met the girls. It shows the same children sitting in their seats in the first Pencils of Promise classroom. "Showing the before and after is incredibly powerful and allows people to go on an emotional journey that elicits a lot of reaction," Braun explains.

Braun's presentation isn't all story; he delivers facts and figures about the organization's financial stability to audiences of potential donors because it's what they think they want to hear. But while the facts and figures might draw a nod of affirmation, they have yet to elicit a standing ovation. The video does—every time.

Neuroscience research in the lab explains why Braun's video triggers a standing ovation. It's all thanks to the neurochemical oxytocin, which I discussed earlier. "Oxytocin is produced when we are trusted or shown a kindness, and it motivates cooperation with others. It does this by enhancing the sense of empathy, our ability to experience others' emotions,"[6] says Paul Zak, professor at Claremont Graduate University.

Zak discovered that oxytocin levels in a person's brain can be "hacked" to motivate people to cooperate. Storytelling is the key to doing so. Zak and his team of researchers found that stories captured on video raised the oxytocin level in the brains of those subjects who watched the videos. Zak says, "By taking blood draws before and after the narrative, we found that character-driven stories do consistently cause oxytocin synthesis. Further, the amount of oxytocin released by the brain predicted how much people were willing to help others; for example, donating money to a charity associated with the narrative."

Zak took his storytelling research one step further to figure out *why* stories have the effect they do. His research in neurobiology helps to explain why every storyteller in this book has either experienced hardship directly, or leverages stories of struggle to move their audiences. "We discovered that, in order to motivate a desire to help others, a story must first sustain attention—a scarce resource in the brain—by developing tension during the narrative. If the story is able to create that tension then it is likely that attentive viewers/listeners will come to share the emotions of the characters in it, and after it ends, likely to continue mimicking the feelings and behaviors of those characters," writes Zak. "Enduring stories tend to share a dramatic arc in which a character struggles and eventually finds heretofore unknown abilities and uses these to triumph over adversity; my work shows that the brain is highly attracted to this story style."

Adam Braun hasn't done any lab research, but he's a student of persuasion. He knows the human brain has an emotional and a logical, or "rational," side. "The rational center leads us to make conclusions and the emotional center leads us to action,"[7] says Braun. "A great pitch must acknowledge the viability of the product or service, but the focus must be on igniting the person's emotional core." Thanks to Braun's ability to ignite the emotional core of an audience, more than 30,000 impoverished children have access to schools they otherwise wouldn't have. It's a lesson worth repeating.

The Storyteller's Secret

Persuasive storytellers ignite the emotional core of their listeners by sharing stories of real people overcoming real hardships. To trigger a release of oxytocin, the stories must follow the narrative arc of struggle and triumph. If a storyteller cannot bring the audience face-to-face with the subject of the narrative, video works nearly as well. Facts and figures inform, but stories move people to action.

31

The Ice Bucket Challenge Melts the Hearts of Millions

What an amazing opportunity we have to change the world.
—Pete Frates, six hours after being diagnosed with ALS

In the summer of 2011 Pete and his mom, Nancy, were sitting at the dinner table when Pete confided something that had been eating at him. "I just don't feel like I'm living up to my potential. Selling insurance is not my passion,"[1] he said.

Pete would find his life's mission, though it wasn't something he'd sought or something he'd wish on his worst enemy. Pete, a former outfielder and captain for the Boston College baseball team, was playing recreational baseball in an intercity league when a 90-mile-an-hour fastball struck him in the left hand. His wrist went limp and never returned to normal. For six months Pete visited doctors to figure out what had gone wrong. Finally a neurologist said he had found an answer and called Pete into his office.

On March 13, 2012, Pete called his mother, Nancy, to see if she'd like to go to the appointment with him. The nurse showed them into a waiting room, and shortly after, not one, but four doctors walked into the room. Nancy later recalled that she knew then that it wouldn't be a normal office visit. "It's not a sprained wrist. It's not a broken wrist. It's not an infection," the doctor said. The doctor then looked Pete in the eye and said, "I don't know how to tell this to a 27-year-old kid. Pete, you have ALS . . . I'm sorry to tell you this but there's no treatment and there's no cure."

Amyotrophic lateral sclerosis, also known as Lou Gehrig's disease, after the baseball player who succumbed to the disease over 75 years ago, is a progressive neurological disease that's hard to diagnose because the symptoms can be quite different. In most patients, however, the disease quickly degenerates into muscle weakness and paralysis. There is no cure, and indeed little progress has been made in the decades since Gehrig died from the disease.

But Pete would not be daunted by his prognosis. Only six hours after the doctors delivered their grim news Pete, his girlfriend Julie, his parents, and his siblings all gathered at his parents' house in Boston. "We're not looking back, we're looking forward,"[2] Pete instructed. "What an amazing opportunity we have to change the world. I'm going to change the face of ALS. I'm going to get it in front of philanthropists like Bill Gates."

The mission had become personal and Pete, the former baseball captain, was determined to lead it. He now knew the answer to the question he had asked his mom several months earlier: *What's my mission in life?* Pete's mission would be to bring attention to the disease, and he would accomplish the mission through sharing his story.

Pete Frates began speaking publicly about the need to raise awareness of the disease. He shared his story with all who would listen: civic groups, medical professionals, drug companies, and with governmental agencies such as the Food and Drug Administration in Washington, D.C.

On July 4, 2014, Frates wrote an article for MLB.com to commemorate the seventy-fifth anniversary of Lou Gehrig's retirement speech, known as "The Luckiest Man" speech. In the 1,700-word article, Frates shared his heartbreaking but inspirational story with the same vivid details he brought to his public speeches. "I once prided myself on my strong hands," he began. "They helped me grip the bat, fire the barrel through the zone and squeeze a fly ball safely into my outfield mitt. Today, they are unable to type this very story, as I depend on eye-tracking technology to deliver the message that my sturdy voice and fingers once did."

Frates traces the steps of his childhood, growing up in Beverly, Massachusetts, playing division one college baseball, and hitting home runs at Boston's historic Fenway Park. Frates also shares the details of how his body began to show signs of the disease, which would eventually take his voice. The article ends with a call to action and Frates's commitment to raise money to fight the disease. "My dream is for this article to be found by someone in a Google search one day and for he or she to wonder how anyone ever could have died from something treated so easily."

Twenty-three days after Frates published his story, the ice began to fall.

Frates did not start the ALS Ice Bucket Challenge. The credit goes to his former roommate who, inspired by Frates's courageous story, recorded himself pouring ice over his head, challenging others to do the same, and posting it on social media.

The challenge succeeded beyond anyone's wildest dreams: by the fourth day thousands of people had joined the challenge and posted their videos to Facebook. Within weeks 2.5 million videos had been posted on Facebook alone and YouTube videos had been posted from 150 countries. Sports stars like LeBron James, musicians like Justin Timberlake and Taylor Swift, and movie stars like Tom Cruise accepted the challenge and encouraged millions of others to do the same. And on August 16, 2014, Frates had accomplished the goal he set out to achieve on the day of his diagnosis, getting the message to philanthropists like Bill Gates. Gates accepted the challenge from Mark Zuckerberg and poured a bucket of ice water over his head on a YouTube video (Gates, in turn, challenged Elon Musk, Ryan Seacrest, and TED talks curator Chris Anderson).

The viral phenomenon raised more than $100 million in donations for the ALS Association in the summer of 2014, compared to $2.8 million for the comparable period the year before. By March 2015, it had generated more than $220 million for the nonprofit association, which allowed them to fast track medical trials that otherwise would have taken years to begin. Although the ALS Ice Bucket Challenge will go down as a case study in social media, the phenomenon would never have happened had it not been for Pete Frates's skill as a communicator and storyteller. "Social media is a tool, but Pete's story galvanized a generation,"[3] Nancy Frates told me.

The Storyteller's Tools

Pete Frates majored in communication at Boston College, a field of study his mother encouraged him to pursue because he was really, really good at it. "Pete could always command a room, a skill his teachers noticed as early as the sixth grade," Nancy told me.

In the sixth grade Pete gave a book report about one of his favorite baseball players, Tony Conigliaro, who played for the Boston Red Sox. Pete already showed a knack for performance and knew how to bring a story to life. Nancy told me that Pete wrote the presentation himself, and showed up on performance day dressed in a baseball uniform. His teacher still talks about it as the most memorable presentation she had ever seen a student deliver.

In the ninth grade Pete ran for class president. "He wrote the speech himself and it had everything you want in a presentation. It had humor, it was relatable, and a call to action. He mesmerized the room," recalls Nancy.

Pete Frates accepted the diagnosis as an opportunity to be the voice for tens of thousands of people who live with ALS each day, and who often lose their voices as the disease progresses. Pete realized that a story had to be relatable. People had to see themselves in Pete's story. Pete wanted them to know that if it could happen to him, it could happen to them. And to do so, he had to make the story as specific as possible.

"Life before my diagnosis was very normal,"[4] Pete told television host Charlie Rose. "I was a three-sport athlete in high school. I went on to play baseball at Boston College where I captained the team in '07. I was 6 foot 2, 225 pounds and, as someone said, cut out of granite and ready to roll."

Speaking to the staff at Biogen Idec, a Massachusetts company specializing in therapies to improve the lives of patients with neurological problems, Pete gave very specific details about the decline in his performance leading up to the fastball that hit his wrist.

Last summer, I was playing inner city baseball down the street in Lexington. My batting average had come down from .400 to .270. It was the second to last game of the year. There's a kid from UMass throwing. He's bringing about 90, mostly fastballs. Ninety should have been no big deal. I struck out and was really frustrated. I was one of the best players in the league. I could hear the other bench taunting me: "We finally got him." During the second to last inning I checked a swing and, being a left-hander, the ball hit me in the left wrist. That's the moment my life changed forever.[5]

In a documentary on the Ice Bucket Challenge shown on ESPN, the host of the show asks the question, "How does a movement start?" The answer, of course, is an inspiring story. But not just any story. A story that transports people into another person's shoes must be vividly told, with specific and concrete details.

"The hallmark of narrative is assurance,"[6] says literary scholar Gerald

Prince. "It lives in certainty. This happened then that. This happened because of that. This happened and it was related to that." Let's break down the structure that Prince says gives stories their specificity and apply it to the story that Pete Frates told.

This happened: Pete's at-bat performance was declining.
Then that: Pete was struck with a fastball.
This happened because of that: Pete's wrist went limp.
This happened and it was related to that: It never recovered.
  Six months later Pete learned he had ALS.

A story, says Prince, is a specific event carried out by specific characters in a specific place at a specific time. Why do we listen for specifics? Prince and other scholars who study the evolution of narrative believe we have a built-in radar to protect ourselves from dishonesty and falsehoods. We're not always accurate, of course, and some people have better "BS" detectors than others. But the more specific a story, the more evidence we have against which to measure a story's truthfulness. People want to believe that you're telling a true story. We listen for specifics to help us distinguish between fact and fiction.

Persuasive Stories Have Specific, Vivid Details

For more than 100 years the *New York Times* has offered its readers the opportunity to contribute to its Neediest Cases Fund, a program that assists troubled families and children. The newspaper doesn't simply solicit the abstract "donations for needy people." Instead the newspaper runs very specific—and heartbreaking—stories of people in need. Again, it's very hard for most people to donate money to a faceless entity, but they'll open their wallets for 21-year-old Carlos Montanez, who grew up in public housing in New York's Lower East Side and wants to go to college. "His family had very little money. Their main source of income is a $600 Social Security disability check that his mother receives every month. She has Charcot-Marie-Tooth disease, a neurological disorder that causes muscle weakness, and she is unable to work."[7]

  Abstractions don't bring in $6 million a year for the Neediest Cases Fund; stories of real people do.

  The *New York Times* reporters are excellent storytellers. Most articles about complex, abstract topics begin with very specific stories of one person, one family, or one organization impacted by the issue. For example, an article about the struggles of the American middle class began with this story:

> The bills arrive as regularly as a heartbeat at the Vories's cozy bi-level brick house just across the Ohio River from Cincinnati. It's the paychecks that are irregular. These days, Alex Vories, 37, is delivering pizzas for LaRosa's, though he has to use his parents' car since he wrecked his own 1997 Nissan van on a rainy day last month. In the spring and autumn, he had managed to snag several weeks of seasonal work with the Internal Revenue Service, sorting tax returns for $14 an hour. But otherwise the family had to make do with the $350 a week his wife, Erica, brought home from her job as a mail clerk for the I.R.S. . . . The financial volatility that the Vories grapple with is a feature of life for millions of workers.[8]

"Millions of workers" is simply too big a number and too vague for our mind's eye to visualize. We can all empathize with Alex Vories, however. We feel his pain as he's forced to deliver pizzas in his parents' car to make ends meet. Abstractions don't motivate people to take action. Abstractions don't inspire people to open their wallets for a cause.

It's well established in the neuroscience literature that our brains do not process abstractions and generalities very well. Persuasive storytelling requires specific and vivid details; even 10-year-old girls know it.

Former PIMCO co-CEO Mohamed El-Erian resigned his position at the giant bond firm after his 10-year-old daughter confronted him with a list of events he missed because he spent too much time at work.

The girl's argument was persuasive because it was specific, concrete, and tangible. She didn't say, "Dad, you need work-life balance." El-Erian's daughter never took a communication course, but she intuitively understands that generic concepts like "work-life" are not as persuasive as specific examples. She created a 22-point list to make her case. "Talk about a wake-up call,"[9] El-Erian wrote in an essay explaining his decision. "The list contained 22 items, from her first day at school and first soccer match of the season to a parent-teacher meeting and a Halloween parade. And the school year wasn't yet over."

Children do not speak in abstractions to get what they want. They know that to be persuasive, they'd better be specific. In much the same way, consumers don't buy solutions; they buy products that will improve their lives in a very specific way. Donors don't contribute to "causes"; they give money to help specific people attain specific goals. And people don't join movements to cure a disease; they spark movements to help one person who they feel connected to through story.

The Storyteller's Secret

Movements don't start themselves. Leaders inspire movements and they do so with stories that provide specific, tangible, and concrete details.

32

His Finest Hour—180 Words That Saved the World

> Short words are best.
>
> —Winston Churchill

The talk started well enough. But just as the newly elected representative, all of 29 years of age, thought he'd hit his stride, he experienced a moment feared by anyone who has ever had to address a large group: He had forgotten the rest of the speech. As he stood frozen in front of his peers for a period that lasted three whole minutes, but must have felt like an eternity, he felt his career begin to unravel. The fog of that moment wasn't thick enough to prevent him from observing his political enemies snicker and laugh openly. Worse, his supporters whispered to one another and looked at the floor in an attempt to disassociate themselves from the catastrophe unfolding in front of them. The speaker finally gave up, returned to his seat in despair, and covered his head with his hands. He thought his career was finished.

The next morning the newspapers called the fiasco a "shipwreck." A famous doctor publicly speculated that the speaker was the victim of "defective cerebration," or early senility.

But the young man wasn't senile. In fact he was one of the sharpest minds in his country. He vowed that he would never make the mistake again. From then on, he worked tirelessly to refine every word of every speech and made sure the only words he spoke were those he wrote himself and believed in with all his heart. Thirty-six years later Winston Churchill's time would come. He had become such a master of his craft that he single-handedly convinced the British people to stand up against Adolf Hitler and to fight to the death. Churchill became known as one of the greatest orators of the twentieth century and changed the course of history.

Winston Churchill proves that one speaker armed with one carefully crafted speech can trigger a movement that defeats unconscionable evil.

The day of the speech was May 28, 1940. Former prime minister Neville Chamberlain had paid the price of trying to appease Adolf Hitler. Nazi Germany had conquered much of Europe. British soldiers were trapped at Dunkirk, and France was about to fall as German soldiers were marching toward Paris. The British island was alone and the Nazi gains seemed irreversible. "Make a deal with Hitler," the majority of the British cabinet pleaded with Churchill, the newly appointed prime minister. The majority of the British people agreed that only an agreement with Hitler would save them.

Churchill called a meeting of the entire cabinet. He would not accede to popular sentiment. "If this long island story of ours is to end at last, let it end only when each one of us lies choking in his own blood upon the ground,"[1] Churchill said. The cabinet members stood, cheered, and shouted their support. Within one year of Churchill's speech, 30,000 British men, women, and children had died at the hands of the Nazis. And yet they fought. They fought through relentless German air assaults on London. They fought on the beaches of Normandy. They fought in the hills, on the beaches, and in the air. Winston Churchill's indomitable courage and persuasive storytelling skill carried Britain and its allies through the greatest crisis the world has ever known.

If you read the history of the period, you realize just how close the British were to making a deal with Hitler. If they had, Hitler would have remained unchecked and democracy would have been dethroned in much of the world, replaced with unconscionable evil, "the abyss of a new Dark Age," in Churchill's words. But in the span of two weeks and six speeches, Churchill successfully turned around public opinion. An entire population ready to cave to Hitler's demands was motivated to pick up their arms and fight to the death.

London mayor Boris Johnson, a prolific writer, details Churchill's remarkable transformation as a storyteller in *The Churchill Factor*. "He wasn't a natural,"[2] Johnson told me. "We think of him as somehow supernaturally gifted, as if he had sprung from a union of Zeus and Polyhymnia the very Muse of Rhetoric. I am afraid we are only partly right." Churchill did learn to develop speeches that ignited the passion of a nation, but it was due to "a triumph of effort and preparation" and not an innate skill with words, according to Johnson.

> To lead the country in time of war, to keep people together at a moment of profound anxiety, you need to connect with them in a deep and emotional way. It was not enough to appeal to the logic of defiance. He couldn't just exhort them to be brave. He needed to engage their attention, to cheer them, to boost them; if necessary to make them laugh and, better still, to laugh at their enemies. To move the British people, he needed at some level to identify with them—with those aspects of their characters that he, and they, conceived to be elemental to the national psyche.[3]

Several stylistic storytelling devices helped Churchill make the connection, but one in particular stands out. Churchill replaced long words with short ones.

The Storyteller's Tools

"The shorter words of a language are usually the more ancient,"[4] Churchill once said. "Their meaning is more ingrained in the national character and they appeal to greater force." Churchill's words motivated millions of people because he crafted his speeches in language that was instantly understandable to the greatest number of people. And the greatest number of people prefer short words they hear in everyday conversation.

On June 18, 1940, France fell to Germany. It was one of the darkest moments of World War II. Churchill gave a radio address on that day; a photocopy of the original speech still exists. The manuscript shows longer words crossed out and replaced with short ones. For example, he replaces "liberated" with "freed."

The ending paragraph of the speech became a rallying cry for the British people. In 180 words, Churchill lays out his argument for war. Note that three quarters of the words are one syllable.

> What General Weygand called the Battle of France is over. I expect that the Battle of Britain is about to begin. Upon this battle depends the survival of Christian civilization. Upon it depends our own British

life, and the long continuity of our institutions and our Empire. The whole fury and might of the enemy must very soon be turned on us. Hitler knows that he will have to break us in this Island or lose the war. If we can stand up to him, all Europe may be free and the life of the world may move forward into broad, sunlit uplands. But if we fail, then the whole world, including the United States, including all that we have known and cared for, will sink into the abyss of a new Dark Age made more sinister, and perhaps more protracted, by the lights of perverted science. Let us therefore brace ourselves to our duties, and so bear ourselves that, if the British Empire and its Commonwealth last for a thousand years, men will still say, "This was their finest hour."[5]

Churchill edited relentlessly, cutting unnecessary words and sentences. He packed a lot of content in a few well-chosen words, using simple language to tell complex stories.

At a crucial point of the Battle of Britain, when German warplanes were bombing London daily, every available British aircraft was in the sky to stop the planes from reaching the city. As Churchill sat in a car with his military secretary he said, "Don't speak to me. I have never been so moved." Churchill sat quietly for five minutes. He then turned to his secretary and asked him to write down a thought that would become one of the most famous quotes of World War II: "Never in the field of human conflict has so much been owed by so many to so few."[6] Only four words in that sentence are more than one syllable and, in six words, Churchill told the entire story of British courage and what it meant to the rest of the world: **so much, so many, so few**. Those six words summarize stories that fill entire books.

"So much" stands for freedom, democracy, and liberty—much of which would have been eliminated if Hitler had not been stopped.

"So many" represents the entire population of the British empire at the time and those who lived in the countries Hitler invaded.

"So few" is a reference to a small number of English pilots, many of whom were killed in the skies as they defended their homeland.

"For millions of people—sophisticated and unsophisticated—he deployed his rhetorical skills to put courage in their hearts and to make them believe they could fight off a threat more deadly than any they had ever known,"[7] writes Boris Johnson. "Churchill showed how it [the art of rhetoric] could help to save humanity."

According to *Wall Street Journal* columnist Sue Shellenbarger, "While trying to look intelligent, a lot of people do things that make them look dumb."[8] The article summarized a growing body of research on how we form impressions of others. Many people believe that if they use big words—capacious, voluminous, consequential language—others will find their use of such words to be a sign of intelligence. The exact opposite is true. If you want to sound smart and confident, replace big words with small ones. Big words don't impress people; big words frustrate people.

Leaders who launch movements don't "implement" a plan. They carry it out. Leaders who start movements don't offer "remuneration" for carrying out the plan. They reward people for doing it. Leaders who launch movements don't carry out a plan from "inception to termination." They see it through from start to finish.

Churchill proved that one person can make a difference. One person can save a civilization. But no person has a chance to persuade the greatest number of people if they cannot explain their ideas with short, well-chosen words.

The Storyteller's Secret

Storytellers motivate the largest numbers of people with the fewest words possible.

PART V

Storytellers Who Launch Movements

33

Great Storytellers Are Made, Not Born

> Don't address their brains. Address their hearts.
> —Nelson Mandela

It's Tuesday, August 27, 1963. At 10:00 p.m. Clarence Jones returns to his room at the Willard Hotel in Washington, D.C. Clarence's task is to compile the pages and pages of handwritten notes he had taken during a meeting in the hotel lobby and turn the notes into a cohesive speech for his boss.

Clarence returned to the lobby less than two hours later. His boss and a group of key advisers listened to Clarence explain and defend the speech he had written. They peppered Clarence with questions: *Why didn't you include this? Why did you say that?* Clarence's boss interrupted the discussion. He had heard enough and decided to go to his room.

On Wednesday, August 28, Clarence's phone rang at 7:00 a.m. The speech was done and copies were being placed in press kits for an event later that day.

The next time Clarence saw a copy of the speech it was sitting on the lectern where his boss, Dr. Martin Luther King Jr., would soon speak.

As the crowd on the Washington Mall swelled to 250,000, King took his place behind the microphone on the steps of the Lincoln Memorial, glanced down at the prepared text in front of him and began to speak: "Five score years ago, a great American, in whose symbolic shadow we stand today, signed the Emancipation Proclamation . . ."

A smile washed upon Clarence's face as he realized that King had kept the opening paragraphs that Clarence had written. Maybe Clarence had finally discovered King's voice. If so, it would have been the first time King read Clarence's speeches word for word. "When it came to my speech drafts, he [King] often acted like an interior designer: I would deliver four strong walls and he would use his God-given abilities to furnish the place so it felt like home."[1] King breathed life into Clarence's narrative. "Clarence, it's as tight an argument as I can imagine, but where's the humanity?" King would often say. As King continued to deliver the speech and Clarence grew more pleased that the civil rights leader was reading the words he had put to paper, something happened that would transform the speech and the future of a nation along with it.

The gospel singer, Mahalia Jackson, who was standing near King, shouted "Tell 'em about the dream, Martin!"

Few people heard the shout, but King did. And he knew exactly what she meant.

King had used the metaphor of a dream in previous speeches, but he had no intention of revisiting it on the mall in Washington. It was not included in the copy of the speech handed to the press.

"Martin clutched the speaker's podium, a hand on each side, leaned back, and looked at the throng of 250,000 or more assembled in front of the Lincoln Memorial,"[2] Clarence remembers. He watched as King set aside the prepared remarks. Clarence knew what would happen next. "These people out there today don't know it yet, but they're about ready to go to church," Clarence whispered to the person next to him.

"I have a dream . . ." King exclaimed. And with those words King channeled three generations of Baptist preachers before him. Clarence had seen it before. King had an "incredible ability to improvise, re-imagine his own polished text, and even recall and, if it felt right, insert other ways he'd presented the material previously."[3]

The sequence that made Martin Luther King Jr.'s "Dream Speech" the greatest speech of the twentieth century had all been improvised. The words "I have a dream" are not in the original copy of the speech!

To "improvise" doesn't mean to create something out of nothing. It means to assemble from whatever materials are readily available. King's materials were available—in his head.

You may have heard about the "10,000-hour" rule. Experts believe it requires about 10,000 hours of practice to be world class in a skill such as playing a sport, mastering music, or performing surgery. This concept directly applies to storytelling and public speaking.

Martin Luther King was on his high school debate team. He had been ordained a minister 16 years before delivering the Dream Speech. If we start doing the math we can see that King was honing his public speaking ability for at least 20 years before he delivered the words that would transform a nation.

It's believed that King gave 2,500 speeches in his lifetime. If we assume two hours of writing and rehearsals for each one (and in many cases he spent much more time), we arrive at the conservative estimate of 5,000 hours. But those are speeches. They don't take into account high school debates and hundreds of sermons. You get the point. King had easily reached 10,000 hours of practice by the twenty-eighth of August 1963.

Martin Luther King Jr. was a master of improvisation because he had put in the time to master his craft. Great storytellers are made, not born.

The Storyteller's Tools

Storytellers don't take shortcuts because there aren't any to take. Inspiration takes practice. Hours and hours of practice. Some famous TED speakers rehearsed their presentation up to 200 times before they delivered it on a TED stage. You'll recall pastor Joel Osteen from Part I. Osteen told me that he rehearses each sermon for six hours before delivering the first time on Saturday night. He then delivers it twice on Sunday. The third sermon is the one that millions of people see on television. Viewers see a polished storyteller, but they don't see the hours of polish that went into crafting an inspiring story. Steve Jobs meticulously rehearsed every keynote for weeks ahead of his famous product launches. The billionaire Warren Buffett enrolled in a Dale Carnegie course and volunteered to teach a business class at the University of Omaha to get over his fear of public speaking. Today his Dale Carnegie certificate is the only diploma he proudly hangs on his office wall. In 1964 Ronald Reagan gave a rousing speech to support then Republican candidate Barry Goldwater. Goldwater lost the election, but voters were inspired by Reagan, who went on to become California's governor and the fortieth president of the United States. The audience saw a magnificent storyteller on the stage beginning in 1964 but they didn't witness Reagan delivering hundreds of speeches to 250,000 General Electric employees over the course of eight years when GE sponsored a television show that Reagan hosted.

In much the same way, Martin Luther King had years and years of practice before giving the speech that captivated the world. And it's only through practice that King was able to skillfully use two classical rhetorical techniques which, as we've discussed, are the building blocks of storytelling: metaphor and anaphora.

The Master of Metaphor

"In a sense we've come to the nation's capital to cash a check,"[4] King said. The architects of the U.S. constitution and the Declaration of Independence had drafted a "promissory note," King said, that guaranteed all of its citizens unalienable rights to life, liberty, and the pursuit of happiness. "It is obvious today that America has defaulted on this promissory note," he said.

Storytellers like King make a conscious effort to incorporate metaphor into their speeches and presentations—the "promissory note" being just one of many metaphors in King's speech.

Metaphor gave King the tool to "breathe life" into abstract concepts:

- "Let us not seek to satisfy our *thirst* for freedom by drinking from the *cup of bitterness and hatred*."
- "Now is the time to rise from the *dark and desolate valley* of segregation to the *sunlit path* of racial justice."
- "I have a dream that one day even the state of Mississippi, a *desert* state, sweltering with *the heat* of injustice and oppression, will be transformed into an *oasis* of freedom and justice."
- No, no, we are not satisfied, and we will not be satisfied until *justice rolls down like waters* and *righteousness like a mighty stream*."

Metaphor is a critical component of the storyteller's toolbox. "Metaphor systematically disorganizes the common sense of things—jumbling together the abstract with the concrete, the physical with the psychological, the like with the unlike—and reorganizes it into uncommon combinations,"[5] writes author James Geary. "Metaphorical thinking—our instinct not just for describing but for comprehending one thing in terms of another, for equating I with an another—shapes our view of the world, and is essential to how we communicate, learn, discover, and invent."

We often think and explain our feelings in metaphor. Have you ever suffered from a "broken heart"? Hopefully you've found the "light of your life." Have you ever taken on a project so intimidating it feels like an "800-pound gorilla"? Maybe it's not that heavy, and it's just an "albatross" around your neck. Entrepreneurs "bootstrap" their companies while others get "cold feet." Either way they're all shooting for the "brass ring." Sometimes you must address the "elephant in the room" before it has a "domino effect." Just be careful not to "jump the shark." Some people sell "snake oil." They're "slippery as an eel." Some people are "smart as a fox" and keep themselves "busy as bees." They have the "heart of a lion," just as long as they don't get on their "soapbox" or get "tunnel vision."

In sales, metaphors are often used to simplify complexity. For example, in technical terms a "dual core" chip has two performance engines that process data at a faster rate. Does it motivate you to buy one? Of course not. It's abstract to nonengineers. What if I told you that a chip is the "brain" of a computer and, with dual-core chips, you get the equivalent of two brains in one computer? You'd be more likely to be intrigued, making it easier for me to explain the specific benefits of the product. That's what metaphor does. Metaphors and analogies are more likely to lead to sales because they bring clarity to abstraction.

Some metaphors will resonate with your audience, while others fall flat. Writing metaphors is not a skill that comes naturally to most people. It's an acquired storytelling technique, so don't hesitate to ask your peers or colleagues for feedback. Even one of the greatest storytellers of the twentieth century—Dr. Martin Luther King Jr.—asked trusted advisers to write portions of his speeches. King made the final edits, but he had the confidence to let others lend him a hand.

Can You Repeat That?

"I have a dream that one day this nation will rise up and live out the true meaning of its creed," Martin Luther King Jr. declared as he began the most cited sequence of the twentieth century. He continued:

> **"I have a dream** that one day on the red hills of Georgia, the sons of former slaves and the sons of former slave owners will be able to sit down together at the table of brotherhood."
> **"I have a dream** that one day . . ."

"I have a dream that one day . . ."

"I have a dream today."

In the Dream Speech King puts on a master class in the use of anaphora. Anaphora is a storytelling device where a word or phrase is repeated at the beginning of successive clauses and sentences. In politics Democratic and Republican leaders share one big love—anaphora.

In January 2015 Democratic president Barack Obama asked the nation:

"Will we accept an economy where only a few of us do spectacularly well? Or will we commit ourselves to an economy that generates rising incomes and chances for everyone who makes the effort?"[6]

"Will we approach the world . . . ?"

"Will we allow ourselves to be . . . ?"

Earlier the same day newly elected Republican Texas governor Greg Abbott told mini-stories of struggle and success within anaphoric paragraphs. "To this day Texas has been filled with legends who started humbly and succeeded spectacularly . . ."[7]

"Where a boy like Dan Duncan who grew up dirt poor in East Texas started a business with two trucks and $10,000, but with hard work and true grit he went on to become one of the wealthiest Texans ever."

"Where people like Colleen Barrett can climb the ladder from executive assistant to being listed as one of the most powerful women in America as President of Southwest Airlines."

"Where a 13-year-old daughter of immigrants from Mexico worked nights in a drapery factory but never gave up on her dreams. Now Eva Guzman is the first Latina to serve as a Justice on the Texas Supreme Court."

Anaphora is effective in the building of a movement because it increases the intensity of an idea, and intense ideas sear themselves into our brain. There's a reason why Winston Churchill chose anaphora as his go-to rhetorical device to rally the British people in World War II:

We shall fight in France, **we shall fight** on the seas and oceans, **we shall fight** with growing confidence and growing strength in the air, we shall defend our Island, whatever the cost may be, **we shall fight** on the beaches, **we shall fight** on the landing grounds, **we shall fight** in the fields and in the streets, **we shall fight** in the hills; we shall never surrender.

Business leaders often shy away from anaphora because they believe it's a tool reserved for political speeches. Actually, anaphora can be seamlessly and comfortably incorporated into business presentations meant to inspire audiences to see the world differently.

For example, Leonard Walker, a division manager for Wells Fargo in Atlanta, spoke at a quarterly meeting of Atlanta Business Banking. His theme was the need for leadership and his key message was that the people in the room had the obligation to step up as leaders to help the local economy out of a recession. "Where are the leaders?"[8] Walker asked. "Do we even need them now? The answers are yes—and in this room. **We are** the leaders today. **We are** the ones we've been waiting for. **We are** the ones upon whose shoulders recovery rests."

When you find your dream moment, practice relentlessly to strike the right chord and, when you can, include stylistic tools like metaphor and anaphora to transform a functional presentation into a soul-stirring event.

The Storyteller's Secret

Great storytellers are made, not born. They take every opportunity to hone their public-speaking skills and to work on the art of inspiring audiences. They experiment with every rhetorical device at their disposal, and often become expert at using the building blocks of narrative—analogy and metaphor.

34

Millions of Women "Lean In" After One Woman Dares to Speak Out

When you want to motivate, persuade, or be remembered, start with
a story of human struggle and eventual triumph. It will capture
people's hearts—by first attracting their brains.

—Paul Zak

Fifteen minutes is enough time to spark a movement. That's how much time Sheryl had to give a talk on the subject of women in the workplace. Some people didn't think she should do it. "It will end your business career. You will never be taken seriously again," they told the high-level business executive. But Sheryl was convinced that she had to speak out about a persistent problem in the business world. For all of women's gains in the workplace, there were still far too few of them in leadership positions.

In December 2010, at the TEDWomen conference in Washington, D.C., she would tackle the problem head on. In preparing for the speech, Sheryl did what came naturally to her. The former management consultant amassed mountains of statistics on things like how many heads of state are women and how many women make up the C-suite in corporate America.

Just before she took the stage, Sheryl found herself unable to focus on the speech. She confided to her friend Pat that she was troubled about something that had happened before boarding the plane for the conference. Her three-year-old daughter, upset at the fact that her mother was leaving, clung to her leg, pleading, "Mommy, don't go." Pat suggested to Sheryl that she should share the story with the mostly female audience.

"Are you kidding?"[1] Sheryl responded. "I'm going to get on a stage and admit my daughter was clinging to my leg?"

"If you want to get women into leadership roles, you have to be honest about how hard it is," Pat said.

Sheryl took Pat's advice.

> Now, at the outset, I want to be very clear that this speech comes with no judgments. I don't have the right answer. I don't even have it for myself. I left San Francisco, where I live, on Monday, and I was getting on the plane for this conference. And my daughter, who's three, when I dropped her off at preschool, did that whole hugging-the-leg, crying, "Mommy, don't get on the plane" thing. This is hard. I feel guilty sometimes. I know no women, whether they're at home or whether they're in the workforce, who don't feel that sometimes. So I'm not saying that staying in the workforce is the right thing for everyone.
>
> My talk today is about what the messages are if you do want to stay in the workforce, and I think there are three. One, sit at the table. Two, make your partner a real partner. And three, don't leave before you leave.[2]

Sheryl Sandberg's talk at TEDWomen went viral. The popularity of the topic and the stories she received from women who were inspired by it convinced the Facebook COO to write a book. The book quickly rose to bestseller status and inspired a movement with the same name: *Lean In*. By accident, Sandberg had discovered what Paul Zak had discovered in the lab: Stories alter brain chemistry that in turn triggers empathy in your audience.

The Storyteller's Tools

Although Sandberg introduced important data points in her now famous TED talk, personal stories made just over 70 percent of the content. Statistics don't spark movements; stories do.

But while Sandberg had discovered the power of story to bring data to life, she reverted back to her training in data analysis as she began to write her book. Sandberg got another wake-up call.

> I wrote a first chapter, I thought it was fabulous. It was chock-full of data and figures, I had three pages on matrilineal Maasai tribes, and

their sociological patterns. My husband read it and he was like, this is like eating your Wheaties. No one—and I apologize to Wheaties—no one, no one, no one will read this book. And I realized through the process that I had to be more honest and more open, and I had to tell my stories. My stories of still not feeling as self-confident as I should, in many situations. My first and failed marriage. Crying at work. Feeling like I didn't belong there, feeling guilty to this day.[3]

Sandberg's friend Pat Mitchell—the same woman who pulled Sandberg aside before her TEDx talk—commented to Sheryl on why she believes *Lean In* took off: "I think that one of the most striking parts about the book, and in my opinion, one of the reasons it's hit such a nerve and is resonating around the world, is that you are personal in the book. You do make it clear that you've had the same challenges that many of us have."[4]

Sandberg says that by being open and honest with her story, she gives other women permission to be open and honest about theirs and together they can achieve equality. The message resonated with one young woman at Facebook, an exceptionally bright engineer who was afraid to speak up.

A Shy Girl Builds a Piazza to Give Students a Voice

Pooja Sankar's journey to Facebook was as unlikely as the prospects she faced growing up in a traditional village in India. A woman's role was to cook, clean, and prepare for marriage. "All through my middle and high school years I grew up in a culture where it was taboo—unheard of, actually—to speak to a boy or see eye to eye with them,"[5] Sankar told me.

Although Sankar grew up in a traditional family in a traditional town, her father took a strong stand on education. In 1998, Sankar enrolled in the Indian Institute of Technology, one of the most competitive schools in the world, with a 1 percent acceptance rate. She had earned one of 2,000 spots awarded to an applicant pool *100* times that size.

Upon entering college, Sankar felt intimidated despite the accomplishments that had gotten her there. "The number one hurdle to overcome was my shyness," she said. "I had to become confident to approach classmates (mostly men), TAs, professors with questions about the course material."

After college, at the age of 22, Sankar came to America where she continued her studies, receiving two master's degrees at the University of

Maryland, College Park and an MBA from Stanford. Just prior to entering Stanford, Pooja worked as an engineer at Facebook in Silicon Valley, where she had the good fortune to attend an internal presentation by Sheryl Sandberg. She told me, "I remember many women who stood up and said they didn't feel like they had a support group or who were sometimes scared or intimidated to raise their hands or ask questions of male classmates. It was eye opening that the problem wasn't just for women in Northern India, but at many of the top colleges in America. There were many other women like myself."

At Stanford, Sankar would often hear the stories of other entrepreneurs and what drove them to start their businesses: "All the stories had a common theme of working on a problem that you were deeply passionate about. For me, the problem I was deeply passionate about was helping shy students connect to classmates and their instructors in a way that enhances their learning experience."

After graduating from business school, Sankar decided to combine her central struggle as a student with her skill in the field of computer science. She created Piazza, an online tool for college students and professors. Piazza is an Italian word for "city square," where people come together to share knowledge and ideas; the online version created a space for students and professors to collaborate.

Sankar found that investors, professors, students, and other target audiences responded instantly to the way in which her personal story of overcoming shyness connects with Piazza's mission, and she now features the story prominently on the Piazza website. "I started Piazza because I wish I had it,"[6] Sankar says in the video introduction.

I was one of three women in my undergraduate Computer Science class at IIT [Indian Institute of Technology in Kanpur, India]. I had grown up in an all-girl high school, and my 50 male classmates had grown up mostly in all-boy high schools. We were too shy to interact with one another. My first year at IIT was challenging. Our professors would give us programming assignments, intending for us to learn a lot of the computer programming basics. Except, most nights, I'd be up until 6:00 a.m. stuck on nuances of the assignment . . . I'd sit in a corner of the computer lab, too shy to ask the guys in my class. They'd all talk to one another, ask each other questions, and learn a lot by working together. I missed out on this learning . . . I started Piazza so every student can have that opportunity to learn from her classmates. Whether she's too shy to ask, whether she's working alone in her dorm room, or whether her few friends in her class don't know the answer either. I want Piazza to be a remedy for students who are not given the intellectual space, freedom, or support to fulfill their educational potential and desire for learning. And I want Piazza to empower instructors to have a positive, personal impact on more students. Piazza is designed to connect students, TAs, and professors so every student can get help when she needs it—even at 2:00 a.m.

Sankar discovered that professors, especially, love to hear the founder's story: "They get pitched for tools that don't have an authentic story behind it. This way they know the tool was created by an entrepreneur who was shy and who doesn't want other shy students to struggle in class. It creates a lot of trust with professors."

Today hundreds of thousands of students across hundreds of campuses are using Piazza including half of all Stanford undergrads and half of MIT students. Sankar approaches storytelling as she approached software development—constantly improving the product: "I go back to the philosophy I live and breathe by in terms of building products. Get that first product out there. It's never going to be the right product out of the gate. It's all about iteration. What's the first message, reaction, non-reaction, iterate. It's taken me thousands of iterations before I was able to deliver what we do in one or two sentences and capture the audience's attention."[7]

Tension and Triumph

Inspiring stories must have two elements: tension and triumph. Today's new breed of storytellers—entrepreneurs like Sandberg and Sankar—openly share the lessons they've learned to triumph over adversity.

"At the age of twenty-two I entered a traditional arranged marriage," Sankar reveals. "For the next four years I had a hard test of my values and my character. I had to dig deep into who I am. I struggled in an extremely traditional relationship where women held a certain role and did not speak up nor hold opinions. I realized that after four years of giving that relationship my very best, that it was not me and I was someone who had strong dreams and strong hopes and who wanted to speak up."

Sankar started Piazza to give students a voice; a voice she didn't have in school.

Sandberg and Sankar both speak of failed marriages and how they learned valuable lessons that were essential to their growth as leaders. Their personal stories of tension and triumph resonate with audiences because people see a part of themselves in the narrative and are transported to another world—the founder's world. And since emotion drives much of our decision-making, audiences are more likely to be swept up in the founder's vision and to embrace that vision as their own.

In *Leadership and the Art of Struggle* author Steven Snyder reminds us that history is replete with stories of leaders who fail—some in spectacular fashion (Steve Jobs getting fired or John F. Kennedy at the Bay of Pigs)—and who emerge stronger and more resilient because of it. "A new perspective dawns when struggle is recognized as an intrinsic aspect of leadership and an opportunity for leaders to realize their full potential,"[8] writes Snyder. "When struggle is viewed as an art to be mastered, a new set of strategies and practices emerges, enabling leaders to elevate their skills to ever-greater heights."

Proverbs 24:16 reads, "For a righteous man falls seven times, and rises again." At first reading the wisdom seems to suggest that a successful person gets up *despite* being knocked down time and time again. The world's most inspiring leaders know the true meaning of the proverb: Successful people rise *because* they've fallen seven times. Failure and struggle are the two best teachers on the planet. They are what great stories are made of.

The Storyteller's Secret

Leaders don't move mountains with mountains of data. They do it by giving their audiences a piece of their heart.

35

The 60-Second Story That Turned the Wine World on Its Side

A great story invites an expansion of understanding, a self-transcendence.

— Maria Popova

'␣ve never eaten as much cheese as I did when I visited Paris. There's a cheese shop on every corner, selling hundreds of varieties. It's not "light" cheese, either. French cheeses are very high in fat and the French eat a lot of it, about 40 pounds of cheese per person each year. In fact the French eat about 60 percent more cheese than Americans. They also consume more high-fat, high-cholesterol meats. Why then, do Americans suffer from heart disease at a much higher rate than the French?

On November 17, 1991, the popular news program *60 Minutes* revealed a possible answer. Host Morley Safer looked into the camera, held up a glass of red wine, and declared, "The answer to France's low rate of heart disease may lie in this inviting glass."[1] In that instant the "French Paradox" was born. Prior to the segment, the medical community had focused on alcohol as a risk factor in a person's diet. Overnight the medical community (and federal dietary guidelines) began to suggest that moderate amounts of red wine could be part of a healthy lifestyle. Later a substance in red wine called resveratrol was found to give wine its heart-protecting properties.

The *60 Minutes* segment triggered a wine boom. Within one year consumption of red wine in America increased more than 40 percent. Americans drank more wine than ever. They bought more Cabernet Sauvignon and Merlot, two varietals that were easy to grow and had appealing price points. The one varietal that did not participate in the boom was Pinot Noir.

Pinot was a considered a "tough sell." It's a very difficult grape to grow. A good Pinot Noir will set back consumers at least $20 and some become cult classics, carrying a price of over $100. It also has a different taste profile than many of the red wines most Americans are used to drinking. Pinot's time would come, however, and it would arrive in the form of a story.

In the 2004 movie, *Sideways,* Paul Giamatti plays Miles Raymond. Miles is a divorced, depressed, and unsuccessful writer. He's a high school English teacher who dreams of selling a novel, but publishers keep turning him down. As his personal and professional life flounders, Miles takes his soon-to-be-married friend on a weekend of wine tasting in Santa Barbara County. Miles is a wine connoisseur. He's a bit of a wine snob, actually, but likable—funny, caring, and passionate.

On the trip Miles meets an attractive waitress, Maya, played by Virginia Madsen. Miles and Maya share a love of wine. In the pivotal scene of the movie, the two stroll outside to the porch with wineglasses in hand.

"Why are you so into Pinot?"[2] Maya asks.

In the next 60 seconds of the movie, the character of Miles Raymond tells a story which would set off a boom in sales of Pinot Noir.

It's a hard grape to grow. It's thin-skinned, temperamental, ripens early. It's not a survivor like Cabernet, which can just grow anywhere and thrive even when it's neglected. No, Pinot needs constant care and attention. In fact it can only grow in these really specific, tucked away corners of the world. And only the most patient and nurturing of growers can do it, really. Only somebody who really takes the time to understand Pinot's potential can coax it into its fullest expression. Its flavors are the most haunting and brilliant and thrilling and subtle and ancient on the planet.

Miles is describing himself in the dialogue and using Pinot as a metaphor for his personality. In this one scene moviegoers projected themselves on the character, feeling his longing and his quest to be understood. *Sideways* was a hit and won an Oscar for Best Adapted Screenplay. It also launched a movement, turning the misunderstood Pinot Noir into the must-have wine of the year.

In less than one year after the movie's 2004 fall release date, sales of Pinot Noir had risen 18 percent. Winemakers began to grow more of the grape to meet demand. In California alone 70,000 tons of Pinot Noir grapes were harvested and crushed in 2004. Within two years the volume had topped 100,000 tons. Today California wine growers crush more than 250,000 tons of Pinot Noir each year.

Interestingly, the Japanese version of the movie did not have the same "*Sideways* Effect" on wine sales. One reason is that the featured grape is Cabernet, a varietal already popular in Japan. But even more critical and relevant to the discussion on storytelling is that Japanese audiences didn't see the "porch scene" because there wasn't one. The scene was not included in the movie. No story, no emotional attachment to a particular varietal. You see, the movie *Sideways* didn't launch a movement in Pinot Noir; the story that Miles told triggered the boom. In 60 seconds Maya fell in love with Miles and millions of Americans fell in love with an expensive wine they knew little about.

The Storyteller's Tools

We're all familiar with what it's like to "get lost" in a good book. Neuroscientists are finding that when we read a page-turning novel, we are immersing ourselves into the body of the protagonist. Researchers examining the brains of people while they read a book can see activity in the areas of the brain associated with the activity or experience the book's characters are having at the time. We have stepped into the characters' shoes, and, as far as the brain is concerned, we've done it for real. The Pinot story that Miles shares with Maya in *Sideways* transports the audience to another place. Viewers lost themselves in the story.

Professors Melanie Green and Timothy Brock study the role "transportation theory" plays in persuading people to change their beliefs. "The power of narratives to change beliefs has never been doubted,"[3] they say. When people are absorbed in a story it impacts the beliefs they hold. The more emotionally involved they are with the characters, the more empathy they feel for the hero and the more likely they are to buy into the hero's view. "Highly transported participants showed beliefs more consonant with the story conclusions as well as more positive evaluations of the story's protagonist . . . individuals altered their real-world beliefs in response to experiences in a story world. Transported individuals may have a greater affinity for story characters and thus may be more likely swayed by the feelings or beliefs expressed by those characters."

Green and Brock found that some stories and characters work better than others at changing beliefs. Audiences are more likely to be "highly transported" in a story if two conditions are met—the characters are likable and have had to endure struggle. "The most powerful tales tend to be those that involve negative aspects, such as dilemmas to be overcome or obstacles to be surmounted." Miles is a bit of a snob, but he's quite likable. He's funny, which psychologists say is a highly valued personality trait. He's loyal, generous, and passionate about his work and hobby. He's also vulnerable and authentic. Miles is human and we care about him. Using the Pinot Noir grape's journey as a metaphor, Miles tells a story about suffering and redemption. The grape overcomes its struggle to reach its fullest expression.

According to professors Green and Brock "transportation" is not limited to the written form. Yes, as we discussed earlier, a good book can transport a reader to another world, but so can movies, conversations, pitches, and presentations. Any "recipient of narrative information" can be transported if they're attached to the character (they like the person) and they hear a compelling story with a dose of human suffering.

A Field Ripe for Storytelling

The wine industry is ripe for storytelling. Sitting in a wine bar at the Seattle airport I once met a California wine distributor who was flying home after meeting with merchants in the Pacific Northwest. "Why can't you just send them samples?" I asked. He said, "Nothing beats sitting down with my customer face-to-face and sharing the story of where the wine is grown and the people who grow it. When I send samples, I get a few orders. When I meet with my customers and share the wine's story, I get so many orders that it makes up for the price of the trip." The distributor hadn't used the word "transportation," but that's exactly what he was doing—transporting his customers to another place through the stories he told.

I was invited to deliver a keynote speech on communication skills to the Court of Master Sommeliers, an exclusive group of the top wine experts in the world. The designation of Master Sommelier is very difficult to achieve. A Master "Somm" must know more than how to serve wine or which varietal goes best with which dish. They are steeped in the world of wine. With one sniff or taste they must be able to identify what kind of wine is in the glass, where it was grown, how many months it aged in the barrel, what year the grapes were harvested, etc. In many cases it takes up to five years of study before a person passes all the tests. The courses are taught by instructors who have already achieved Master Somm status.

Prior to the event I had spoken to three people who were rated the best presenters among the instructors. I asked each of them to send me their PowerPoint presentations and to point out the section of the deck that received the most positive feedback. Each of the instructors highlighted slides that allowed them to tell a story, stories that transported their audiences to a different time and place. For example, one instructor sent me a slide called "Intro to Champagne." The slide showed a map of France with the Champagne region highlighted in color. The instructor's story went like this:

> The region of Champagne lies just to the east of Paris. This part of France has seen just about every invader and battle to pass through Europe. The Huns sacked it, the Gauls passed through here, and both world wars ravaged the area. In fact, the worst parts of the trench warfare of World War I took place in the Marne Valley. Bullets and unexploded bombs are still found in the vineyards. On the other hand, this is a region that is key for celebration. All the kings of France were coronated in the Reims Cathedral.

Another instructor sent me a slide with a simple photo of a vineyard. A sign at the entrance read, "Côte-Rôtie." The instructor said:

> History is alive in this place. Do you see the rock walls? The Romans built them. The Romans had figured out that grapevines would grow almost anywhere there were fruit trees, including the incredibly steep slopes along the Rhône River in Côte-Rôtie. We walked into the vineyards and Philippe, our guide, reached down and said, "Has anyone ever held Roman pottery in their hand before?" We found 10 terra cotta pieces: Roman roof tiles and shards of pots. It's changed so much and so little at the same time in the thousands of years the Northern Rhône has been cultivated for wine grapes. It's an amazing place.

These stories are important because they evoke emotions and, in the early classes of the Master Sommelier course, it's just as important to get students excited about the wine industry as it is to provide the facts needed to pass a test.

"I still remember the first day of my first class," one Master Sommelier recalled. "When I got home my wife asked how I liked the program. I told her, 'I can't explain it, but I want to be friends with these people.'" This is yet another example of the power of story. Most people who watch a presentation with compelling stories and narratives are at loss to explain why the presentation inspired them. They just know they were moved. They want to be "friends" with the speaker. They want to be part of the journey.

The Storyteller's Secret

Storytellers who trigger movements know better than to barrage their audience with an endless litany of facts, figures, and data. Facts are a necessary component of persuasion, but facts must be balanced with the skillful use of narrative to transport listeners to another time and place. Once listeners are figuratively walking in the shoes of the protagonist—the hero—they feel as though they have a stake in the outcome and are willing to do whatever is necessary to help the hero reach his or her final destination.

36

From My Heart Rather Than from a Sheet of Paper

There are some realities that you can only see through eyes that have been cleansed by tears.

—Pope Francis

Tuesday, October 9, 2012, began the same way as most other days for the 15-year-old schoolgirl on her way to class. She boarded a "school bus," a rickety truck with a cover and three wooden benches in the back. The bus was making its way down a muddy road alongside a dirty, smelly stream, when it suddenly came to a halt, and two masked men boarded. One addressed the group, asking them to identify the girl, and then pulled out a Colt .45 and fired three shots at her in quick succession. The first hit the girl in the left eye and exited her left shoulder. She slumped over, blood draining from her ear.

The young girl was treated at a hospital in England and survived. She still lives in the United Kingdom because the risk of returning to her home country of Pakistan is too great. Her first name alone has become a symbol of resilience and courage: Malala.

Malala Yousafzai isn't alone. At any one time there are 66 million girls out of school around the world. Every three seconds a girl becomes a child bride, and 4 out of 5 victims of human trafficking are girls.[1] Those numbers are staggering, but as we know the human mind doesn't handle abstraction very well. And that's why one face, one story, can humanize a global atrocity and give voice to millions who cannot speak for themselves. And when the face belongs to a brilliant storyteller, a movement begins.

The Storyteller's Tools

Malala is a teenager who speaks with timeless wisdom. An exceptional communicator, Malala grew up in a storytelling family. People would come to her family's house in the Swat Valley of northwest Pakistan to hear Malala's father tell stories. They loved to hear him talk, as did Malala: "I would listen, rapt, as he told stories of warring tribes, Pashtun leaders and saints, often through poems that he read in a melodious voice, crying sometimes as he read."[2] Malala recalls that her grandfather was also famous for his speeches. As an imam at a local mosque his sermons were so popular, "people would come down from the mountains by donkey or on foot to hear him."

Listening to her family's stories made Malala want to be a great storyteller, too. She entered a public-speaking competition and, consistent with her cultural tradition, delivered a speech written by her father. Malala finished second and learned a valuable lesson: "I started writing my own speeches and changing the way I delivered them, from my heart rather than from a sheet of paper."

One year after the attack that nearly took her life, Malala delivered a speech at the United Nations to draw attention to the millions of girls around the world who are denied access to education. She received several standing ovations and sparked a global movement to unlock the potential in young girls.

Malala's public-speaking skills gave voice to the millions of girls who are denied an education because of social, political, and economic factors. Celebrities were moved to action. Actress Angelina Jolie donated $200,000 to the Malala Fund. Pop singer Madonna dedicated a song to Malala in her concert tour and displayed a Malala tattoo on her back. The movement had begun. Malala's book, *I Am Malala,* spent more than one year on the *New York Times* bestseller list.

On December 10, 2014, at the age of 17, Malala took the stage in Oslo as the youngest recipient of the Nobel Peace Prize. Her story put a face on the faceless and gave a voice to those who are kept silent.

The human mind simply cannot process the fact that 66 million girls are denied an education. The number is completely lost in the 340 million tweets people send every day or the 55 million Facebook updates that are posted each day. How is it possible for, in Malala's words, "One child, one teacher, one book and one pen" to change the world? If the one pen belongs to one extraordinary storyteller, anything can happen. A tragic story can bring people to tears. A beautifully crafted story can inspire a movement.

If you've read this far, then you know that a good story must have a protagonist, a hero. When the hero has a clearly defined goal—and must triumph over adversity to reach the goal—you get a hit.

Give the Audience Something to Cheer For

Austin Madison is an animator and story artist for such Pixar movies as *Ratatouille*, *WALL-E*, *Toy Story 3*, *Brave*, and others. In a revealing presentation Madison outlined the 7-step process that all Pixar movies follow.

1. Once there was a ___.[3]
   [A protagonist/hero with a goal is the most important element of a story.]
2. Every day he ___.
   [The hero's world must be in balance in the first act.]
3. Until one day ___.
   [A compelling story introduces conflict. The hero's goal faces a challenge.]
4. Because of that ___.
   [This step is critical and separates a blockbuster from an average story. A compelling story isn't made up of random scenes that are loosely tied together. Each scene has one nugget of information that compels the next scene.]
5. Because of that ___.
6. Until finally ___.
   [The climax reveals the triumph of good over evil.]
7. Ever since then ___.
   [The moral of the story.]

The steps are meant to immerse an audience into a hero's journey and give the audience someone to cheer for. This process is used in all forms of storytelling: journalism, screenplays, books, presentations, speeches. Madison uses a classic hero/villain movie to show how the process plays out—*Star Wars*. Here's the story of Luke Skywalker.

Once there was a farm boy who wanted to be a pilot. *Every day he* helped on the farm. *Until one day* his family is killed. *Because of that* he joins legendary Jedi Obi-Wan Kenobi. *Because of that* he hires the smuggler Han Solo to take him to Alderaan. *Until finally* Luke reaches his goal and becomes a starfighter pilot and saves the day. *Ever since then* Luke's been on the path to be a Jedi knight.

Like millions of others, I was impressed with Malala's Nobel Peace prize–winning acceptance speech. While I appreciated the beauty and power of her words, it wasn't until I did the research for this book that I fully understood why Malala's words inspired me. Malala's speech perfectly follows Pixar's 7-step storytelling process. I doubt that she did this intentionally, but it demonstrates once again the theme in this book—there's a difference between a story, a good story, and a story that sparks movements.

Below is Pixar's storytelling process overlayed on Malala's Nobel Prize acceptance speech:

Once there was a little girl who lived in a "paradise home" in Pakistan's Swat Valley, "a place of tourism and beauty."[4]

Every day she had "a thirst for education" and would go to class "to sit and learn and read."

Until one day the Swat Valley "turned into a place of terrorism."

Because of that girls' education became a crime and "girls were stopped from going to school."

Because of that Malala's priorities changed: "I decided to speak up."

Until finally the terrorists attacked Malala. She survived. "Neither their ideas nor their bullets could win."

Ever since then Malala's voice "has grown louder and louder" because Malala is speaking for the 66 million girls deprived of an education. "I tell my story, not because it is unique, but because it is not," Malala said. "It is the story of many girls . . . I am those 66 million girls who are deprived of education."

According to Pixar's Austin Madison, the 7-step storytelling outline works best once you've grabbed the audience's attention with an opening scene "that slams you into the back of your seat."

The first sentence of Malala's book, *I Am Malala,* slams its readers in their seats. The first scene begins with these words: "I come from a country that was created at midnight. When I almost died it was just after midday. One year ago I left my home for school and never returned. I was shot by a Taliban bullet . . ."[5]

Only after Malala slams you to the back of your seat with her opening sequence does she go back in time to introduce you to the characters "before the Taliban, a time where everything is in balance."

Stories don't inspire movements. Well-told stories do.

Malala delivered her Nobel Prize speech at the age of 17. Great storytelling knows no age and yet it's timeless. If you go back far enough, you'll find a story behind every movement and a story behind that story.

For example, a story inspired Malala. "All Pashtun children grow up with the story of how Malalai inspired the Afghan army to defeat the British in 1880 in one of the biggest battles of the Second Anglo-Afghan war,"[6] Malala writes. Malalai of Maiwand was a teenage girl who tended to the wounded on the battlefield. According to the story a lead flag bearer was killed and Malalai used her veil as a flag and walked toward her opponents. She was killed and became a symbol for bravery and a voice for the oppressed. Malalai is known as the Afghan "Joan of Arc" and many institutions are named after her.

Is it merely a coincidence that prominent Afghan women's rights activists, including Malala, are named after the battle hero, including Malala and Malalai Joya? Or is it possible that the story of Malalai of Maiwand shaped the young girls, their perception of themselves, and the impression they leave on others? We may never know for sure, but do we know that stories stay in your soul and shape the person you are today. Stories build confidence. Stories inspire people to dream bigger—the audience and the storyteller. "Once I had asked God for one or two extra inches in height, but instead he made me as tall as the sky, so high that I could not measure myself,"[7] Malala once said. Malala stands at just five feet (five feet two "in heels" as she likes to joke), yet she towers over her foes. Our future rests with storytellers like Malala who we admire for their courage and who inspire us with their words.

The Storyteller's Secret

If you're going to share a story, make it great. A good story can bring one to tears; a great one can start a movement.

37

Story, Story, Story

Your voice is worthwhile. Have faith in it.

—John Lasseter

John loved to draw. He drew everywhere, even in church. He filled sketchpads with pages and pages of cartoons, often well into the night. And so John's parents had a tough time getting him up in the morning for school. But Saturday mornings were different. John woke himself up at the crack of dawn so he wouldn't miss a minute of his beloved Saturday morning cartoons, especially Bugs Bunny and the Road Runner.

In high school John's passion for animation was further fueled when he read *The Art of Animation*, a book that explored the history of Disney animation. John's mother, Jewell, an art teacher who considered art a noble profession, supported John when he transferred out of Pepperdine to be enrolled as one of the first students in a new art course at the California Institute of the Arts (CalArts). Some of Disney's most important animation veterans, known as the "Nine Old Men," taught the program. After graduation, John was thrilled to survive the ultracompetitive selection process to become an animator with Walt Disney. He had won his dream job, or so he thought.

John was one of the first animators to recognize the potential of computer animation. Excited by its potential, he began working on a film to demonstrate the new technology to his colleagues. But John's boss was decidedly less excited by it, and one day he abruptly canceled the project and fired John. To this day John can't talk about what happened without getting a tear in his eye, particularly as he relates the moment when one of his supervisors turned to him and said, "We don't want to hear your ideas. Just do what you're told."

In 1983 John and his wife headed north to the San Francisco Bay Area, where John got a job at the Lucasfilm's computer division, a group tasked with developing computer technology for the film industry. In 1986 a visionary named Steve Jobs bought the division for $10 million and established the division as an independent company called Pixar. Over the next five years Pixar would nearly run out of money several times; Jobs invested up to $50 million of his own money to keep the dream alive. Jobs was certain Pixar would revolutionize the movie industry.

John remembers his very first meeting with Steve Jobs: "We wanted to do a short film. I had to pitch it to him. I pitched the short film that became *Tin Toy*. Steve had his classic pose with fingers together, thinking. He was thinking—not about the drawings on the board I was pitching—he was staring off into the future. At the end of that meeting, he asked me to do something and it was the only thing Steve ever asked me to do. He said, 'John, make it great.'"[1]

Tin Toy went on to win the Academy Award for Best Animated Short Film, the first Oscar ever given to computer animation. Steve Jobs, John Lasseter, and Ed Catmull had transformed Pixar from a computer technology company to an animation studio. *Tin Toy* served as the inspiration for Pixar's *Toy Story*. Other hits followed, including: *A Bug's Life, Cars, Monsters, Inc., Ratatouille, Finding Nemo, Tangled,* and, of course, one of the biggest animated movies of all time, *Frozen.* Lasseter's life had come full circle when Disney bought Pixar, turning Jobs's original investment of $10 million into a $7.5 billion windfall. Lasseter was named chief creative officer of both Pixar and Walt Disney Animation Studios.[2]

Those three words of advice Steve Jobs gave Lasseter—make it great—would go on to inspire every frame of every movie Lasseter created from that day forward. Everything had to be great. Every product. Every story. Every time.

The Storyteller's Tools

John Lasseter will be the first to say that audiences are not entertained by technology alone. The technology supports the story. The story *always* comes first. And there's no story without heart. He says, "As we develop a story, the plot changes dramatically, characters come and go, but . . . the heart of the film—that's like the foundation of the building, you've got to get that right upfront because everything builds off that. You can't add that later. You can't punch up the heart."[3]

Lasseter has also said that the emotion comes from the main character. "What does the character learn? How do they change?" Everything in the film must support the main character's journey. The film revolves around the narrative.

Technology *Complements* the Story, but the Story Always Comes First

Many business professionals are enamored of PowerPoint. There are an estimated 40 million PowerPoint presentations delivered each and every day. Meanwhile a growing number of communicators are using presentation tools such as Prezi or Apple Keynote, tools that are attempting to reinvent the field of presentations. What I hope this book—and John Lasseter's story—has taught you is that presentation software is wonderful and should be used to illustrate a story, as long as it *complements* the story. But the story—the tension and triumph—must always come first.

Pixar cofounder Ed Catmull called Lasseter the first storyteller to join the company, even when it was primarily a technology hardware firm. Lasseter's role was to make sure technology didn't overwhelm the company's purpose—to make great films. "We took pride in the fact that reviewers talked mainly about the way *Toy Story* made them feel and not about the computer wizardry that enabled us to get it up on the screen,"[4] according to Catmull.

Steve Jobs was once asked why many films are dreadful while Pixar seems to have one hit after another. He explained that animation is so expensive a studio cannot afford to create too many scenes that ultimately are left on the cutting-room floor. Walt Disney solved this problem by editing the film before it was created and he did it with storyboards. Animators draw each scene on boards and use a "scratch track" to put in the voices and the music. "Basically we build the movie before we make it,"[5] Jobs explained. "One of the things I'm proudest about at Pixar is—we have a story crisis on every movie—and production is rolling and there's mouths to feed and something's just not working. And we stop. We stop and we fix the story. Because John Lasseter instilled a culture of story, story, story. Even though

Pixar is the most technologically advanced studio in the world, John has a saying that's really stuck and that's this—no amount of technology will turn a bad story into a good story."

Steve Jobs and John Lasseter bonded over a shared passion for creating stories that would outlive them and be watched for generations to come.

Elsa's Badass Song

Without Steve Jobs there is no Pixar, and without Pixar and Disney John Lasseter would not have had the platform to bring us some of the most beloved movies of our time. *Frozen* is one of them.

If you're a parent of young children, then you probably have every song to Disney's *Frozen* stuck in your head. The movie's heroine, Elsa, was originally written to be a villain. One song forced the writers to rewrite the entire movie.

In the original draft of the script based on the adaptation of Hans Christian Andersen's fairy tale, "The Snow Queen," Elsa had magical powers that she used for evil. The Elsa in *Frozen* was quite different. Instead of a villain, she was misunderstood protagonist, someone who had awesome power, made a mistake, and learned to harness the power for good.

Husband and wife songwriting team Robert Lopez and Kristen Anderson-Lopez were brainstorming the music for the movie on a walk in Brooklyn's Prospect Park. They threw questions at each other: "What would it feel like to be a perfect exalted person, but only because you've held back this secret?" Robert said it would feel like "a kingdom of isolation." He wanted to feel Elsa's emotion when she finally decided to reveal her hidden talent, and so he jumped on a picnic table with his arms held wide and recited some of the lyrics that would eventually become famous for their message of empowerment.

When producers and screenwriters heard the song, they realized they had to rewrite the entire movie. Everything changed—the plot, the dialogue, even Elsa's appearance, because Elsa was no longer the villain. "Let It Go" won the Academy Award for best original song.

Frozen's composers said "Let It Go" was Elsa's "badass song" because it helped them find their true north for the rest of the story.

You can only reach the fullness of your potential when you find your true north and become comfortable with expressing who you really are. The storytellers in this book have all embraced their past, unleashed the treasure they hold inside, and have used their gifts to create their own stories. By doing so they've captured our imagination, stirred our souls, and inspired us to dream bigger than we've ever imagined.

Storytelling is not something we do. Storytelling is who we are, and there's a storyteller in each of us. Your story can change the world. Let it out.

The Storyteller's Secret

Story is king. Presentation software serves to illustrate the narrative; but the story *always* comes first.

Conclusion

The Storyteller's Universe

If you're going to have a story, have a big story, or none at all.
— Joseph Campbell

Storytelling is not a luxury, wrote novelist Robert Stone: "It's almost as necessary as bread. We cannot imagine ourselves without it, because the self is a story."[1] If the self is a story, then we're all storytellers. The sooner you accept it, the sooner you can get started on the work of shaping your future.

Storytelling strengthens cultures and, more importantly, preserves the culture for future generations. The Jewish people are said to be "a nation of storytellers" because they have a rich tradition of passing along parables, fables, folktales, and sacred tales that are handed down from generation to generation. "Stories, especially told face-to-face, transmit the experiences, history, wisdoms, and lessons of past generations. In other words, the voice, a person's exquisite musical instrument, carries the message on wings of a story from one heart to another,"[2] says speech professor and storyteller Peninnah Schram. The Jewish people don't tell stories only for entertainment. They are "commanded" to teach younger generations the story of their people. "The messages in the tales are passed along in the most beautiful and imaginative way, namely, through a story. Those images will remain in the memory longer than any lecture or sermon," says Schram.

A business is also a culture of people, men and women who are bound together to sell products and services that improve the lives of their customers and move the world forward. "Great brands and great businesses have to be great storytellers,"[3] says Apple Store chief Angela Ahrendts. "We have to tell authentic, emotive, and compelling stories because we're building relationships with people and every great relationship has to be built on trust."

Ahrendts has a point. A healthy relationship in based on trust and stories build trust. Stories also connect people in a profound way. Storytellers influence one another to dream bigger and move mountains. The end of one story is the start of another. The ancient Greek philosopher Plato once said, "Come then, and let us pass a leisure hour in storytelling, and our story shall be the education of our heroes." Plato meant that the stories themselves create, inspire, and guide others to play the hero in their own life narrative.

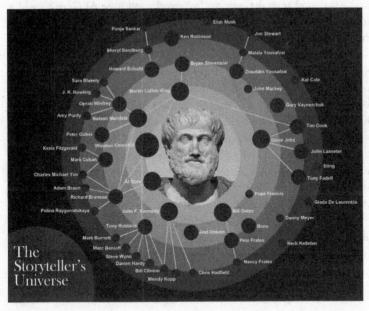

courtesy: Carolyn Kilmer

The poet Muriel Rukeyser once said, "The universe is made of stories, not of atoms." Think about the universe of connections in this book alone.

Nelson Mandela inspired the world with his words and actions, but his approach to public speaking was inspired by Winston Churchill, whose books Mandela "devoured." Mandela also remembered his father as an "excellent orator who captivated his audiences by entertaining them as well as teaching them." Mandela was skilled at the art of persuasion because he had a keen understanding that the way to a person's mind is through his heart. Mandela's courage and character, his values and vision all combined to create an iconic symbol of freedom and racial equality. But it was Mandela's gift as a storyteller that moved people to tear down the wall of injustice.

Storytellers by the names of Oprah Winfrey, Peter Guber, and Bryan Stevenson were among the millions of people whom Mandela inspired. Oprah, in turn, directly inspired Amy Purdy, Sara Blakely, and millions of others to own their stories. In the business world Steve Jobs inspired Jony Ive, Tony Fadell, Tim Cook, and countless entrepreneurs who are selling products that change the way we live, work, and play. Al Gore created a presentation that he showed to Richard Branson on the topic of climate change. Titled "An Inconvenient Truth," the presentation was structured as a visual narrative. Richard Branson told me that he was so moved by the presentation he made a commitment to invest a portion of Virgin's profits in projects to combat global warming. One presentation can change the world. Mark Burnett, Marc Benioff, and Bill Clinton all cite Tony Robbins as a storyteller who influenced the way they see the world. Robbins was inspired by the storytellers before him.

The world's youngest Nobel Peace Prize winner, Malala Yousafzai, has inspired a generation of women to stand up against oppression. Malala traces her courage back to the stories her father told her, especially the stories of Malalai the warrior princess.

Show me an inspiring leader and I'll show you a storyteller who influenced the way that leader sees the world. What do storytellers do? According to Walt Disney, they "instill hope again, and again, and again." Storytellers give us hope, and hope is a universal desire.

The Storyteller's Toolkit

The Storyteller's Secrets at a Glance

- **Identify your brand's core purpose. (**Steve Jobs, Richard Branson)
- **Dream in moonshots.** (Mark Burnett, Howard Schultz, Elon Musk)
- **Reframe the story you tell yourself.** (Joel Osteen, Darren Hardy)
- **Share the backstory of your life.** (Sting, Kat Cole, Sara Blakely)
- **Tell stories of struggle and the lessons learned.** (Tony Robbins, Amy Purdy, Adam Braun)
- **Introduce a "hero"—person or product—who triumphs over adversity.** (Oprah, *Sideways,* Darren Hardy, Peter Guber, Steve Jobs)
- **Consistently and publicly frame your vision in a founder's story.** (Howard Schultz, Walnut Hill Medical Center, John Mackey, Herb Kelleher)
- **Make stories at least 65 percent of your presentation.** (Bryan Stevenson, Sheryl Sandberg)
- **Violate expectations.** (Bill Gates, Elon Musk)
- **Use simple words and analogies to hide complexity.** (Dr. Ed Hallowell, Martin Luther King Jr., Elon Musk)
- **Enrich your story with specific and relevant details.** (Sara Blakely, Pete Frates)
- **Unleash your best storytellers.** (Tokyo 2020, Steve Wynn, Danny Meyer)
- **Deliver serious topics with a side of humor.** (Sir Ken Robinson)
- **Tell authentic and personal stories tailored to your audience.** (Gary Vaynerchuk, Giada De Laurentiis)
- **Be succinct; use a few well-chosen words.** (Richard Branson, Charles Yim, Winston Churchill)

- **Break up your story into three parts.** (Pope Francis, Steve Jobs, Sheryl Sandberg)
- **Use pictures to illustrate your story.** (Chris Hadfield)
- **Wrap data in stories to make a personal connection.** (Sheryl Sandberg, John Lasseter)
- **Take every opportunity to hone your presentation skills.** (Martin Luther King Jr., Winston Churchill, Richard Branson)
- **Inspire employees to be the hero of their own customer stories**. (Danny Meyer, Steve Wynn)
- **Don't make your story good; make it great.** (Malala Yousafzai, John Lasseter)

The Storyteller's Checklist

Be inspired. Share your passion.
Inspiring storytellers are inspired themselves. They are very clear on their motivation and they enthusiastically share their passion with their audience.

☐ **Why did you start your company? Why are you in your role?**

☐ **How does your company, product, service, or cause improve the lives of its customers?**

☐ **What are you passionate about?**

☐ **What makes your heart sing?**

Reframe the story you tell yourself before telling your story to others.
The story you choose to tell yourself exerts a powerful influence over your ability to captivate people. Some beliefs limit your potential. If you don't believe you'll ever master the art of public speaking, you're probably right.

What's your internal narrative? Check the boxes by the following statements you typically "run" in your head, then rewrite the statement in a positive frame.

☐ **I'm terrible at giving presentations.**
Reframe:

☐ **I got nervous once and it ruined me. I'm a horrible public speaker.**
Reframe:

☐ **Nobody wants to listen to me. I'm boring.**
Reframe:

☐ _____ .
Reframe:

Introduce a relatable hero who overcomes hardship and learns a valuable lesson.

Oprah uses a classic narrative technique to inspire her audience: start with humble beginnings, help your audience see themselves in the story, and turn the experience into a lesson.

- ☐ Do you have a three-part storytelling structure that naturally exists in your presentation content?
- ☐ What is the Trigger Event—that humbling moment when all goes wrong and failure occurs?
- ☐ What is the Transformation—that moment where you rise above the failure and benefits result?
- ☐ What is the Life Lesson—that lesson learned from the experience?

Build a story in three steps.

According to Peter Guber, anyone can build a story in three steps:

1. Grab your listener with a question or unexpected challenge.
2. Tell a story around the struggle that will ultimately lead to conquering the challenge.
3. Galvanize listeners with a call to action.

- ☐ What's your presentation topic?
- ☐ What is the challenge you can present?
- ☐ What is the struggle surrounding that challenge?
- ☐ What is the resolution and call to action?

See the big picture before you dive into the details.

Every great story needs a title. In a business pitch, the title is the headline—the one sentence that's going to grab your listeners' attention and put the narrative into context. It should be specific, succinct, and "Twitter friendly" (140 characters or less).

- ☐ What is the one thing I want people to know when they walk away from my presentation?
- ☐ Do you reveal your headline in the very beginning of the presentation? If not, decide when you will introduce your headline within the first 60 seconds.

Stick to the Rule of Three.
Beginning with Aristotle and continuing through to Pope Francis today, the world's greatest storytellers stick to the rule of three because it accomplishes three things:

- It offers a simple template to structure your story.
- It simplifies your story so your audience can remember its key messages.
- It leads to the ultimate goal of persuasion—action!

☐ Can you divide your key points into a category of three? Where else in your presentation can you package content into three key points?

☐ What stories are you going to use? Can you identify one story to align with each of your three key points?

Video is a storyteller's friend.
If you plan to tell your story on video, remember three things: passion, smiles, and conversation.

☐ Passion leads to energy and without energy and enthusiasm, it becomes difficult to hold attention. Authentic passion comes across on video. What are you passionate about? Make sure your content taps into that passion.

☐ Remember that storytelling is all about emotion and smiling has been associated with the strongest emotional reaction. Authentic smiles come from genuine interest in your topic. If you're passionate about your topic, your enthusiasm will be more authentic.

☐ Have you internalized your story? Reading from a teleprompter or directly from notes results in an unnatural delivery with a slower rate of speech. Practicing your script is an important step toward becoming more conversational on camera. Remember to use short, simple words. They are easier to remember and more conversational.

Pictures trump words.

One image—for example, a photograph of a human face—activates up to 30 million neurons in the visual cortex, according to neuroscientist Uri Hasson. PowerPoint slides that have a lot of "noise" are complicated and cluttered with extraneous text, charts, or numbers that are nonessential to the one idea that the speaker is trying to get across. Replacing words with pictures helps listeners recall and recognize your content.

☐ Crafting your story comes first. Then you need to visualize your story. Identify those key points in your presentation that need to "hit home." Those key points need to be illustrated so the listener will be able to recall them better and take action.

☐ What images, videos, or photos can you use in your presentation to replace what you would normally present as text for your key points?

How readable is your story?

The Flesch-Kincaid readability formula is a tool intended to measure how easy it is to read and to understand a passage or a book. It weighs sentence structure, word length, and other factors to arrive at a grade level at which students should be able to comprehend books and text. Ernest Hemingway and Steve Jobs's content bring in readability scores a fourth- to sixth-grader can understand. Simplifying your language adds power to your content's ability to persuade.

☐ Test your presentation content. Go to www.readability-score.com. Cut and paste a sample of your story or presentation content in the text box at the home page. At the right of the text box, the readability level of your text will calculate automatically.

☐ What's your average grade level score? If your score puts you above fourth to sixth grade, you might want to reconsider the wording (for a consumer audience). There's more influential power in being simple than being complex.

Share stories to strengthen cultures.

Culture stories are more impactful when they are shared among employees. When an employee gets a handwritten note or a call from the boss, that person tells another, who tells another, who tells another. Stories perpetuate themselves and bolster a company's culture.

☐ Do you have opportunities in your company to share stories?

☐ Share a success story about a teammate or client in your next staff meeting. How can you tie this story into your larger theme?

Short words have long-lasting impact.

Churchill the storyteller was a student of language. He obsessed over capturing just the right words to stir his audience to action and his experience with language taught him one thing—use short words for maximum effect. A photocopy of Churchill's original speech for a radio address during World War II when France fell to Germany shows longer words crossed out and replaced with shorter ones. For example, he replaced "liberated" with "freed."

☐ Do a majority of the words you use have more than 2 syllables? Are there longer words you can replace with shorter ones?

☐ Have a friend read your story or presentation content and ask him or her to highlight those parts of the content that seem awkward or too wordy. Having an outside perspective will help you identify those parts that need refining . . . or trimming.

Analogies and metaphors work like magic.

In communication circles, we like to use Shakespeare to explain metaphor. If you say, "Juliet is like the sun," you are making an analogy [A is like B]. If you say, "Juliet is the sun," you are creating a metaphor [A is B]. In both cases, B is the concrete thing that people recognize, and it makes A [whatever it is] easier to understand.

☐ Do you have an abstract idea or concept in your presentation that would benefit from using an analogy or metaphor? What is it?

☐ **Analogy: A is like B.**

_____ is like

My idea or concept (A)

_____ .

A concrete thing that most people recognize (B)

☐ **Metaphor: A is B.**

_____ is

My idea or concept (A)

_____ .

A concrete thing that most people recognize (B)

The storyteller's love for anaphora.

In the Dream Speech, Martin Luther King Jr. puts on a master class in the use of anaphora. Anaphora is a storytelling device where a word or phrase is repeated at the beginning of successive clauses and sentences. Anaphora is effective in the building of a movement because it increases the intensity of an idea, and intense ideas sear themselves into our brain.

☐ Not all stories need to include anaphora in the language. If your story or presentation's sole purpose is to inspire and motivate your listeners to rally behind your cause, you might want to experiment with anaphora in those key points of your presentation.

☐ Rhetorical questions often work well in anaphora. For example: "Will we do this? Will we do that? Will we . . . ?" or "Have you ever this? Have you ever that? Have you ever . . . ?"

☐ Using "we" in an assertive style also works well in anaphora. For example, "We are this. We are that. We . . ." or "We will this. We will that. We will . . ."

Give your audience something to cheer for . . . in 7 steps.

Austin Madison is an animator and story artist for such Pixar movies as *Ratatouille, WALL-E, Toy Story 3, Brave,* and others. In a revealing presentation, Madison outlined the 7-step process that all Pixar movies follow (see the steps to the right). These steps are meant to immerse an audience into a hero's journey and give the audience someone to cheer for. This process is used in all forms of storytelling: journalism, screenplays, books, presentations, and speeches.

Apply Pixar's 7-step process to your presentation should it be a good fit for your content:

☐ **Step 1: Once there was a _____.** (A protagonist/hero with a goal is the most important element of a story.)

☐ **Step 2: Every day he _____.** (The hero's world must be in balance in the first act.)

☐ **Step 3: Until one day _____.** (A compelling story introduces conflict. The hero's goal faces a challenge.)

☐ **Step 4: Because of that _____.**
(This step is critical and separates a
blockbuster from an average story.
A compelling story isn't made up of
random scenes that are loosely tied
together. Each scene has one nugget of
information that compels the next scene.)

☐ **Step 5: Because of that _____.**

☐ **Step 6: Until finally _____.**
(The climax reveals the triumph of good
over evil.)

☐ **Step 7: Ever since then _____.**
(The moral of the story.)

Notes

Introduction: Richard Branson, Dopamine and the Kalahari Bushmen

1. Richard Branson, "Great Balls of Fire and the Power of Storytelling," Virgin .com, April 13, 2015, http://www.virgin.com/richard-branson/great-balls-of-fire -and-the-power-of-storytelling (accessed June 15, 2015).

2. Polly Wiessner, "Embers of Society: Firelight Talk Among the Ju/'hoansi Bushmen," *PNAS* (Early Edition), vol. 111, no. 39, September 30, 2014, 14027–14035.

3. Ibid.

1. What Makes Your Heart Sing?

1. Kevin Gale, "Palm Beach Resident Sculley issues statement on Jobs' death, The Business Journals, October 6, 2011, http://www.bizjournals.com/southflorida /news/2011/10/06/sculley-issues-statement-on-jobs-death.html (accessed April 1, 2015).

2. "Apple Confidential-Steve Jobs on 'Think Different'-Internal Meeting Sept. 23, 1997," YouTube, November 5, 2013, https://www.youtube.com/watch?v =9GMQhOm-Dqo (accessed April 27, 2015).

3. Chris Gardner, founder and CEO of Gardner Rich & Co, in discussion with the author, July 18, 2007.

2. From T-Shirt Salesman to Mega Producer

1. Mark Burnett, *Jump In!: Even If You Don't Know How to Swim* (New York: Ballantine Books, 2005), 28.

2. Ibid., 83.

3. Ibid., 93.

4. Ibid., 82.

5. Mark Burnett, executive and television producer and author, in discussion with the author, February 24, 2014.

6. Carlin Flora, "The X-Factors of Success," *Psychology Today,* May 1, 2005, https:// www.psychologytoday.com/articles/200505/the-x-factors-success (accessed April 27, 2015).

7. Mark Burnett, executive and television producer and author, in discussion with the author, February 24, 2014.

3. Conquering Stage Fright to Sell Out Yankee Stadium

1. Joel Osteen, pastor of Lakewood Church in Houston, Texas, in discussion with the author, September 22, 2014.
2. Ibid.
3. Ibid.
4. "Inside the Psychologist's Studio with Albert Bandura," YouTube, https://www.youtube.com/watch?v=-_U-pSZwHy8 (accessed April 2, 2015).
5. Albert Bandura, "Self-efficacy: Toward a Unifying Theory of Behavioral Change," *Psychological Review,* vol. 84, no. 2, 1977, 191–215.
6. "It's Too Small—Joel Osteen," YouTube, July 25, 2014, https://m.youtube.com/watch?v=53d1uZEfVXU (accessed June 16, 2015).

4. A Rock Star Rediscovers His Gift in the Backstory of his Youth

1. Sting, "How I Started Writing Songs Again," TED.com, May 2014, http://www.ted.com/talks/sting_how_i_started_writing_songs_again/transcript?language=en#t-1202075 (accessed April 2, 2015).
2. Ibid.
3. Ibid.
4. Ibid.
5. Ibid.
6. Bobby Herrera, president of Populus Group, gave permission for author to use letter on May 29, 2015.
7. Bobby Herrera, president of Populus Group, in discussion with the author on May 12, 2015.

5. Change Your Story, Change Your Life

1. "Tony Robbins, The Secret of His Success," *Biography,* DVD, released December 27, 2005.
2. Ibid.
3. "Peter Guber Interviews Tony (Until Tony Turns the Tables and Starts Interviewing Him)," *Anthony Robbins Business and Finance Blog,* March 7, 2011, http://business.tonyrobbins.com/peter-guber-interviews-tony-until-tony-turns-the-tables-and-starts-interviewing-him/ (accessed April 2, 2015).
4. Ibid.
5. Tom Hawker, "25 Things You (Probably) Didn't Know About Sylvester Stallone," IGN, January 30, 2013, http://www.ign.com/articles/2013/01/30/25-things-you-probably-didnt-know-about-sylvester-stallone (accessed April 27, 2015).

6. The Power in Your Personal Legend

1. Colleen McElroy, "How to Tell a Captivating Story," *O, The Oprah Magazine,* March 2003, http://www.oprah.com/spirit/Storytelling-Tell-a-Story-How-to-Tell-a-Story (accessed June 16, 2015).
2. "Oprah Talks to Maya Angelou," *O, The Oprah Magazine,* December 2000, http://www.oprah.com/omagazine/Oprah-Interviews-Maya-Angelou (accessed June 16, 2015).

3. "Oprah Winfrey on Career, Life and Leadership," YouTube, April 28, 2014, https://www.youtube.com/watch?v=6DlrqeWrczs (accessed April 27, 2015).
4. Ibid.
5. Ibid.
6. Ibid.
7. "Oprah Receives Bob Hope Humanitarian Award. VOB," YouTube, June 1, 2012, https://www.youtube.com/watch?v=FQxrZ7jT0iM (accessed April 2, 2015).
8. "Oprah Winfrey on Career, Life and Leadership," YouTube, April 28, 2014, https://www.youtube.com/watch?v=6DlrqeWrczs (accessed April 27, 2015).
9. "J. K. Rowling Harvard Commencement Speech/Harvard Commencement 2008," YouTube, December 1, 2014, https://www.youtube.com/watch?v=Uibf DUPJAEU (accessed April 2, 2015).

7. A Coffee King Pours His Heart into His Business

1. Howard Schultz and Dori Jones Young, *Pour Your Heart into It: How Starbucks Built a Company One Cup at a Time* (New York: Hyperion, 1999), 3.
2. *The Big Idea with Donny Deutsch,* October 6, 2006, property of CNBC.
3. Howard Schultz and Dori Jones Young, *Pour Your Heart into It: How Starbucks Built a Company One Cup at a Time* (New York: Hyperion, 1999), 4.
4. "Coffee Culture Howard Schultz Wanted to Bring to America /Super Soul Sunday /Oprah Winfrey Network," YouTube, December 8, 2013, https://www.youtube.com/watch?v=-oXDiZ42zvs (accessed April 27, 2015).
5. "The Man Behind Starbucks Reveals How He Changed the World," YouTube, January 23, 2015, https://www.youtube.com/watch?v=LnA7n9qSB7E (accessed April 27, 2015).
6. Howard Schultz and Dori Jones Young, *Pour Your Heart into It: How Starbucks Built a Company One Cup at a Time* (New York: Hyperion, 1999), 7.
7. Greg J. Stephens, Lauren J. Silbert, and Uri Hasson, "Speaker-Listener Neural Coupling Underlies Successful Communication," *PNAS,* August 10, 2010, 107 (32), 14425–14430, http://www.ncbi.nlm.nih.gov/pmc/articles/PMC2922522/ (accessed April 3, 2015).
8. Howard Schultz and Dori Jones Young, *Pour Your Heart into It: How Starbucks Built a Company One Cup at a Time* (New York: Hyperion, 1999), 35.

8. We're Not Retailers with a Mission, We're Missionaries Who Retail

1. John Mackey and Rajendra Sisodia, *Conscious Capitalism: Liberating the Heroic Spirit of Business* (Boston, MA: Harvard Business Review Press, 2013), 7.
2. Ibid., 82.
3. Ibid., 260.
4. Dan Levy, "The Purpose-Driven Company: Q&A with Whole Foods' John Mackey," *Sparksheet,* June 12, 2013, http://sparksheet.com/the-purpose-driven-company-qa-with-whole-foods-john-mackey/ (accessed April 3, 2015).
5. Robert Safian, "Generation Flux's Secret Weapon," *Fast Company,* October 14, 2014, http://www.fastcompany.com/3035975/generation-flux/find-your-mission (accessed April 3, 2015).

6. Rick Wartzman, "What Unilever Shares with Google & Apple," *Fortune,* January 7, 2015, http://fortune.com/2015/01/07/what-unilever-shares-with-google-and-apple/ (accessed April 3, 2015).

7. Jo Confino, "Paul Polman: 'The Power Is in the Hands of the Consumer,'" *Guardian,* November 21, 2011, http://www.theguardian.com/sustainable-business/unilever-ceo-paul-polman-interview (accessed April 3, 2015).

8. Doug McMillon, President & CEO, Wal-Mart Stores, Inc. "One Customer at a Time," Walmart.com, June 5, 2015, http://news.walmart.com/executive-viewpoints/one-customer-at-a-time (accessed June 16, 2015).

9. If You Can't Tell It, You Can't Sell It

1. Peter Guber, *Tell to Win: Connect, Persuade, and Triumph with the Hidden Power of Story* (New York: Crown Business, 2011), 3.

2. Ibid., 48.

3. Ibid., 59.

4. Ibid., 21.

5. Ibid, 101.

6. "Steve Jobs Introducing the iPhone at Macworld 2007," YouTube, December 2, 2010, https://www.youtube.com/watch?v=x7qPAY9JqE4 (accessed April 3, 2015).

7. Peter Guber, *Tell to Win: Connect, Persuade, and Triumph with the Hidden Power of Story* (New York: Crown Business, 2011), vii.

10. How a Spellbinding Storyteller Received TED's Longest Standing Ovation

1. Bryan Stevenson, "We Need to Talk About an Injustice," TED.com, March 2012, http://www.ted.com/talks/bryan_stevenson_we_need_to_talk_about_an_injustice/transcript?language=en (accessed April 3, 2015).

2. Ibid.

3. Bryan Stevenson, founder and director of the Equal Justice Initiative, in discussion with the author, December 17, 2012.

4. Paul Barrett, "Bryan Stevenson's Death Defying Acts," *NYU Law Magazine* (2007), September 15, 2011, http://blogs.law.nyu.edu/magazine/2007/bryan-stevenson's-death-defying-acts/ (accessed April 3, 2015).

5. Bryan Stevenson, "We Need to Talk About an Injustice," TED.com, March 2012, http://www.ted.com/talks/bryan_stevenson_we_need_to_talk_about_an_injustice/transcript?language=en (accessed April 3, 2015).

6. Paul Barrett, "Bryan Stevenson's Death Defying Acts," *NYU Law Magazine* (2007), September 15, 2011, http://blogs.law.nyu.edu/magazine/2007/bryan-stevenson's-death-defying-acts/ (accessed April 3, 2015).

7. Bryan Stevenson, founder and director of the Equal Justice Initiative, in discussion with the author, December 17, 2012.

8. Paul Zak, "How Stories Change the Brain," *Greater Good,* December 17, 2013, http://greatergood.berkeley.edu/article/item/how_stories_change_brain (accessed April 27, 2015).

11. Turning Sewage into Drinking Water

1. "Bill Gates Releases Malaria Mosquitoes TED!! Must See," YouTube, February 6, 2009, http://www.youtube.com/watch?v=tWjpVJ8YNtk (accessed April 11, 2013).

2. A. K. Pradeep, author of *The Buying Brain: Secrets for Selling to the Subconscious Mind,* in discussion with the author, September 2, 2010.

3. "Cisco Telepresence Magic," YouTube, November 6, 2007, https://www.youtube.com/watch?v=rcfNC_x0VvE (accessed April 27, 2015).

4. "Macworld 2007—Steve Jobs Introduces iPhone—Part 1," YouTube, http://www.youtube.com/watch?v=PZoPdBh8KUs&feature=related (accessed January 30, 2009).

5. Jerome Bruner, "The Narrative Construction of Reality," *Critical Inquiry,* vol. 18, no. 1, Autumn 1991, 1–21.

12. What You Don't Understand Can (and Does) Hurt You

1. Keath Low, "Adam Levine Talks About ADHD," About.com, December 4, 2014, http://add.about.com/od/famouspeoplewithadhd/a/Adam-Levine-Talks-About-Adhd.htm (accessed April 27, 2015).

2. Ibid.

3. Edward Hallowell and John Raley, *Driven to Distraction: Recognizing and Coping with Attention Deficit Disorder from Childhood Through Adulthood* (New York: Anchor Books, 1994), 45.

4. Edward Hallowell, author and world-renowned ADHD expert, in discussion with the author, July 28, 2014.

5. Ibid.

6. Adam Jackson, cofounder and CEO of Doctor on Demand, in discussion with the author, January 28, 2015.

7. Edward Hallowell, author and world-renowned ADHD expert, in discussion with the author, July 28, 2014.

8. Zachary Meisel and Jason Karlawish, "Narrative vs. Evidence-Based Medicine—And, Not Or," *Journal of the American Medical Association,* vol. 306, no. 18, November 9, 2011, .

9. Eun Kyung Kim, "President Obama on Measles: 'You Should Get Your Kids Vaccinated,'" *Today,* February 2, 2015, http://www.today.com/news/president-obama-measles-you-should-get-your-kids-vaccinated-2D80467430 (accessed April 27, 2015).

10. Zachary Meisel and Jason Karlawish, "Narrative vs. Evidence-Based Medicine—And, Not Or," *Journal of the American Medical Association,* vol. 306, no. 18, November 9, 2011, .

11. Rahel Gebreyes, "Melinda Gates Speaks Out Against The Anti-Vaccine Movement," *Huffington Post,* January 22, 2015, http://www.huffingtonpost.com/2015/01/22/melinda-gates-anti-vaccine_n_6519464.html (accessed April 27, 2015).

13. The $98 Pants That Launched an Empire

1. Adam Bluestein, "How to Tell Your Company's Story," *Inc.*, February 2014, http://www.inc.com/magazine/201402/adam-bluestein/sara-blakely-how-i-got-started.html (accessed April 27, 2015).
2. "Seth Combs: SOL REPUBLIC, Co-Founder/ Revolution Season 4/ Brian Solis TV," YouTube, December 23, 2013, https://www.youtube.com/watch?v=IJCCKTmLYpc (accessed June 16, 2015).
3. Ibid.
4. "Content Marketing World Conference Keynote Speech/ Kevin Spacey," YouTube, October 8, 2014, https://www.youtube.com/watch?v=udQXwyuUnn4 (accessed June 16, 2015).

14. Japan Unleashes Its Best Storytellers to Win Olympic Gold

1. Mami Sato, Tokyo2020 Presentation IOC Session in Buenos Aires, http://www.japanportal.jp/T2020_Final%20Presentation%20Script.pdf (accessed April 27, 2015).
2. Ibid.
3. Owen Gibson, "Japanese Bid's Passion Earns Tokyo the 2020 Olympic Games," *Guardian,* September 7, 2013, http://www.theguardian.com/sport/2013/sep/07/tokyo-2020-olympic-games (accessed April 17, 2015).
4. Kaz Nagatsuka, "Sato Shines as Role Model," *Japan Times,* October 4, 2012, http://www.japantimes.co.jp/sports/2014/10/04/more-sports/track-field/sato-shines-role-model/#.VLqhYFsnUah (accessed April 17, 2015).
5. "No. 9: Tokyo Lands 2020 Paralympic Games," December 23, 2013, International Paralympic Committee, http://www.paralympic.org/feature/no-9-tokyo-lands-2020-paralympic-games (accessed April 17, 2015).
6. Owen Gibson, "Japanese Bid's Passion Earns Tokyo the 2020 Olympic Games," *Guardian,* September 7, 2013, http://www.theguardian.com/sport/2013/sep/07/tokyo-2020-olympic-games (accessed April 17, 2015).
7. Julie Roehm, Chief Storyteller, SVP Marketing for SAP, in discussion with the author, April 17, 2014.

15. A Funny Look at the Most Popular TED Talk of All Time

1. NPR/TED Staff, "How Do Schools Kill Creativity?" TED Radio Hour, October 7, 2014, http://health.wusf.usf.edu/post/how-do-schools-kill-creativity (accessed April 27, 2015).
2. Ibid.
3. John Medina, *Brain Rules* (Seattle, WA: Pear Press, 2008), 2.
4. Ken Robinson, "Ken Robinson Says Schools Kill Creativity," TED.com, June 2006, http://www.ted.com/talks/ken_robinson_says_schools_kill_creativity.html?qsha=1&utm_expid=166907-20&utm_referrer=http%3A%2F%2Fwww.ted.com%2Fsearch%3Fcat%3Dss_all%26q%3Dken%2Brobinson (accessed May 18, 2013).
5. "Ken Robinson: Education Innovation—Conversations from Penn State,"

Penn State News, http://news.psu.edu/video/223269/2011/06/10/ken-robinson -education-innovation-conversations-penn-state (accessed April 27, 2015).

6. John Medina, *Brain Rules* (Seattle, WA: Pear Press, 2008), 80.

7. Ernest Lim Kok Seng and Catheryn Khoo-Lattimore, "Up Close and Personal: Employing In-Depth Interviews to Explore International Students' Perceptions of Quality Learning Environment at a Private University in Malaysia," *International Handbook of Academic Research and Teaching, Proceedings of Intellectbase International Consortium,* vol. 22, Spring 2012.

8. Polly Wiessner, "Embers of Society: Firelight Talk Among the Ju/'hoansi Bushmen," *PNAS* (Early Edition), vol. 111, no. 39, September 30, 2014, 14027–14035.

9. "Apple Special Event, June 2, 2014," Apple.com, http://www.apple.com/apple -events/june-2014/ (accessed April 28, 2015).

10. Ken Robinson, "Ken Robinson Says Schools Kill Creativity," TED.com, June 2006, http://www.ted.com/talks/ken_robinson_says_schools_kill_creativity .html?qsha=1&utm_expid=166907-20&utm_referrer=http%3A%2F%2Fwww .ted.com%2Fsearch%3Fcat%3Dss_all%26q%3Dken%2Brobinson (accessed May 18, 2015).

11. Ken Robinson, *The Element: How Finding Your Passion Changes Everything* (New York: Penguin Books, 2009), 22.

16. Dirt, Cigars, and Sweaty Socks Put a Marketer on the Map

1. Gary Vaynerchuk, *Why Now Is the Time to Crush It! Cash In on Your Passion* (New York: Penguin Books, 2009), 18.

2. Ibid., 54.

3. Ibid., 31.

4. "Episode 1—Verite," Wine Library TV, February 21, 2006, http://tv.winelibrary .com/2006/02/21/episode-1-verite/ (accessed April 28, 2015).

5. Gary Vaynerchuk, *Why Now Is the Time to Crush It! Cash In on Your Passion* (New York: Penguin Books, 2009), 86.

6. Ibloggedthis.com, "Conan Eats Dirt, Cigars, and Wet Rocks," Funny or Die, August 3, 2007, http://www.funnyordie.com/videos/87d3bf2270/conan-eats -dirt-cigars-and-wet-rocks-from-ibloggedthis (accessed, April 21, 2015).

7. Ibid.

8. Gary Vaynerchuk, *Why Now Is the Time to Crush It! Cash In on Your Passion* (New York: Penguin Books, 2009), 101.

9. Ibid., 104.

10. Gary Vaynerchuk, "Gary Vaynerchuk on How to Tell Stories in an ADHD World," SpeakTips, August 1, 2014, http://www.speaktips.com/home/gary -vaynerchuck-on-how-to-tell-stories-in-an-adhd-world (accessed April 21, 2015).

17. A Burger with a Side of Story

1. Danny Meyer, CEO of the Union Square Hospitality Group, in discussion with the author, February 16, 2015.

2. Danny Meyer, *Setting the Table: The Transforming Power of Hospitality in Business* (New York: HarperCollins, 2006), 6.

3. Danny Meyer, CEO of the Union Square Hospitality Group, in discussion with the author, February 16, 2015.

4. Ibid.

5. Danny Meyer, *Setting the Table: The Transforming Power of Hospitality in Business* (New York: HarperCollins, 2006), 142.

6. Steve Marsh, "The Tao of Danny," *Delta Sky* (magazine), December 2014, http://deltaskymag.delta.com/Sky-Extras/Favorites/The-Tao-of-Danny.aspx (accessed April 21, 2015).

7. Danny Meyer, CEO of the Union Square Hospitality Group, in discussion with the author, February 16, 2015.

8. Danny Meyer, *Setting the Table: The Transforming Power of Hospitality in Business* (New York: HarperCollins, 2006), 95.

18. If Something Can't Be Explained on the Back of an Envelope, It's Rubbish

1. Richard Branson, *Losing My Virginity: How I Survived, Had Fun, and Made a Fortune Doing Business My Way* (New York: Crown Publishing Group), 25.

2. "Richard Branson—Anderson Cooper Interview," Newslines, May 21, 2004, http://newslines.org/richard-branson/anderson-cooper-interview-2/ (accessed April 28, 2015).

3. Richard Branson, *Losing My Virginity: How I Survived, Had Fun, and Made a Fortune Doing Business My Way* (New York: Crown Publishing Group), 34.

4. Richard Branson, "Complexity is your enemy," Virgin.com, http://www.virgin.com/richard-branson/complexity-is-your-enemy (accessed April 28, 2015).

5. Sir Richard Branson, founder of Virgin Group, in discussion with the author, April 22, 2013.

6. Richard Branson, *The Virgin Way: Everything I Know About Leadership* (New York: Portfolio, 2014), 249.

7. "Back to the Future at Apple," *Bloomberg Businessweek,* May 24, 1998, http://www.bloomberg.com/bw/stories/1998-05-24/back-to-the-future-at-apple (accessed April 28, 2015).

8. Richard Branson, "How to inspire change," Virgin.com, June 3, 2014, http://www.virgin.com/richard-branson/how-to-inspire-change (accessed April 28, 2015).

19. The Evangelizer in Chief

1. Carol Glatz, "Short, Sweet, Simple: Francis and the Rule of Three," Catholic News Service, September 24, 2013, https://cnsblog.wordpress.com/2013/09/24/short-sweet-simple-francis-the-rule-of-three/ (accessed April 22, 2015).

2. Francis X. Rocca, "Pope, at Mass with Millions, Tells Filipinos to Protect the Family," Catholic News Service, January 18, 2015, https://cnsblog.wordpress.com/2015/01/18/pope-at-mass-with-millions-tells-filipinos-to-protect-the-family/ (accessed April 28, 2015).

3. Pope Francis, "Midnight Mass: Solemnity of the Nativity of the Lord, Homily of Pope Francis," Vatican Basilica, December 24, 2014, http://w2.vatican.va /content/francesco/en/homilies/2014/documents/papa-francesco_20141224 _omelia-natale.html (accessed April 28, 2015).

4. Pope Francis, "Holy Mass, Blessing and Imposition of the Ashes, Homily of Pope Francis," Basilica of Santa Sabina, February 18, 2015, http://w2.vatican.va/content /francesco/en/homilies/2015/documents/papa-francesco_20150218_omelia -ceneri.html (accessed April 28, 2015).

20. A Film Mogul's Granddaughter Cooks Up Her Own Recipe for Success

1. Lindsay Powers, "Giada De Laurentiis: Grandfather Dino 'Was a True Inspiration,' " *Hollywood Reporter,* November 11, 2010, http://www.hollywoodreporter .com/news/giada-de-laurentiis-grandfather-dino-44543 (accessed April 28, 2015).

2. Scott Stump, "Celeb Chef Giada De Laurentiis to Release Series of Children's Books," *Today,* March 21, 2013, http://www.today.com/books/celeb-chef-giada -de-laurentiis-release-series-childrens-books-1C9002346 (accessed April 22, 2015).

3. James Mottram, "Dino De Laurentiis, Hannibal," BBC Home, http://www.bbc .co.uk/films/2001/02/12/dino_de_laurentis_hannibal_120201_interview .shtml (accessed April 28, 2015).

4. "UCLA Department of Anthropology, Commencement 2009: Speaker Giada De Laurentiis," YouTube, https://www.youtube.com/watch?v=Sojqm9FUmEc (accessed April 28, 2015).

5. Ibid.

6. Ibid.

7. Ibid.

8. Melissa Row, "You Are Never Fully Dressed Without a Smile," Women of Worth, January 8, 2015, http://www.womenofworth.co/you-are-never-fully-dressed -without-a-smile/ (accessed April 28, 2015).

21. The Storytelling Astronaut Wows a TED Audience

1. Chris Hadfield, *An Astronaut's Guide to Life on Earth: What Going to Space Taught Me About Ingenuity, Determination, and Being Prepared for Anything* (New York: Macmillan, 2013).

2. Chris Hadfield, first Canadian to walk in space, in conversation with the author, November 14, 2014.

3. Ibid.

4. Ifat Levy, Uri Hasson, and Rafael Malach, "One Picture Is Worth at Least a Million Neurons," *Current Biology,* vol. 14, 996–1001, June 8, 2004, https://psych .princeton.edu/~psych/psychology/research/hasson/pubs/Levy_CurrentBiology _2004.pdf (accessed April 27, 2015).

5. "Worth a Thousand Words," Brain Rules, December 10, 2009, http://brainrules .blogspot.com/2009/12/worth-thousand-words.html (accessed April 28, 2015).

6. Chris Hadfield, "What I Learned from Going Blind in Space," TED.com, March 2014, http://www.ted.com/talks/chris_hadfield_what_i_learned_from _going_blind_in_space?language=en (accessed April 27, 2015).

7. Julio Gonzalez, Alfonso Barros-Loscertales, Friedemann Pulvermuller, Vanessa Meseguer, Ana Sanjuan, Vincente Belloch, and Ceasar Avila, "Reading Cinnamon Activates Olfactory Brain Regions," *NeuroImage*, 32, 906–912, 2006, http:// www3.uji.es/~gonzalez/neuroimage.pdf (accessed April 27, 2015).

8. James Geary, *I Is an Other: The Secret Life of Metaphor and How It Shapes the Way We See the World* (New York: Harper Perennial, 2011), 175.

22. "Dude's Selling a Battery" and Still Inspires

1. Ashlee Vance, *Elon Musk: Tesla, SpaceX, and the Quest for a Fantastic Future* (New York: Ecco, 2015), 30.

2. "Powerwall Tesla Home Battery," Tesla Powerwall Launch Event in LA, Tesla Motors, April 30, 2015, http://www.teslamotors.com/powerwall (accessed June 16, 2015).

3. "Elon Musk Debuts the Tesla Powerwall," YouTube, May 1, 2015, https://www .youtube.com/watch?v=yKORsrlN-2k (accessed June 16, 2015).

4. T. C. Sottek, "Watch Elon Musk Announce Tesla Energy in the Best Tech Keynote I've Ever Seen," *Verge,* http://www.theverge.com/2015/5/1/8527543/elon -musk-tesla-battery-feels (accessed June 16, 2015).

5. "Apple Music Event 2003-iTunes Music Store Introduction," YouTube, https://m .youtube.com/watch?v=B2n86TROxzY (accessed June 16, 2015).

6. Ronald E. Reggio, "What Is Charisma and Charismatic Leadership?," *Psychology Today,* October 7, 2012, https://www.psychologytoday.com/blog/cutting-edge -leadership/201210/what-is-charisma-and-charismatic-leadership (accessed April 1, 2015).

23. An Entrepreneur Makes *Shark Tank* History

1. "Shark Tank, $1 Million Deal from ALL Sharks, Breathometer [update]," YouTube, January 28, 2015, https://www.youtube.com/watch?v=4690Nxgobrw (accessed April 28, 2015).

2. Charles Yim, CEO of Breathometer, in discussion with the author, February 19, 2015.

3. Ibid.

4. Jill Rosen, "Super Bowl Ads: Stories Beat Sex and Humor, Johns Hopkins Researcher Finds," John Hopkins News Network, January 31, 2014, http://hub .jhu.edu/2014/01/31/super-bowl-ads (accessed April 27, 2015).

24. Find Your Fight

1. "Darren Hardy-How Did I Develop My Message, Brand and Skills," YouTube, December 11, 2011, https://www.youtube.com/watch?v=0T6LXuzfRwQ (accessed April 28, 2015).

2. Darren Hardy, publisher and founding editor of *Success* magazine, in discussion with the author, March 12, 2015.

3. Darren Hardy, *The Entrepreneur Roller Coaster: Why Now Is the Time to #Join-TheRide* (Lake Dallas, TX: Success, 2015), 46.

4. Ibid., 47.

5. Lawrence Calhoun and Richard Tedeschi, *The Foundations of Posttraumatic Growth: An Expanded Framework: Handbook of Posttraumatic Growth, Research and Practice* (Mahwah, NJ: Lawrence Erlbaum Associates, 2006), 4.

6. Dan McAdams, *The Stories We Live By: Personal Myths and the Making of the Self* (New York: The Guilford Press, 1993), 28.

7. Darren Hardy, *The Entrepreneur Roller Coaster: Why Now Is the Time to #Join-TheRide* (Lake Dallas, TX: Success, 2015), 53.

8. Ibid., 51.

9. Chris Matthews, *Jack Kennedy, Elusive Hero* (New York: Simon & Schuster Paperbacks, 2011), 65.

10. Ibid.

25. The Hospital Steve Jobs Would Have Built

1. Rich Guerra Jr., M.D., internist and cardiologist at North Texas Heart Center, in discussion with the author (a video link was shared with author), February 20, 2015.

2. The Disney Institute and Theodore Kinni, *Be Our Guest: Perfecting the Art of Customer Service* (New York: Disney Enterprises, 2011), 69.

3. Rob Gill, "An Integrative Review of Storytelling: Using Corporate Stories to Strengthen Employee Engagement and Internal and External Reputation," *PRism,* 8 (1), 2011, 1–15.

4. Howard Leonhardt, founder of Leonhardt Ventures, in discussion with the author, January 20, 2015.

5. "Dr. Oliver Sacks-Narrative and Medicine: The Importance of the Case History," YouTube, March 20, 2013, https://www.youtube.com/watch?v=7PYAnB5Jx-k (accessed April 27, 2015).

6. Oliver Sacks, *The Man Who Mistook His Wife for a Hat and Other Clinical Tales* (New York: Touchstone, 1970), 110.

7. Kezia Fitzgerald, CEO and cofounder of CareAline Products, in discussion with the author, March 27, 2015.

8. Ibid.

26. A Hotel Mogul Turns 12,000 Employees into Customer Service Heroes

1. "Part I: Steve Wynn Discusses His Journey into the Las Vegas Hotel and Casino Business," YouTube, July 17, 2014, https://www.youtube.com/watch?v=m9Lg7uKhTMs (accessed April 27, 2015).

2. Ibid.

3. Ibid.

4. Ibid.

5. Ibid.

27. A Revolutionary Idea That Took Off on the Back of a Napkin

1. Chuck Lucier, "Herb Kelleher: The Thought Leader Interview," *Strategy+business,* June 1, 2004 http://www.strategy-business.com/article/04212?pg=all (accessed April 28, 2015).

2. "Herb and His Airline," *60 Minutes,* October 15, 1989, http://www.cbsnews.com/videos/herb-and-his-airline/ (accessed April 28, 2015).

3. Chuck Lucier, "Herb Kelleher: The Thought Leader Interview," *Strategy+business,* June 1, 2004, http://www.strategy-business.com/article/04212?pg=all (accessed April 27, 2015).

4. "Herb Kelleher: People Are Your Competitive Advantage," YouTube, March 9, 2012, https://www.youtube.com/watch?v=Fw6_LpI0BDQ (accessed April 28, 2015).

5. Chuck Lucier, "Herb Kelleher: The Thought Leader Interview," *Strategy+business,* June 1, 2004, http://www.strategy-business.com/article/04212?pg=all (accessed April 27, 2015).

6. Carmine Gallo, "Southwest Airlines Motivates Its Employees with a Purpose Bigger Than a Paycheck," Forbes.com, January 21, 2014, http://www.forbes.com/sites/carminegallo/2014/01/21/southwest-airlines-motivates-its-employees-with-a-purpose-bigger-than-a-paycheck/ (accessed April 28, 2015).

7. "Southwest Purpose and Vision," YouTube, December 19, 2013, https://www.youtube.com/watch?v=eGxMf88I5g4 (accessed April 28, 2015).

8. Ibid.

9. Ibid.

10. Rob Marsh, "9 Inspirational Quotes on Business by Herb Kelleher," Logo-Maker, May 21, 2012, http://www.logomaker.com/blog/2012/05/21/9-inspirational-quotes-on-business-by-herb-kelleher/ (accessed April 28, 2015).

11. Ibid.

28. When Amy Lost Her Legs, She Found Her Voice

1. Amy Purdy, 2014 Paralympic Bronze Medalist and cofounder of Adaptive Action Sports, in discussion with the author, February 17, 2015.

2. Amy Purdy, *On My Own Two Feet: From Losing My Legs to Learning the Dance of Life* (New York: HarperCollins, 2014), 156.

3. Amy Purdy, 2014 Paralympic Bronze Medalist and cofounder of Adaptive Action Sports, in discussion with the author, February 17, 2015.

4. Ibid.

5. Amy Purdy, *On My Own Two Feet: From Losing My Legs to Learning the Dance of Life* (New York: HarperCollins, 2014), 170.

6. Amy Purdy, "Living Beyond Limits," TED.com, May 2011, https://www.ted.com/talks/amy_purdy_living_beyond_limits/transcript?language=en (accessed April 28, 2015).

7. Amy Purdy, 2014 Paralympic Bronze Medalist and cofounder of Adaptive Action Sports, in discussion with the author, February 17, 2015.

8. Ibid.

29. From Hooters to the C-Suite—A Former Waitress Shares Her Recipe for Success

1. "Inspirational Leaders Luncheon with Kat Cole, President of Cinnabon," You-Tube, https://www.youtube.com/watch?v=etULbJaEwsw (accessed April 27, 2015).
2. Ibid.
3. Kat Cole, president and COO of Cinnabon, in discussion with the author, June 27, 2014.
4. "Inspirational Leaders Luncheon with Kat Cole, President of Cinnabon," YouTube, https://www.youtube.com/watch?v=etULbJaEwsw (accessed April 27, 2015).
5. Ibid.
6. Howard Gardner and Emma Laskin, *Leading Minds: An Anatomy of Leadership* (New York: Basic Books, 2011), 30.
7. "Inspirational Leaders Luncheon with Kat Cole, President of Cinnabon," You-Tube, https://www.youtube.com/watch?v=etULbJaEwsw (accessed April 27, 2015).

30. Trading Wall Street Riches for the Promise of a Pencil

1. Adam Braun, *The Promise of a Pencil: How an Ordinary Person Can Create Extraordinary Change* (New York: Scribner, 2014), 35.
2. Ibid., 152.
3. Ibid., 64.
4. Ibid., 25.
5. Adam Braun, founder of Pencils of Promise, in discussion with the author, March 25, 2014.
6. Paul Zak, "Why Your Brain Loves Good Storytelling," *Harvard Business Review,* October 28, 2014, https://hbr.org/2014/10/why-your-brain-loves-good-story telling/ (accessed Aprils 27, 2015).
7. Adam Braun, founder of Pencils of Promise, in discussion with the author, March 25, 2014.

31. The Ice Bucket Challenge Melts the Hearts of Millions

1. Nancy Frates, inspirational speaker and ALS advocate, in discussion with the author, September 3, 2014.
2. Ibid.
3. Ibid.
4. "Brain Series 2 Episode 10: Disorders of Motor Neurons," *Charlie Rose,* July 19, 2012, http://www.charlierose.com/watch/60100481 (accessed April 28, 2015).
5. "Pete Presents to the Staff at Biogen Idec," YouTube, June 14, 2014, https://www.youtube.com/watch?v=GvkUWQtQvyk&feature=youtu.be (accessed April 28, 2015).
6. Marie-Laure Ryan, *Narrative Across Media: The Languages of Storytelling (Frontiers of Narrative)* (Lincoln, NE: University of Nebraska Press, 2004), 147.
7. John Otis, "Despite Making Sacrifices for Family, a College Student Still Pursues His Dream," *New York Times,* December 11, 2014, http://www.nytimes.com

/2014/12/12/nyregion/despite-making-sacrifices-for-family-a-college-student
-still-pursues-his-dream.html?rref=collection%2Fundefined%2Fundefined
(accessed April 28, 2015).

8. Patricia Cohen, "Unsteady Incomes Keep Millions Behind on Bills," *New York Times,* December 3, 2014, http://www.nytimes.com/2014/12/04/business/unsteady-incomes-keep-millions-of-workers-behind-on-bills-.html?_r=2 (accessed April 27, 2015).

9. Mohamed El-Erian, "Father and Daughter Reunion," *Worth,* May/June 2014, http://www.worth.com/index.php?option=com_content&view=article&id=6722:father-and-daughter-reunion&catid=4:live (accessed April 29, 2015).

32. His Finest Hour—180 Words That Saved the World

1. "May 1940 War Cabinet Crisis," *Wikipedia,* https://en.wikipedia.org/wiki/May_1940_War_Cabinet_Crisis (accessed June 16, 2015).

2. Boris Johnson, mayor of London, in discussion with the author, November 13, 2014.

3. Boris Johnson, *The Churchill Factor: How One Man Made History* (New York: Riverhead Books, 2014), 129.

4. Ibid.

5. Winston Churchill, "Their Finest Hour: June 18, 1940, House of Commons, Listen to an Excerpt Here at the BBC Archives," The Churchill Centre, http://www.winstonchurchill.org/resources/speeches/1940-the-finest-hour/their-finest-hour (accessed April 29, 2015).

6. Boris Johnson, *The Churchill Factor: How One Man Made History* (New York: Riverhead Books, 2014), 94–95.

7. Ibid., 97.

8. Sue Shellenbarger, "How to Look Smarter: The Tactics People Use to Look Intelligent Often Backfire: Fancy Words Don't Work," *Wall Street Journal,* January 13, 2015, http://www.wsj.com/articles/how-to-look-smarter-1421189631?autologin=y (accessed April 29, 2015).

33. Great Storytellers Are Made, Not Born

1. Clarence Jones and Stuart Connelly, *Behind the Dream: The Making of the Speech That Transformed a Nation* (New York: Palgrave Macmillan, 2011), 76.

2. Ibid., 110.

3. Ibid., 106.

4. Philip Kennicott, "Revisiting King's Metaphor About a Nation's Debt," *Washington Post,* August 24, 2011, http://www.washingtonpost.com/lifestyle/style/revisiting-kings-metaphor-about-a-nations-debt/2011/07/26/gIQArshBaJ_story.html (accessed June 16, 2015).

5. James Geary, *I Is an Other: The Secret Life of Metaphor and How It Shapes the Way We See the World* (New York: Harper Perennial, 2011), 3.

6. President Barack Obama, "President Obama's 2015 State of the Union Address," WhiteHouse.gov, https://www.whitehouse.gov/sotu (accessed April 29, 2015).

7. Greg Abbott, "Greg Abbott Delivers 2015 Texas Inaugural Speech," Office of the Governor Greg Abbott, January 20, 2015, http://gov.texas.gov/news/speech /20415 (accessed April 28, 2015).

8. "Winner: Banking and Financial Services, 'We Are The Cavalry,'" Vital Speeches of the Day, http://vsotd.com/sites/default/files/2014_CiceroAwardsWinnersF.pdf (accessed April 29, 2015).

34. Millions of Women "Lean In" After One Woman Dares to Speak Out

1. Sheryl Sandberg, "Sheryl Sandberg: So We Leaned In . . . Now What?" TED .com, December 2013, http://www.ted.com/talks/sheryl_sandberg_so_we_leaned _in_now_what?language=en (accessed April 29, 2015).

2. Sheryl Sandberg, "Sheryl Sandberg: Why We Have Too Few Women Leaders," TED.com, December 2010, http://www.ted.com/talks/sheryl_sandberg_why_we _have_too_few_women_leaders/transcript?language=en (accessed April 29, 2015).

3. Sheryl Sandberg, "Sheryl Sandberg: So We Leaned In . . . Now What?" TED .com, December 2013, http://www.ted.com/talks/sheryl_sandberg_so_we _leaned_in_now_what?language=en (accessed April 29, 2015).

4. Ibid.

5. Pooja Sankar, founder of Piazza, in discussion with the author, July 14, 2014.

6. "Our Story," Piazza, https://piazza.com/about/story (accessed April 29, 2015).

7. Pooja Sankar, founder of Piazza, in discussion with the author, July 14, 2014.

8. Steven Snyder, Leadership and the Art of Struggle: How Great Leaders Grow Through Challenge and Adversity (San Francisco, CA: Berrett-Koehler Publishers, 2013), xi.

35. The 60-Second Story That Turned the Wine Industry on Its Side

1. "The French Paradox," 60 Minutes, November 17, 1991, http://www.cbsnews .com/videos/the-french-paradox/ (accessed April 29, 2015).

2. "Sideways Movie Scene," November 11, 2012, YouTube, https://www.youtube .com/watch?v=PhUnqhMsm7g (accessed April 29, 2015).

3. Melanie Green and Timothy Brock, "The Role of Transportation in the Persua- siveness of Public Narratives," Journal of Personality and Social Psychology, vol. 79, no. 5, 2000, 701–721.

36. From My Heart Rather Than from a Sheet of Paper

1. Malala.org, http://www.malala.org (accessed April 29, 2015).

2. Malala Yousafzai, I Am Malala: The Girl Who Stood Up for Education and Was Shot by the Taliban (New York: Little Brown and Company, 2013), 67.

3. "Pixar's Story Process," YouTube, https://www.youtube.com/watch?v =whnJSSkR_B0 (accessed April 29, 2015).

4. Malala Yousafzai, "Nobel Lecture by Malala Yousafzai (28 minutes)," Nobelprize .org, December 10, 2014, http://www.nobelprize.org/mediaplayer/index.php?id =2424&view=2 (accessed April 29, 2015).

5. Malala Yousafzai, I Am Malala: The Girl Who Stood Up for Education and Was Shot by the Taliban (New York: Little Brown and Company, 2013), 1.

6. Ibid., 10.
7. Malala Yousafzai, "Nobel Lecture by Malala Yousafzai (28 minutes)," Nobelprize
.org, December 10, 2014, http://www.nobelprize.org/mediaplayer/index.php?id
=2424&view=2 (accessed April 29, 2015).

37. Story, Story, Story

1. "Steve Jobs Disney Legends Award Accepted by John Lasseter at the 2013
D23 Expo," YouTube, August 11, 2013, https://www.youtube.com/watch?v
=6RcicFebqRE (accessed April 29, 2015).
2. Ibid.
3. Stephanie Goodman, "Pixar's John Lasseter Answers Your Questions," *New York
Times,* November 1, 2011, http://artsbeat.blogs.nytimes.com/2011/11/01/pixars
-john-lasseter-answers-your-questions/?_r=0 (accessed April 29, 2015).
4. Ed Catmull with Amy Wallace, *Creativity, Inc.: Overcoming the Unseen Forces That
Stand in the Way of True Inspiration* (New York: Random House, 2014), 371.
5. "Steve Jobs on Pixar Success, Hollywood & Storytelling-D3 2005 [HQ]," You-
Tube, https://www.youtube.com/watch?v=Oi2VlxdNuWU&app=desktop (accessed April 29, 2015).

Conclusion: The Storyteller's Universe

1. Spencer Raymond, "The Archive Project—March 18, 2005," OPB, March 18,
2015, http://www.opb.org/radio/programs/literary-arts-archive-project/segment
/the-archive-project-march-18-2015/ (accessed April 29, 2015).
2. Peninnah Schram, professor emerita of speech and drama at Yeshiva University,
in discussion with the author, March 27, 2015.
3. Omar Kattan, "Lessons from Angela Ahrendts on Brand Storytelling," Brand
Stories: New Age Brand Building, http://www.brandstories.net/2014/09/13
/angela-ahrendts-great-brands-great-storytellers/ (accessed April 29, 2015).

Index